"... Throughout the ages men have been moved by great songs and roused by dramatic poems. Long before scribes wrote them down, primitive bards...celebrated heroic battles and glorified gallant deeds in verse.... Poems which tell stories [have always been] popular because they reach down into the heart of the folk.... Ancient singers put the history of the period into galloping measures and ringing rhymes; they embroidered legends with highly colored figures and turned the news of the day into literature.

"The poems in this book span several centuries; many of them are among the glories of English literature. But the emphasis here is on the poem, not on the poet; it is on the power and persuasion of the tale rather than on the reputation of the writer. Here is a book of narratives in many keys, mingling the classic and the contemporary, the popular and the not-yet-familiar—for readers who respond to romance, humor and adventure."

— *From the Introduction by Louis Untermeyer*

Other anthologies edited by Louis Untermeyer

*Published in a PERMABOOK edition.
†Published in a WASHINGTON SQUARE PRESS edition.

STORY POEMS

An Anthology of Narrative Verse

REVISED AND ENLARGED

Selected and Edited by
LOUIS UNTERMEYER

WASHINGTON SQUARE PRESS, INC.　　•　　NEW YORK

STORY POEMS: An Anthology of Narrative Verse

Washington Square Press edition published 1961

2nd printing...................November, 1962

A new edition of a distinguished
literary work now made available in
an inexpensive, well-designed format

Story Poems contains much of the narrative
verse which appeared in Louis Untermeyer's
Pocket Book of Story Poems, published in 1945.

L

Published by
Washington Square Press, Inc.: Executive Offices, 630 Fifth Avenue;
University Press Division, 32 Washington Place, New York, N.Y.

Washington Square Press editions are distributed
in the U.S. by Affiliated Publishers, a division of Pocket
Books, Inc., 630 Fifth Avenue, New York 20, N.Y.

ACKNOWLEDGMENTS

For permission to reprint copyright material controlled by them, the editor
thanks the following publishers and agents:

ERNEST BENN LIMITED (ENGLAND)—for "The Cremation of Sam Mc-
Gee" and "The Shooting of Dan McGrew" from *Songs of a Sourdough* by
Robert W. Service. Reprinted by permission of the publishers and copy-
right owners, Ernest Benn Limited.

BRANDT & BRANDT—for "The Ballad of William Sycamore" and "Metropolitan Nightmare" from *Selected Works of Stephen Vincent Benét,* published by Rinehart & Company; copyright, 1922, by Stephen Vincent Benét;
copyright renewed, 1950, by Rosemary Carr Benét. "The Ballad of the
Harp-Weaver" from *Collected Poems* by Edna St. Vincent Millay, published by Harper & Brothers; copyright, 1922, 1950, by Edna St. Vincent
Millay.

DODD, MEAD & COMPANY—for "The Cremation of Sam McGee" and
"The Shooting of Dan McGrew" from *The Collected Poems of Robert W.
Service.*

DOUBLEDAY & COMPANY, INC.—for "Ballad of East and West" and
"Gunga Din" from *Barrack-Room Ballads* by Rudyard Kipling; copyright,
1899, by Rudyard Kipling.

HARCOURT, BRACE & COMPANY—for the translations from *Heinrich
Heine: Paradox and Poet* by Louis Untermeyer; copyright, 1937. Reprinted
by permission of the author and publisher.

HARPER & BROTHERS—for "Old Christmas" from *Lonesome Water* by
Roy Helton, published by Harper & Brothers; copyright, 1930, by Harper
& Brothers.

ACKNOWLEDGMENTS   V

HENRY HOLT AND COMPANY, INC.—for "The Listeners" from *Collected Poems* by Walter de la Mare and "Bredon Hill" from *A Shropshire Lad* by A. E. Housman. "The Code," "The Witch of Coös," and "The Death of the Hired Man" from *Complete Poems of Robert Frost;* copyright, 1930, 1949, by Henry Holt and Company, Inc.; copyright, 1936, 1948, by Robert Frost. Reprinted by permission of the publishers.

HOUGHTON MIFFLIN COMPANY—for "A Turkish Legend" from *Collected Poems* by Thomas Bailey Aldrich; "The Menagerie" from *Poems and Poetic Dramas* by William Vaughn Moody; the selections from *The Complete Poems of Ralph Waldo Emerson, The Complete Poems of Oliver Wendell Holmes, The Complete Poems of Henry Wadsworth Longfellow,* and *The Complete Poems of John Greenleaf Whittier.*

JOSEPH LAUREN—"The Butterfly and the Caterpillar," "The Fox and the Grapes," and "The Frogs Who Wanted a King" are copyright by the author and reprinted with his permission.

J. B. LIPPINCOTT COMPANY—for "The Highwayman" from *Collected Poems: Volume I* by Alfred Noyes, published by J. B. Lippincott Company; copyright, 1906, 1934, by Alfred Noyes.

LITTLE, BROWN & COMPANY—for "Adventures of Isabel" from *The Face Is Familiar* by Ogden Nash. Reprinted by permission of Little, Brown & Company.

MACMILLAN & COMPANY, LTD. (ENGLAND)—for "Father Gilligan" from *The Collected Poems of William Butler Yeats.*

THE MACMILLAN COMPANY—for "The Stone" from *Collected Poems* by W. W. Gibson; "The Man He Killed" and "Ah, Are You Digging on My Grave?" from *Collected Poems* by Thomas Hardy; "Father Gilligan" from *Collected Poems* by William Butler Yeats; "Spanish Waters" from *Collected Poems: Volume I,* copyright, 1925, by John Masefield.

THE MACMILLAN COMPANY OF CANADA, LTD.—for "Ballad of East and West" and "Gunga Din" from *Barrack-Room Ballads* by Rudyard Kipling.

THE RYERSON PRESS (CANADA)—for "The Shooting of Dan McGrew" and "The Cremation of Sam McGee" from *The Collected Poems of Robert W. Service,* published in Canada by The Ryerson Press, Toronto.

CHARLES SCRIBNER'S SONS—for "The Dinkey-Bird" from *The Collected Poems of Eugene Field* and "Juggling Jerry" from *The Complete Poems of George Meredith.*

THE SOCIETY OF AUTHORS (ENGLAND)—for "Spanish Waters" by John Masefield. Reprinted by permission of The Society of Authors and Dr. John Masefield, O.M.

LOUIS UNTERMEYER—for the translation of "The Erl-King" by Johann Wolfgang von Goethe.

A. P. WATT & SONS (ENGLAND)—for "Ballad of East and West" and "Gunga Din" from *Barrack-Room Ballads* by Rudyard Kipling, reprinted by permission of Mrs. George Bambridge; "Father Gilligan" from *The Collected Poems of William Butler Yeats,* reprinted by permission of Mrs. W. B. Yeats; "The Highwayman" from *Collected Poems* by Alfred Noyes, reprinted by permission of Alfred Noyes and William Blackwood and Sons, Ltd.

CONTENTS

PEOPLE

THE HEART SPEAKS

PRAISE AND PATRIOTISM

FABLE AND FANTASY

LAUGHTER IN RHYME

OF MYSTERY AND TERROR

HEROES AND LEGENDS OF
THE NEW WORLD

INTRODUCTION

Throughout the ages men have been moved by great songs and roused by dramatic poems. Long before scribes wrote them down, primitive bards sang their chants, celebrated heroic battles and glorified gallant deeds in verse. Narrative poetry has always enjoyed the widest range and the greatest appeal. Poems which tell stories are popular because they reach down into the heart of the folk; they originated among the people. The old tales in verse were made for crowds in market places, sung in taverns and repeated on street corners. The ancient singers put the history of the period into galloping measures and ringing rhymes; they embroidered legends with highly colored figures and turned the news of the day into literature.

The poems in this book span several centuries; many of them are among the glories of English literature. But the emphasis here is on the poem, not on the poet; it is on the power and persuasion of the tale rather than on the reputation of the writer. Great names are scattered through this collection, but they are matched by little-known and anonymous singers.

The plan of the book emphasizes the design. It dispenses with chronology for the sake of contrast. The editor hopes to surprise the reader with several novelties and, by virtue of the arrangement, to make even the old favorites take on new life.

L.U.

STORY POEMS:

An Anthology of Narrative Verse

BRAVE HEARTS AND HIGH ADVENTURES

The poems in this section depict life in action: vivid records of memorable events as well as mythical exploits. Some of them are transcripts of history. Tennyson's "The Charge of the Light Brigade" is founded on the suicidal gallantry of a British division at the battle of Balaclava during the Crimean war of 1854. Byron's "Waterloo" is tense with the excitement and apprehension in the midst of gayety on the eve of Napoleon's final defeat by Wellington in 1815. Halleck's "Marco Bozzaris" is a tribute to the desperate heroism of a Greek patriot in the struggle for independence against the Turks. Browning's "Hervé Riel" celebrates a common Breton sailor whose expert piloting saved a French squadron from destruction, and who, told to name his reward, asked for a day off so he could see his wife.

Browning's two other poems are more fictional. The narrator of "Incident of the French Camp" is supposedly one of Napoleon's aides who recalls the storming of Ratisbon, a town which Lannes, one of Napoleon's generals, was attacking; but the episode of the brave young messenger is Browning's invention. "How They Brought the Good News from Ghent to Aix" has even less foundation on fact. The story is only suggested—we do not know what good news is being delivered, nor why the riders are

spurring their horses with such urgency; but we feel
the drama and sense the background in the clattering rhythm of the ride. Kipling is not explicit about
the setting of "Gunga Din" and "Ballad of East and
West"; but we know that the scene is India and
that, in spite of the tradition that "East is East and
West is West, and never the twain shall meet," the
distance has been spanned by men of good will and
an understanding between two kinds of civilization
has been accomplished.

Ballad of East and West

*Oh, East is East, and West is West, and never the twain shall
    meet,*
*Till Earth and Sky stand presently at God's great Judgment
    Seat;*
*But there is neither East nor West, Border, nor Breed, nor
    Birth,*
*When two strong men stand face to face, tho' they come from
    the ends of the earth!*

Kamal is out with twenty men to raise the Borderside,
And he has lifted the Colonel's mare that is the Colonel's
    pride:
He has lifted her out of the stable-door between the dawn
    and the day,
And turned the calkins upon her feet, and ridden her far
    away.
Then up and spoke the Colonel's son that led a troop of the
    Guides:
"Is there never a man of all my men can say where Kamal
    hides?"

Then up and spoke Mahommed Khan, the son of the
    Ressaldar:
"If ye know the track of the morning-mist, ye know where
    his pickets are.
At dusk he harries the Abazai—at dawn he is into Bonair,
But he must go by Fort Bukloh to his own place to fare,
So if ye gallop to Fort Bukloh as fast as a bird can fly,
By the favour of God ye may cut him off ere he win to the
    Tongue of Jagai.
But if he be past the Tongue of Jagai, right swiftly turn ye
    then,
For the length and the breadth of that grisly plain is sown
    with Kamal's men.
There is rock to the left, and rock to the right, and low lean
    thorn between,
And ye may hear a breech-bolt snick where never a man is
    seen."
The Colonel's son has taken a horse, and a raw rough dun
    was he,
With the mouth of a bell and the heart of Hell and the head
    of the gallows-tree.
The Colonel's son to the Fort has won, they bid him stay to
    eat—
Who rides at the tail of a Border thief, he sits not long at his
    meat.
He's up and away from Fort Bukloh as fast as he can fly,
Till he was aware of his father's mare in the gut of the
    Tongue of Jagai,
Till he was aware of his father's mare with Kamal upon her
    back,
And when he could spy the white of her eye, he made the
    pistol crack.

He has fired once, he has fired twice, but the whistling ball
    went wide.
"Ye shoot like a soldier," Kamal said. "Show now if ye can
    ride."
It's up and over the Tongue of Jagai, as blown dust-devils go,

The dun he fled like a stag of ten, but the mare like a barren
    doe.
The dun he leaned against the bit and slugged his head above,
But the red mare played with the snaffle-bars, as a maiden
    plays with a glove.
There was rock to the left, and rock to the right, and low
    lean thorn between,
And thrice he heard a breech-bolt snick tho' never a man
    was seen.
They have ridden the low moon out of the sky, their hoofs
    drum up the dawn,
The dun he went like a wounded bull, but the mare like a
    new-roused fawn.
The dun he fell at a water-course—in a woful heap fell he,
And Kamal has turned the red mare back, and pulled the
    rider free.
He has knocked the pistol out of his hand—small room was
    there to strive,
" 'Twas only by favour of mine," quoth he, "ye rode so long
    alive:
There was not a rock for twenty mile, there was not a clump
    of tree,
But covered a man of my own men with his rifle cocked on
    his knee.
If I had raised my bridle-hand, as I have held it low,
The little jackals that flee so fast were feasting all in a row:
If I had bowed my head on my breast, as I have held it high,
The kite that whistles above us now were gorged till she
    could not fly."
Lightly answered the Colonel's son: "Do good to bird and
    beast,
But count who come for the broken meats before thou makest
    a feast.
If there should follow a thousand swords to carry my bones
    away,
Belike the price of a jackal's meal were more than a thief
    could pay.

They will feed their horse on the standing crop, their men
    on the garnered grain,
The thatch of the byres will serve their fires when all the
    cattle are slain.
But if thou thinkest the price be fair,—thy brethren wait to
    sup,
The hound is kin to the jackal-spawn,—howl, dog, and call
    them up!
And if thou thinkest the price be high, in steer and gear and
    stack,
Give me my father's mare again, and I'll fight my own way
    back!"
Kamal has gripped him by the hand and set him upon his
    feet.
"No talk shall be of dogs," said he, "when wolf and grey
    wolf meet.
May I eat dirt if thou hast hurt of me in deed or breath;
What dam of lances brought thee forth to jest at the dawn
    with Death?"
Lightly answered the Colonel's son: "I hold by the blood of
    my clan:
Take up the mare for my father's gift—by God, she has carried
    a man!"
The red mare ran to the Colonel's son, and nuzzled against
    his breast;
"We be two strong men," said Kamal then, "but she loveth
    the younger best.
So she shall go with a lifter's dower, my turquoise studded
    rein,
My broidered saddle and saddle-cloth, and silver stirrups
    twain."
The Colonel's son a pistol drew and held it muzzle-end,
"Ye have taken the one from a foe," said he; "will ye take
    the mate from a friend?"
"A gift for a gift," said Kamal straight; "a limb for the risk
    of a limb.
Thy father has sent his son to me, I'll send my son to him!"

With that he whistled his only son, that dropped from a
    mountain-crest—
He trod the ling like a buck in spring, and he looked like a
    lance in rest.
"Now here is thy master," Kamal said, "who leads a troop
    of the Guides,
And thou must ride at his left side as shield on shoulder rides.
Till Death or I cut loose the tie, at camp and board and bed,
Thy life is his—thy fate it is to guard him with thy head.
So, thou must eat the White Queen's meat, and all her foes
    are thine,
And thou must harry thy father's hold for the peace of the
    Border-line,
And thou must make a trooper tough and hack thy way to
    power—
Belike they will raise thee to Ressaldar when I am hanged
    in Peshawur."

They have looked each other between the eyes, and there
    they found no fault,
They have taken the Oath of the Brother-in-Blood, on
    leavened bread and salt:
They have taken the Oath of the Brother-in-Blood on fire and
    fresh-cut sod,
On the hilt and the haft of the Khyber knife, and the Won-
    drous Names of God.
The Colonel's son he rides the mare and Kamal's boy the
    dun,
And two have come back to Fort Bukloh where there went
    forth but one.
And when they drew to the Quarter-Guard, full twenty
    swords flew clear—
There was not a man but carried his feud with the blood of
    the mountaineer.
"Ha' done! ha' done!" said the Colonel's son. "Put up the steel
    at your sides!
Last night ye had struck at a Border thief—to-night 'tis a man
    of the Guides!"

*Oh, East is East, and West is West, and never the twain shall
    meet,*
*Till Earth and Sky stand presently at God's great Judgment
    Seat;*
*But there is neither East nor West, Border, nor Breed, nor
    Birth,*
*When two strong men stand face to face, tho' they come
    from the ends of the earth!*

—RUDYARD KIPLING

Gunga Din

You may talk o' gin an' beer
When you're quartered safe out 'ere,
An' you're sent to penny-fights an' Aldershot it;
But when it comes to slaughter
You will do your work on water,
An' you'll lick the bloomin' boots of 'im that's got it.
Now in Injia's sunny clime,
Where I used to spend my time
A-servin' of 'Er Majesty the Queen,
Of all them black-faced crew
The finest man I knew
Was our regimental *bhisti*,[1] Gunga Din.

It was "Din! Din! Din!
You limping lump o' brick-dust, Gunga Din!
Hi! *slippy hitherao!*
Water, get it! *Panee lao!*[2]
You squidgy-nosed old idol, Gunga Din!"

The uniform 'e wore
Was nothin' much before,

[1] The *bhisti*, or water-carrier, attached to regiments in India, is often one of the most devoted of the Queen's servants.

[2] Bring water swiftly.

An' rather less than 'arf o' that be'ind,
For a twisty piece o' rag
An' a goatskin water-bag
Was all the field-equipment 'e could find.
When the sweatin' troop-train lay
In a sidin' through the day,
Where the 'eat would make your bloomin' eyebrows crawl,
We shouted "Harry By!"[3]
Till our throats were bricky-dry,
Then we wopped 'im 'cause 'e couldn't serve us all.

    It was "Din! Din! Din!
    You 'eathen, where the mischief 'ave you been?
    You put some *juldee*[4] in it,
    Or I'll *marrow*[5] you this minute,
    If you don't fill up my helmet, Gunga Din!"

'E would dot an' carry one
Till the longest day was done,
An' 'e didn't seem to know the use o' fear.
If we charged or broke or cut,
You could bet your bloomin' nut,
'E'd be waitin' fifty paces right flank rear.
With 'is *mussick*[6] on 'is back,
'E would skip with our attack,
An' watch us till the bugles made "Retire."
An' for all 'is dirty 'ide,
'E was white, clear white, inside
When 'e went to tend the wounded under fire!

    It was "Din! Din! Din!"
    With the bullets kickin' dust-spots on the green.
    When the cartridges ran out,
    You could 'ear the front-files shout:
    "Hi! ammunition-mules an' Gunga Din!"

---

[3] Tommy Atkins' equivalent for "O Brother!"
[4] Speed.
[5] Hit you.
[6] Water-skin.

I sha'n't forgit the night
When I dropped be'ind the fight
With a bullet where my belt-plate should 'a' been.
I was chokin' mad with thirst,
An' the man that spied me first
Was our good old grinnin', gruntin' Gunga Din.
'E lifted up my 'ead,
An' 'e plugged me where I bled,
An' 'e guv me 'arf-a-pint o' water—green;
It was crawlin' an' it stunk,
But of all the drinks I've drunk,
I'm gratefulest to one from Gunga Din.

    It was "Din! Din! Din!
      'Ere's a beggar with a bullet through 'is spleen;
      'E's chawin' up the ground an' 'e's kickin' all around:
      For Gawd's sake, git the water, Gunga Din!"

'E carried me away
To where a *dooli* lay,
An' a bullet come an' drilled the beggar clean.
'E put me safe inside,
An' just before 'e died:
"I 'ope you liked your drink," sez Gunga Din.
So I'll meet 'im later on
In the place where 'e is gone—
Where it's always double drill and no canteen;
'E'll be squattin' on the coals
Givin' drink to pore damned souls,
An' I'll get a swig in Hell from Gunga Din!

    Din! Din! Din!
    You Lazarushian-leather Gunga Din!
    Tho' I've belted you an' flayed you,
    By the livin' Gawd that made you,
    You're a better man than I am, Gunga Din!

                —RUDYARD KIPLING

Hervé Riel

On the sea and at the Hogue, sixteen hundred ninety-two,
   Did the English fight the French,—woe to France!
And, the thirty-first of May, helter-skelter thro' the blue,
Like a crowd of frightened porpoises a shoal of sharks pursue,
   Came crowding ship on ship to St. Malo on the Rance,
With the English fleet in view.

'Twas the squadron that escaped, with the victor in full chase;
   First and foremost of the drove, in his great ship, Dam-
      freville;
   Close on him fled, great and small,
   Twenty-two good ships in all;
And they signalled to the place
"Help the winners of a race!
   Get us guidance, give us harbour, take us quick—or,
      quicker still,
   Here's the English can and will!"

Then the pilots of the place put out brisk and leapt on board;
   "Why, what hope or chance have ships like these to pass?"
      laughed they:
"Rocks to starboard, rocks to port, all the passage scarred and
      scored,
Shall the *Formidable* here with her twelve and eighty guns
   Think to make the river-mouth by the single narrow way,
Trust to enter where 'tis ticklish for a craft of twenty tons,
   And with flow at full beside?
   Now, 'tis slackest ebb of tide.
   Reach the mooring? Rather say,
While rock stands or water runs,
Not a ship will leave the bay!"

Then was called a council straight.
Brief and bitter the debate:

"Here's the English at our heels; would you have them take
        in tow
All that's left us of the fleet, linked together stern and bow,
For a prize to Plymouth Sound?
Better run the ships aground!"
    (Ended Damfreville his speech).
"Not a minute more to wait!
    Let the Captains all and each
    Shove ashore, then blow up, burn the vessels on the beach!
France must undergo her fate.

"Give the word!" But no such word
Was ever spoke or heard;
    For up stood, for out stepped, for in struck amid all these
—A Captain? A Lieutenant? A Mate—first, second, third?
        No such man of mark, and meet
        With his betters to compete!
        But a simple Breton sailor pressed by Tourville for the
            fleet,
    A poor coasting-pilot he, Hervé Riel the Croisickese.

And "What mockery or malice have we here?" cries Hervé
        Riel:
    "Are you mad, you Malouins? Are you cowards, fools, or
        rogues?
Talk to me of rocks and shoals, me who took the soundings,
        tell
On my fingers every bank, every shallow, every swell
    'Twixt the offing here and Grève where the river dis-
        embogues?
Are you bought by English gold? Is it love the lying's for?
    Morn and eve, night and day,
    Have I piloted your bay,
Entered free and anchored fast at the foot of Solidor.
Burn the fleet and ruin France? That were worse than fifty
        Hogues!
    Sirs, they know I speak the truth! Sirs, believe me there's
        a way!

Only let me lead the line,
    Have the biggest ship to steer,
    Get this *Formidable* clear,
Make the others follow mine,
And I lead them, most and least, by a passage I know well,
    Right to Solidor past Grève,
        And there lay them safe and sound;
    And if one ship misbehave,
        —Keel so much as grate the ground,
Why, I've nothing but my life,—here's my head!" cries Hervé
    Riel.

Not a minute more to wait.
"Steer us in, then, small and great!
    Take the helm, lead the line, save the squadron!" cried its
        chief.
Captains, give the sailor place!
    He is Admiral, in brief.
Still the north-wind, by God's grace!
See the noble fellow's face
As the big ship, with a bound,
Clears the entry like a hound,
Keeps the passage as its inch of way were the wide sea's
    profound!
    See, safe thro' shoal and rock,
    How they follow in a flock,
Not a ship that misbehaves, not a keel that grates the ground,
    Not a spar that comes to grief!
The peril, see, is past,
All are harboured to the last,
And just as Hervé Riel hollas "Anchor!"—sure as fate,
Up the English come, too late!

So, the storm subsides to calm:
    They see the green trees wave
    On the heights o'erlooking Grève.
Hearts that bled are stanched with balm.
"Just our rapture to enhance,

Let the English rake the bay,
Gnash their teeth and glare askance
    As they cannonade away!
'Neath rampired Solidor pleasant riding on the Rance!"
How hope succeeds despair on each Captain's countenance!
Out burst all with one accord,
        "This is Paradise for Hell!
        Let France, let France's King
        Thank the man that did the thing!"
What a shout, and all one word,
        "Hervé Riel!"
As he stepped in front once more,
    Not a symptom of surprise
    In the frank blue Breton eyes,
Just the same man as before.

Then said Damfreville, "My friend,
I must speak out at the end,
    Though I find the speaking hard.
Praise is deeper than the lips:
You have saved the King his ships,
    You must name your own reward.
'Faith, our sun was near eclipse!
Demand whate'er you will,
France remains your debtor still.
Ask to heart's content and have! or my name's not Damfreville."

Then a beam of fun outbroke
On the bearded mouth that spoke,
As the honest heart laughed through
Those frank eyes of Breton blue:
"Since I needs must say my say,
    Since on board the duty's done,
    And from Malo Roads to Croisic Point, what is it but a
        run?
Since, 'tis ask and have, I may—
    Since the others go ashore—

Come! A good whole holiday!
    Leave to go and see my wife, whom I call the Belle
        Aurore!"
    That he asked and that he got,—nothing more.

Name and deed alike are lost:
Not a pillar nor a post
    In his Croisic keeps alive the feat as it befell;
Not a head in white and black
On a single fishing-smack,
In memory of the man but for whom had gone to wrack
    All that France saved from the fight whence England bore
        the bell.
Go to Paris: rank on rank
    Search the heroes flung pell-mell
On the Louvre, face and flank!
    You shall look long enough ere you come to Hervé Riel.
So, for better and for worse,
Hervé Riel, accept my verse!
In my verse, Hervé Riel, do thou once more
Save the squadron, honour France, love thy wife the Belle
        Aurore!

                    —ROBERT BROWNING

Incident of the French Camp

You know, we French stormed Ratisbon.
    A mile or so away,
On a little mound, Napoleon
    Stood on our storming-day;
With neck out-thrust, you fancy how,
    Legs wide, arms locked behind,
As if to balance the prone brow
    Oppressive with its mind.

Just as perhaps he mused "My plans
    That soar, to earth may fall,

Let once my army-leader Lannes
　　Waver at yonder wall"—
Out 'twixt the battery smokes there flew
　　A rider, bound on bound
Full-galloping; nor bridle drew
　　Until he reached the mound.

Then off there flung in smiling joy,
　　And held himself erect
By just his horse's mane, a boy:
　　You hardly could suspect—
(So tight he kept his lips compressed,
　　Scarce any blood came through)
You looked twice ere you saw his breast
　　Was all but shot in two.

"Well," cried he, "Emperor, by God's grace
　　We've got you Ratisbon!
The Marshal's in the market-place,
　　And you'll be there anon
To see your flag-bird flap his vans
　　Where I, to heart's desire,
Perched him!" The chief's eye flashed; his plans
　　Soared up again like fire.

The chief's eye flashed; but presently
　　Softened itself, as sheathes
A film the mother-eagle's eye
　　When her bruised eaglet breathes;
"You're wounded!" "Nay," the soldier's pride
　　Touched to the quick, he said:
"I'm killed, Sire!" And, his chief beside,
　　Smiling, the boy fell dead.

　　　　　　　　　　　　—ROBERT BROWNING

How They Brought the Good News from Ghent to Aix

I sprang to the stirrup, and Joris, and he;
I galloped, Dirck galloped, we galloped all three;
"Good speed!" cried the watch, as the gate bolts undrew,
"Speed!" echoed the wall to us galloping through;
Behind shut the postern, the lights sank to rest,
And into the midnight we galloped abreast.

Not a word to each other; we kept the great pace
Neck by neck, stride by stride, never changing our place;
I turned in my saddle and made its girths tight,
Then shortened each stirrup, and set the pique right,
Rebuckled the cheek-strap, chained slacker the bit,
Nor galloped less steadily Roland a whit.

'Twas moonset at starting; but while we drew near
Lokeren, the cocks crew and twilight dawned clear;
At Boom, a great yellow star came out to see;
At Düffeld, 'twas morning as plain as could be;
And from Mecheln church-steeple we heard the half-chime,
So, Joris broke silence with, "Yet there is time!"

At Aershot, up leaped of a sudden the sun,
And against him the cattle stood black every one,
To stare thro' the mist at us galloping past,
And I saw my stout galloper Roland at last,
With resolute shoulders, each butting away
The haze, as some bluff river headland its spray:

And his low head and crest, just one sharp ear bent back
For my voice, and the other pricked out on his track;
And one eye's black intelligence,—ever that glance
O'er its white edge at me, his own master, askance!
And the thick heavy spume-flakes which aye and anon
His fierce lips shook upwards in galloping on.

By Hasselt, Dirck groaned; and cried Joris, "Stay spur!
Your Roos galloped bravely, the fault's not in her,
We'll remember at Aix"—for one heard the quick wheeze
Of her chest, saw the stretched neck and staggering knees,
And sunk tail, and horrible heave of the flank,
As down on her haunches she shuddered and sank.

So, we were left galloping, Joris and I,
Past Looz and past Tongres, no cloud in the sky;
The broad sun above laughed a pitiless laugh,
'Neath our feet broke the brittle bright stubble like chaff;
Till over by Dalhem a dome-spire sprang white,
And "Gallop," gasped Joris, "for Aix is in sight!"

"How they'll greet us!"—and all in a moment his roan
Rolled neck and croup over, lay dead as a stone;
And there was my Roland to bear the whole weight
Of the news which alone could save Aix from her fate,
With his nostrils like pits full of blood to the brim,
And with circles of red for his eye-sockets' rim.

Then I cast loose my buffcoat, each holster let fall,
Shook off both my jack-boots, let go belt and all,
Stood up in the stirrup, leaned, patted his ear,
Called my Roland his pet-name, my horse without peer;
Clapped my hands, laughed and sang, any noise, bad or good,
Till at length into Aix Roland galloped and stood.

And all I remember is—friends flocking round
As I sat with his head 'twixt my knees on the ground;
And no voice but was praising this Roland of mine,
As I poured down his throat our last measure of wine,
Which (the burgesses voted by common consent)
Was no more than his due who brought good news from
     Ghent.

                                        —ROBERT BROWNING

Excelsior

The shades of night were falling fast,
As through an Alpine village passed
A youth, who bore, 'mid snow and ice,
A banner with the strange device—
        Excelsior!

His brow was sad; his eye beneath
Flashed like a falchion from its sheath;
And like a silver clarion rung
The accents of that unknown tongue—
        Excelsior!

In happy homes he saw the light
Of household fires gleam warm and bright:
Above, the spectral glaciers shone,
And from his lips escaped a groan—
        Excelsior!

"Try not the pass," the old man said:
"Dark lowers the tempest overhead;
The roaring torrent is deep and wide!"
And loud that clarion voice replied,
        Excelsior!

"O stay," the maiden said, "and rest
Thy weary head upon this breast!"
A tear stood in his bright blue eye,
But still he answered, with a sigh,
        Excelsior!

"Beware the pine-tree's withered branch!
Beware the awful avalanche!"
This was the peasant's last good-night:
A voice replied, far up the height,
        Excelsior!

At break of day, as heavenward
The pious monks of Saint Bernard
Uttered the oft-repeated prayer,
A voice cried, through the startled air,
   Excelsior!

A traveller, by the faithful hound,
Half buried in the snow was found,
Still grasping in his hand of ice
That banner with the strange device—
   Excelsior!

There in the twilight cold and gray,
Lifeless, but beautiful, he lay,
And from the sky, serene and far,
A voice fell, like a falling star—
   Excelsior!

     —HENRY WADSWORTH LONGFELLOW

The Charge of the Light Brigade

Half a league, half a league,
 Half a league onward,
All in the valley of Death
 Rode the six hundred.
"Forward, the Light Brigade!
Charge for the guns!" he said:
Into the valley of Death
 Rode the six hundred.

"Forward, the Light Brigade!"
Was there a man dismay'd?
Not tho' the soldier knew
 Some one had blunder'd:
Theirs not to make reply,
Theirs not to reason why,
Theirs but to do and die:

Into the valley of Death
  Rode the six hundred.

Cannon to right of them,
Cannon to left of them,
Cannon in front of them
  Volley'd and thunder'd;
Storm'd at with shot and shell,
Boldly they rode and well,
Into the jaws of Death,
Into the mouth of Hell
  Rode the six hundred.

Flash'd all their sabres bare,
Flash'd as they turn'd in air,
Sabring the gunners there,
Charging an army, while
  All the world wonder'd:
Plunged in the battery-smoke
Right thro' the line they broke;
Cossack and Russian
Reel'd from the sabre-stroke
  Shatter'd and sunder'd.
Then they rode back, but not,
  Not the six hundred.

Cannon to right of them,
Cannon to left of them,
Cannon behind them
  Volley'd and thunder'd;
Storm'd at with shot and shell,
While horse and hero fell,
They that had fought so well
Came thro' the jaws of Death
Back from the mouth of Hell,
All that was left of them,
  Left of six hundred.

When can their glory fade?
O the wild charge they made!
    All the world wonder'd.
Honour the charge they made!
Honour the Light Brigade,
    Noble six hundred!

—ALFRED, LORD TENNYSON

Waterloo

There was a sound of revelry by night,
And Belgium's capital had gather'd then
Her beauty and her chivalry, and bright
The lamps shone o'er fair women and brave men;
A thousand hearts beat happily; and when
Music arose with its voluptuous swell,
Soft eyes look'd love to eyes which spake again,
And all went merry as a marriage bell;
But hush! hark! a deep sound strikes like a rising knell!

Did ye not hear it?—No; 'twas but the wind,
Or the car rattling o'er the stony street;
On with the dance! let joy be unconfined;
No sleep till morn, when Youth and Pleasure meet
To chase the glowing hours with flying feet.—
But hark! that heavy sound breaks in once more,
As if the clouds its echo would repeat;
And nearer, clearer, deadlier than before!
Arm! arm! it is—it is—the cannon's opening roar!

Within a window'd niche of that high hall
Sate Brunswick's fated chieftain; he did hear
That sound the first amidst the festival,
And caught its tone with Death's prophetic ear,
And when they smiled because he deem'd it near,
His heart more truly knew that peal too well
Which stretch'd his father on a bloody bier,

And roused the vengeance blood alone could quell.
He rush'd into the field, and, foremost fighting, fell.

Ah! then and there was hurrying to and fro,
And gathering tears, and tremblings of distress,
And cheeks all pale, which but an hour ago
Blush'd at the praise of their own loveliness;
And there were sudden partings, such as press
The life from out young hearts, and choking sighs
Which ne'er might be repeated: who could guess
If ever more should meet those mutual eyes,
Since upon night so sweet such awful morn could rise!

And wild and high the "Cameron's Gathering" rose,
The war-note of Lochiel, which Albyn's hills
Have heard, and heard, too, have her Saxon foes;
How in the noon of night that pibroch thrills
Savage and shrill! But with the breath which fills
Their mountain pipe, so fill the mountaineers
With the fierce native daring which instils
The stirring memory of a thousand years,
And Evan's, Donald's fame rings in each clansman's ears!

And Ardennes waves above them her green leaves,
Dewy with Nature's tear-drops, as they pass,
Grieving, if aught inanimate e'er grieves,
Over the unreturning brave—alas!
Ere evening to be trodden like the grass
Which now beneath them, but above shall grow
In its next verdure, when this fiery mass
Of living valour, rolling on the foe,
And burning with high hope, shall moulder cold and low.

Last noon beheld them full of lusty life,
Last eve in Beauty's circle proudly gay,
The midnight brought the signal-sound of strife,
The morn the marshalling arms—the day
Battle's magnificently stern array!

The thunder-clouds close o'er it, which when rent
The earth is cover'd thick with other clay,
  Which her own clay shall cover, heap'd and pent,
Rider and horse—friend, foe,—in one red burial blent!

—GEORGE GORDON, LORD BYRON

The Destruction of Sennacherib

The Assyrian came down like the wolf on the fold,
And his cohorts were gleaming in purple and gold;
And the sheen of their spears was like stars on the sea,
When the blue wave rolls nightly on deep Galilee.

Like the leaves of the forest when summer is green,
That host with their banners at sunset were seen:
Like the leaves of the forest when autumn hath blown,
That host on the morrow lay withered and strown.

For the Angel of Death spread his wings on the blast,
And breathed in the face of the foe as he passed;
And the eyes of the sleepers waxed deadly and chill,
And their hearts but once heaved, and forever grew still!

And there lay the steed with his nostril all wide,
But through it there rolled not the breath of his pride:
And the foam of his gasping lay white on the turf,
And cold as the spray of the rock-beating surf.

And there lay the rider distorted and pale,
With the dew on his brow, and the rust on his mail;
And the tents were all silent, the banners alone,
The lances unlifted, the trumpet unblown.

And the widows of Ashur are loud in their wail,
And the idols are broke in the temple of Baal;
And the might of the Gentile, unsmote by the sword,
Hath melted like snow in the glance of the Lord!

—GEORGE GORDON, LORD BYRON

Marco Bozzaris

At midnight, in his guarded tent,
   The Turk was dreaming of the hour
When Greece, her knee in suppliance bent,
   Should tremble at his power:
In dreams, through camp and court, he bore
The trophies of a conqueror;
   In dreams his song of triumph heard;
Then wore his monarch's signet ring:
Then pressed that monarch's throne—a king;
As wild his thoughts, and gay of wing,
   As Eden's garden bird.

At midnight, in the forest shades,
   Bozzaris ranged his Suliote band,
True as the steel of their tried blades,
   Heroes in heart and hand.
There had the Persian's thousands stood,
There had the glad earth drunk their blood
   On old Platæa's day;
And now there breathed that haunted air
The sons of sires who conquered there,
With arm to strike and soul to dare,
   As quick, as far as they.

An hour passed on—the Turk awoke;
   That bright dream was his last;
He woke—to hear his sentries shriek,
   "To arms! they come! the Greek! the Greek!"
He woke—to die midst flame and smoke,
And shout, and groan, and sabre-stroke,
   And death-shots falling thick and fast
As lightnings from the mountain cloud;
And heard, with voice as trumpet loud,
   Bozzaris cheer his band:

"Strike—till the last armed foe expires;
Strike—for your altars and your fires;
Strike—for the green graves of your sires;
    God—and your native land!"

They fought—like brave men, long and well;
    They piled that ground with Moslem slain,
They conquered—but Bozzaris fell,
    Bleeding at every vein.
His few surviving comrades saw
His smile when rang their proud hurrah,
    And the red field was won;
Then saw in death his eyelids close
Calmly, as to a night's repose,
    Like flowers at set of sun.

Bozzaris! with the storied brave
    Greece nurtured in her glory's time,
Rest thee—there is no prouder grave,
    Even in her own proud clime.
She wore no funeral-weeds for thee,
    Nor bade the dark hearse wave its plume
Like torn branch from death's leafless tree
In sorrow's pomp and pageantry,
    The heartless luxury of the tomb;
But she remembers thee as one
Long loved and for a season gone;
For thee her poet's lyre is wreathed,
Her marble wrought, her music breathed;
For thee she rings the birthday bells;
Of thee her babe's first lisping tells;
For thine her evening prayer is said
At palace-couch and cottage-bed;
Her soldier, closing with the foe,
Gives for thy sake a deadlier blow;
His plighted maiden, when she fears
For him the joy of her young years,

Thinks of thy fate, and checks her tears;
  And she, the mother of thy boys,
Though in her eye and faded cheek
Is read the grief she will not speak,
  The memory of her buried joys,
And even she who gave thee birth,
Will, by their pilgrim-circled hearth,
  Talk of thy doom without a sigh;
For thou art Freedom's now, and Fame's:
One of the few, the immortal names,
  That were not born to die.

—FITZ-GREENE HALLECK

Sir Galahad

My good blade carves the casques[1] of men,
  My tough lance thrusteth sure,
My strength is as the strength of ten,
  Because my heart is pure.
The shattering trumpet shrilleth high,
  The hard brands[2] shiver on the steel,
The splinter'd spear-shafts crack and fly,
  The horse and rider reel:
They reel, they roll in clanging lists,[3]
  And when the tide of combat stands,
Perfume and flowers fall in showers,
  That lightly rain from ladies' hands.

How sweet are looks that ladies bend
  On whom their favours fall!
For them I battle till the end,
  To save from shame and thrall:
But all my heart is drawn above,
  My knees are bow'd in crypt and shrine:

---

[1] Casques: helmets.
[2] Brands: swords.
[3] Lists: tournaments.

I never felt the kiss of love,
   Nor maiden's hand in mine.
More bounteous aspects on me beam,
   Me mightier transports move and thrill;
So keep I fair thro' faith and prayer
   A virgin heart in work and will.

When down the stormy crescent goes,
   A light before me swims,
Between dark stems the forest glows,
   I hear a noise of hymns:
Then by some secret shrine I ride;
   I hear a voice, but none are there;
The stalls are void, the doors are wide,
   The tapers burning fair.
Fair gleams the snowy altar-cloth,
   The silver vessels sparkle clean,
The shrill bell rings, the censer swings,
   And solemn chaunts resound between.

Sometimes on lonely mountain-meres
   I find a magic bark;
I leap on board: no helmsman steers:
   I float till all is dark.
A gentle sound, an awful light!
   Three angels bear the holy Grail:
With folded feet, in stoles of white,
   On sleeping wings they sail.
Ah, blessed vision! blood of God!
   My spirit beats her mortal bars,
As down dark tides the glory slides,
   And star-like mingles with the stars.

When on my goodly charger borne
   Thro' dreaming towns I go,
The cock crows ere the Christmas morn,
   The streets are dumb with snow.

The tempest crackles on the leads,
    And, ringing, springs from brand and mail;
But o'er the dark a glory spreads,
    And gilds the driving hail.
I leave the plain, I climb the height;
    No branchy thicket shelter yields;
But blessed forms in whistling storms
    Fly o'er waste fens and windy fields.

A maiden knight—to me is given
    Such hope, I know not fear;
I yearn to breathe the airs of heaven
    That often meet me here.
I muse on joy that will not cease,
    Pure spaces clothed in living beams,
Pure lilies of eternal peace,
    Whose odours haunt my dreams;
And, stricken by an angel's hand,
    This mortal armour that I wear,
This weight and size, this heart and eyes,
    Are touch'd, are turn'd to finest air.

The clouds are broken in the sky,
    And thro' the mountain-walls
A rolling organ-harmony
    Swells up, and shakes and falls.
Then move the trees, the copses nod,
    Wings flutter, voices hover clear:
"O just and faithful knight of God!
    Ride on! the prize is near."
So pass I hostel, hall, and grange;
    By bridge and ford, by park and pale,
All-arm'd I ride, whate'er betide,
    Until I find the holy Grail.

                    —ALFRED, LORD TENNYSON

Beth Gêlert

The spearmen heard the bugle sound,
    And cheerily smiled the morn;
And many a brach, and many a hound
    Obeyed Llewellyn's horn.

And still he blew a louder blast,
    And gave a lustier cheer,
"Come, Gêlert, come, wert never last
    Llewellyn's horn to hear.

"O where does faithful Gêlert roam
    The flower of all his race;
So true, so brave—a lamb at home,
    A lion in the chase?"

In sooth, he was a peerless hound,
    The gift of royal John;
But now no Gêlert could be found,
    And all the chase rode on.

That day Llewellyn little loved
    The chase of hart and hare;
And scant and small the booty proved,
    For Gêlert was not there.

Unpleased, Llewellyn homeward hied,
    When, near the portal seat,
His truant Gêlert he espied
    Bounding his lord to greet.

But when he gained the castle-door,
    Aghast the chieftain stood;
The hound all o'er was smeared with gore;
    His lips, his fangs, ran blood.

Llewellyn gazed with fierce surprise;
    Unused such looks to meet,
His favorite checked his joyful guise,
    And crouched, and licked his feet.

Onward, in haste, Llewellyn passed,
    And on went Gêlert too;
And still, where'er his eyes he cast,
    Fresh blood-gouts shocked his view.

O'erturned his infant's bed he found,
    With blood-stained covert rent;
And all around the walls and ground
    With recent blood besprent.

He called his child—no voice replied—
    He searched with terror wild;
Blood, blood he found on every side,
    But nowhere found his child.

"Hell-hound! my child's by thee devoured,"
    The frantic father cried;
And to the hilt his vengeful sword
    He plunged in Gêlert's side.

Aroused by Gêlert's dying yell,
    Some slumberer wakened nigh;
What words the parent's joy could tell
    To hear his infant's cry!

Concealed beneath a tumbled heap
    His hurried search had missed,
All glowing from his rosy sleep
    The cherub boy he kissed.

Nor scathe[1] had he, nor harm, nor dread,
    But, the same couch beneath,

---
[1] Scathe: injury.

Lay a gaunt wolf, all torn and dead,
  Tremendous still in death.

Ah, what was then Llewellyn's pain!
  For now the truth was clear;
His gallant hound the wolf had slain
  To save Llewellyn's heir.

                    —WILLIAM ROBERT SPENCER

Spanish Waters

Spanish waters, Spanish waters, you are ringing in my ears,
Like a slow sweet piece of music from the grey forgotten
    years;
Telling tales, and beating tunes, and bringing weary thoughts
    to me
Of the sandy beach at Muertos, where I would that I could
    be.

There's a surf breaks on Los Muertos, and it never stops to
    roar,
And it's there we came to anchor, and it's there we went
    ashore,
Where the blue lagoon is silent amid snags of rotting trees,
Dropping like the clothes of corpses cast up by the seas.

We anchored at Los Muertos when the dipping sun was red,
We left her half-a-mile to sea, to west of Nigger Head;
And before the mist was on the Cay, before the day was done,
We were all ashore on Muertos with the gold that we had
    won.

We bore it through the marshes in a half-score battered
    chests,
Sinking, in the sucking quagmires, to the sunburn on our
    breasts,

Heaving over tree-trunks, gasping, damning at the flies and
heat,
Longing for a long drink, out of silver, in the ship's cool
lazareet.[1]

The moon came white and ghostly as we laid the treasure
down,
There was gear there'd make a beggarman as rich as Lima
Town,
Copper charms and silver trinkets from the chests of Spanish
crews,
Gold doubloons and double moydores, louis d'ors and porta-
gues,[2]

Clumsy yellow-metal earrings from the Indians of Brazil,
Uncut emeralds out of Rio, bezoar stones from Guayaquil;
Silver, in the crude and fashioned, pots of old Arica bronze,
Jewels from the bones of Incas desecrated by the Dons.

We smoothed the place with mattocks, and we took and
blazed the tree,
Which marks yon where the gear is hid that none will ever
see,
And we laid aboard the ship again, and south away we steers,
Through the loud surf of Los Muertos which is beating in my
ears.

I'm the last alive that knows it. All the rest have gone their
ways,
Killed, or died, or come to anchor in the old Mulatas Cays,
And I go singing, fiddling, old and starved and in despair,
And I know where all that gold is hid, if I were only there.

It's not the way to end it all. I'm old, and nearly blind,
And an old man's past's a strange thing, for it never leaves
his mind.

---

[1] Lazareet, or lazarette: a space between decks.
[2] Doubloons, moydores, louis d'ors, portagues: gold coins.

And I see in dreams, awhiles, the beach, the sun's disc
    dipping red,
And the tall ship, under topsails, swaying in past Nigger
    Head.

I'd be glad to step ashore there. Glad to take a pick and go
To the lone blazed coco-palm tree in the place no others
    know,
And lift the gold and silver that has mouldered there for
    years
By the loud surf of Los Muertos which is beating in my ears.

               —JOHN MASEFIELD

              📖

"A Ballad of a Nun" is based on a legend which
has been retold in different ways by authors of
various nations. The Swiss novelist, Gottfried Keller,
entitled his version "The Statue and the Nun" and
enlarged the romantic element of the story. Maurice
Maeterlinck, the Belgian dramatist, embroidered the
tale in his colorful "Sister Beatrice." The German pro-
ducer, Max Reinhardt, expanded the plot into a
theatrical spectacle, "The Miracle," in which the story
had been rearranged by Karl Vollmöller, with music
by Engelbert Humperdinck, composer of "Hansel
and Gretel." It remained for an English poet of the
late nineteenth century to give it a form which is
both lyrical and dramatic.

              📖

A Ballad of a Nun

From Eastertide to Eastertide
    For ten long years her patient knees
Engraved the stones—the fittest bride
    Of Christ in all the diocese.

She conquered every earthly lust;
  The abbess loved her more and more;
And, as a mark of perfect trust,
  Made her the keeper of the door.

High on a hill the convent hung,
  Across a duchy looking down,
Where everlasting mountains flung
  Their shadows over tower and town.

The jewels of their lofty snows
  In constellations flashed at night;
Above their crests the moon arose;
  The deep earth shuddered with delight.

Long ere she left her cloudy bed,
  Still dreaming in the orient land,
On many a mountain's happy head
  Dawn lightly laid her rosy hand.

The adventurous sun took heaven by storm;
  Clouds scattered largesses of rain;
The sounding cities, rich and warm,
  Smouldered and glittered in the plain.

Sometimes it was a wandering wind,
  Sometimes the fragrance of the pine,
Sometimes the thought how others sinned,
  That turned her sweet blood into wine.

Sometimes she heard a serenade
  Complaining sweetly far away.
She said, "A young man woos a maid";
  And dreamt of love till break of day.

Then would she ply her knotted scourge
  Until she swooned; but evermore

She had the same red sin to purge,
  Poor, passionate keeper of the door!

For still night's starry scroll unfurled,
  And still the day came like a flood:
It was the greatness of the world
  That made her long to use her blood.

In winter-time when Lent drew nigh,
  And hill and plain were wrapped in snow,
She watched beneath the frosty sky
  The nearest city nightly glow.

Like peals of airy bells outworn
  Faint laughter died above her head
In gusts of broken music borne:
  "They keep the Carnival," she said.

Her hungry heart devoured the town:
  "Heaven save me by a miracle!
Unless God sends an angel down,
  Thither I go though it were Hell."

She dug her nails deep in her breast,
  Sobbed, shrieked, and straight withdrew the bar:
A fledgling flying from the nest,
  A pale moth rushing to a star.

Fillet and veil in strips she tore;
  Her golden tresses floated wide;
The ring and bracelet that she wore
  As Christ's betrothed, she cast aside.

"Life's dearest meaning I shall probe;
  Lo! I shall taste of love at last!
Away!" She doffed her outer robe,
  And sent it sailing down the blast.

Her body seemed to warm the wind;
    With bleeding feet o'er ice she ran:
"I leave the righteous God behind;
    I go to worship sinful man."

She reached the sounding city's gate;
    No question did the warder ask:
He passed her in: "Welcome, wild mate!"
    He thought her some fantastic mask.

Half-naked through the town she went;
    Each footstep left a bloody mark;
Crowds followed her with looks intent;
    Her bright eyes made the torches dark.

Alone and watching in the street
    There stood a grave youth nobly dressed;
To him she knelt and kissed his feet;
    Her face her great desire confessed.

He healed her bosom with a kiss;
    She gave him all her passion's hoard;
And sobbed and murmured ever, "This
    Is life's great meaning, dear, my lord.

"I care not for my broken vow;
    Though God should come in thunder soon,
I am sister to the mountains now,
    And sister to the sun and moon."

Through all the towns of Belmarie
    She made a progress like a queen.
"She is," they said, "whate'er she be,
    The strangest woman ever seen.

"From fairyland she must have come,
    Or else she is a mermaiden."

Some said she was a ghoul, and some
　A heathen goddess born again.

But soon her fire to ashes burned;
　Her beauty changed to haggardness;
Her golden hair to silver turned;
　The hour came of her last caress.

At midnight from her lonely bed
　She rose, and said, "I have had my will."
The old ragged robe she donned, and fled
　Back to the convent on the hill.

Half-naked as she went before,
　She hurried to the city wall,
Unnoticed in the rush and roar
　And splendour of the Carnival.

No question did the warder ask:
　Her ragged robe, her shrunken limb,
Her dreadful eyes! "It is no mask;
　It is a she-wolf, gaunt and grim!"

She ran across the icy plain;
　Her worn blood curdled in the blast;
Each footstep left a crimson stain;
　The white-faced moon looked on aghast.

She said between her chattering jaws,
　"Deep peace is mine; I cease to strive.
Oh, comfortable convent laws
　That bury foolish nuns alive!

"A trowel for my passing-bell,
　A little bed within the wall,
A coverlet of stones—how well
　I there shall keep the Carnival!"

Like tired bells chiming in their sleep,
　　The wind faint peals of laughter bore;
She stopped her ears and climbed the steep,
　　And thundered at the convent door.

It opened straight; she entered in,
　　And at the wardress' feet fell prone:
"I come to purge away my sin.
　　Bury me; close me up in stone."

The wardress raised her tenderly;
　　She touched her wet and fast-shut eyes.
"Look, sister; sister, look at me.
　　Look, can you see through my disguise?"

She looked and saw her own sad face,
　　And trembled, wondering, "Who art thou?"
"God sent me down to fill your place:
　　I am the Virgin Mary now."

And with the word, God's mother shone.
　　The wanderer whispered, "Mary, hail!"
The vision helped her to put on
　　Bracelet and fillet, ring and veil.

"You are sister to the mountains now,
　　And sister to the day and night:
Sister to God." And on the brow
　　She kissed her thrice, and left her sight.

While dreaming in her cloudy bed,
　　Far in the crimson orient land,
On many a mountain's happy head
　　Dawn lightly laid her rosy hand.

　　　　　　　　　　　　　—JOHN DAVIDSON

BALLADS OF LONG AGO

Unlike the court poets whose songs glorified their lords and masters, the ballad-makers spoke the language of the common folk. Words and music were often accompanied by choral dancing so that the ballad became a communal affair. The soloist would start his song-story about a romance or a gory incident, and the audience would join in. Later, another singer would add improvisations of his own, the original story would accumulate new details, the locale would be changed—and what started as the creation of an individual became the expression of a community.

Many of the ballads were already old in the fourteenth century. *The Vision of Piers Plowman,* written in about 1370, refers satirically to the prevalence of ballads about Robin Hood. Many of the earliest English ballads came down from the hills of Scotland and were adapted to fit different scenes and situations. Some of them found their way to America, where they acquired local flavor and wide popularity. They took root everywhere—along the seacoast of Maine and the Carolina backwoods, as well as the Ozark Mountains and the hills of Kentucky. The transformations were astonishing; in the single state of Virginia ballad-hunters found ninety-two variants of "Barbara Allen." Although the forms may differ, the substance is the same. The old ballads persist because, in their very simplicity, they have the stuff of permanence.

In the versions that follow many of the more archaic words and spellings have been modernized.

Fair Margaret and Sweet William

As it fell out on a long summer's day,
   Two lovers they sat on a hill:
They sat together that long summer's day,
   And could not talk their fill.

"I'm not the man for you, Margaret;
   You're not the wife for me.
Before tomorrow at eight of the clock,
   A rich wedding you shall see."

Fair Margaret sat in her bower-window
   Combing her yellow hair,
She saw Sweet William and his brown bride
   Unto the church draw near.

Then down she laid her ivory comb,
   And up she bound her hair;
She went out from her bower alive,
   But alive nevermore came there.

When day was gone, and night was come,
   And all men fast asleep,
Came in the ghost of Fair Margaret,
   And stood at William's feet.

"How like ye the lady, Sweet William,
   That lies in your arms asleep?

God give you joy of your gay bride-bed,
    And me of my winding-sheet!"

When night was gone and day was come
    And all men waked from sleep,
Sweet William to his lady said,
    "Alas! I have cause to weep.

"I dreamed a dream, my lady,
    A dream that bodes no good;
I dreamed our bower was full of red swine
    And our bride-bed full of blood."

He callèd up his merry men all,
    By one, by two, by three,
Saying, "I'll away to Fair Margaret's bower,
    With the leave of my ladye."

And when he came to Fair Margaret's bower
    He knockèd at the ring;
And who so ready as her seven brothers
    To rise and let him in?

"O, is she in the parlor?" he said,
    "Or is she in the hall?
Or is she in the long chamber
    Amongst her merry maids all?"

"No, she's not in the parlor," they said,
    "Nor she's not in the hall:
But she is in the long chamber,
    Laid out against the wall."

He turnèd up the covering-sheet,
    And look'd upon the dead.
"Methinks her lips are pale and wan,
    She has lost her cherry red.

"I would do more for thee, Margaret,
  Than would any of thy kin:
And I will kiss thy pale, cold lips
  Though thy smile I cannot win."

With that bespake the seven brothers,
  Making a piteous moan:
"You may go kiss your jolly brown bride,
  And let our sister alone."

"If I do kiss my jolly brown bride,
  I do but what is right;
For I made no vow to your sister dear,
  By day nor yet by night.

"Deal on, deal on, my merry men all,
  Deal on your cake and wine!
For whatever is dealt at her funeral today
  Shalt be dealt tomorrow at mine."

Fair Margaret died on the over-night,
  Sweet William died on the morrow.
Fair Margaret died for pure, pure love;
  Sweet William died for sorrow.

Margaret was buried in the lower chancel,
  Sweet William in the higher;
Out of her breast there sprang a rose-tree,
  Out of his breast a briar.

AUTHOR UNKNOWN

The Two Sisters of Binnorie

There were two sisters sat in a bower;
  Binnorie, O Binnorie;
There came a knight to be their wooer;
  By the bonny mill-dams of Binnorie.

He courted the eldest with gloves and rings,
But he loved the youngest above all things.

The eldest was vexèd to despair,
And much she envied her sister fair.

The eldest said to the youngest one,
"Will ye see our father's ships come in?"

She's taken her by the lily-white hand,
And led her down to the river strand.

The youngest stood upon a stone;
The eldest came and pushed her in.

"O sister, sister, reach your hand,
And you shall be heir of half my land.

"O sister, reach me but your glove
And sweet William shall be all your love."

"Sink on, nor hope for hand or glove!
Sweet William shall surely be my love."

Sometimes she sank, sometimes she swam,
Until she came to the mouth of the dam.

Out then came the miller's son
And saw the fair maid swimming in.

"O father, father, draw your dam!
Here's either a mermaid or a swan."

The miller hasted and drew his dam,
And there he found a drowned womàn.

You could not see her middle small,
Her girdle was so rich withal.

You could not see her yellow hair
For the gold and pearls that clustered there.

And by there came a harper fine
Who harped to nobles when they dine.

And when he looked that lady on,
He sighed and made a heavy moan.

He's made a harp of her breast bone,
Whose sounds would melt a heart of stone.

He's taken three locks of her yellow hair
And with them strung his harp so rare.

He went into her father's hall
To play his harp before them all.

But as he laid it on a stone,
The harp began to play alone.

And soon the harp sang loud and clear,
"Farewell, my father and mother dear.

Farewell, farewell, my brother Hugh,
Farewell, my William, sweet and true."

And then as plain as plain could be,
   (*Binnorie, O Binnorie*)
"There sits my sister who drownèd me
   By the bonny mill-dams of Binnorie!"

AUTHOR UNKNOWN

Lord Randal

"O where have you been, Lord Randal, my son?
O where have you been, my handsome young man?"—
   "I have been to the wild wood; mother, make my bed soon,
   For I'm weary with hunting, and fain would lie down."

"Who gave you your dinner, Lord Randal, my son?
Who gave you your dinner, my handsome young man?"—
   "I dined with my sweetheart; mother, make my bed soon,
   For I'm weary with hunting, and fain would lie down."

"What had you for dinner, Lord Randal, my son?
What had you for dinner, my handsome young man?"—
   "I had eels boiled in broth; mother, make my bed soon,
   For I'm weary with hunting, and fain would lie down."

"And where are your bloodhounds, Lord Randal, my son?
And where are your bloodhounds, my handsome young
      man?"—
   "O they swelled and they died; mother, make my bed soon,
   For I'm weary with hunting, and fain would lie down."

"O I fear you are poisoned, Lord Randal, my son!
O I fear you are poisoned, my handsome young man!"—
   "O yes! I am poisoned; mother, make my bed soon,
   For I'm sick at the heart, and I fain would lie down."

AUTHOR UNKNOWN

Johnnie Armstrong

There dwelt a man in fair Westmoreland,
   Johnnie Armstrong men did him call;
He had neither land nor rents coming in,
   Yet he kept eight score men in his hall.

He had horse and harness for them all,
    Fine steeds all milky white;
The golden bands about their necks,
    And their weapons, were all alike.

News was then brought unto the king,
    That there was such a one as he,
That he lived free as a bold outlaw
    And robbed all the north countree.

The king he wrote a letter then,
    He wrote it large and long;
He signed it with his royal hand
    And promised to do him no wrong.

When this letter came to Johnnie,
    His heart was blithe as birds on the tree.
"Never was an Armstrong sent for by the king;
    Not my father, my grandfather, nor none but me.

"And if we go before the king,
    We must go right orderly;
Each man of you shall have his scarlet coat,
    Laced with silver laces three.

"Each one shall have his velvet coat,
    Laced with silver lace so white,
With the golden bands about your necks,
    Black hats and white feathers alike."

By the morrow morning at ten of the clock
    To Edinburgh gone was he;
And with him all of his eight score men—
    A goodly sight for to see!

When Johnnie came before the king
    He sank down on his knee;

"O pardon, my sovereign liege," he cried.
  "Pardon my eight score men and me."

"Thou shalt have no pardon, thou traitor bold,
  Not thy eight score men nor thee;
Tomorrow morning at ten of the clock
  Thou shalt all hang on the gallows tree."

Johnnie looked over his left shoulder,
  And a grievous look looked he;
Saying, "Asking grace of a graceless face—
  Why there is none for you nor me."

Saying, "Fight on, fight on, my merry men,
  And see that none of you be ta'en;
For rather than men shall say we were hanged,
  Let them say how we were slain."

Then like a madman Johnnie laid about,
  Like a madman then fought he,
Until a coward Scot came at Johnnie behind
  And ran him through his fair bodie.

Johnnie cried, "Fight on, my merry men all,
  And see that none of you be ta'en.
I'll lie me down to bleed for a while,
  Then I'll rise and fight again."

AUTHOR UNKNOWN

True Thomas

True Thomas lay on Huntlie bank;
  A marvel he did see;
For there he saw a lady bright,
  Come riding down by the Eildon tree.[1]

---

[1] The Eildon tree was the tree of magic under which Thomas the Rhymer delivered prophecies.

Her skirt was of the grass-green silk,
    Her mantle of the velvet fine;
On every lock of her horse's mane,
    Hung fifty silver bells and nine.

True Thomas he pulled off his cap,
    And bowed low down on his knee;
"All hail, thou mighty Queen of Heaven!
    For thy peer on earth could never be."

"O no, O no, Thomas," she said,
    "That name does not belong to me;
I'm but the Queen of fair Elfland,
    That hither am come to visit thee.

"Harp and carp,[1] Thomas," she said,
    "Harp and carp along with me;
And if ye dare to kiss my lips,
    Sure of your body I will be!"

"Betide me weal, betide me woe,
    That threat shall never frighten me!"
Then he has kissed her on the lips,
    All underneath the Eildon tree.

"Now ye must go with me," she said,
    "True Thomas, ye must go with me;
And ye must serve me seven years,
    Through weal or woe as may chance to be."

She's mounted on her milk-white steed,
    She's taken True Thomas up behind;
And aye, whene'er her bridle rang,
    The steed flew swifter than the wind.

O they rode on, and farther on,
    The steed flew swifter than the wind;

---

[1] Harp and carp: play and talk lightly.

Until they reached a desert wide,
    And living land was left behind.

"Light down, light down now, Thomas," she said,
    "And lean your head upon my knee;
Light down, and rest a little space,
    And I will show you marvels three.

"O see ye not yon narrow road,
    So thick beset with thorns and briers?
That is the path of righteousness,
    Though after it but few enquires.

"And see ye not yon broad, broad road,
    That stretches o'er the lily leven?[a]
That is the path of wickedness,
    Though some call it the road to heaven.

"And see ye not yon bonny road,
    That winds about the green hillside?
That is the way to fair Elfland,
    Where you and I this night must bide.

"But, Thomas, ye shall hold your tongue,
    Whatever ye may hear or see;
For if ye speak word in Elfin land,
    Ye'll ne'er win back to your own countree!"

O they rode on, and farther on;
    They waded through rivers above the knee,
And they saw neither sun nor moon,
    But they heard the roaring of a sea.

It was mirk, mirk night; there was no star-light;
    They waded through red blood to the knee;
For all the blood that's shed on earth,
    Runs through the springs o' that countree.

[a] Lily leven: lovely lawn.

At last they came to a garden green,
   And she pulled an apple from on high—
"Take this for thy wages, True Thomas;
   It will give thee the tongue that can never lie!"

"My tongue is my own," True Thomas he said,
   "A goodly gift ye would give to me!
I neither could to buy or sell
   At fair or tryst where I may be.

"I could neither speak to prince or peer,
   Nor ask of grace from fair ladye."
"Now hold thy peace!" the lady said,
   "For as I say, so must it be."

He has gotten a coat of the even cloth,
   And a pair of shoes of the velvet green;
And till seven years were gone and past,
   True Thomas on earth was never seen.

                            AUTHOR UNKNOWN

Barbara Allen's Cruelty

All in the merry month of May,
   When green buds they were swelling,
Young Jemmy Grove on his death-bed lay
   For love of Barbara Allen.

He sent his man unto her then,
   To the town where she was dwelling:
"O haste and come to my master dear,
   If your name be Barbara Allen."

Slowly, slowly she rose up,
   And she came where he was lying;
And when she drew the curtain by,
   Says, "Young man, I think you're dying."

"O it's I am sick, and very, very sick,
    And it's all for Barbara Allen."
"O the better for me you'll never be,
    Tho' your heart's blood were a-spilling!

"O do you not mind, young man," she says,
    "When the red wine you were filling,
That you made the healths go round and round,
    And slighted Barbara Allen?"

He turned his face unto the wall,
    And death with him was dealing:
"Adieu, adieu, my dear friends all;
    Be kind to Barbara Allen."

As she was walking o'er the fields,
    She heard the dead-bell knelling;
And every toll the dead-bell struck,
    Cried, "Woe to Barbara Allen!"

"O mother, mother, make my bed,
    To lay me down in sorrow.
My love has died for me today,
    I'll die for him tomorrow."

                                        AUTHOR UNKNOWN

Edward, Edward

"Why does your sword so drip with blood,
            Edward, Edward?
Why does your sword so drip with blood,
    And why so sad are ye, O?"
"O I have killed my hawk so good,
            Mother, mother,
O I have killed my hawk so good
    And I had no more but he, O."

"Your hawk's blood was never so red,
      Edward, Edward,
Your hawk's blood was never so red,
   My dear son, I tell thee, O."
"O I have killed my red-roan steed,
      Mother, mother,
O I have killed my red-roan steed,
   That was so fair and free, O."

"Your steed was old and your stable's filled,
      Edward, Edward,
Your steed was old and your stable's filled,
   Now say what may it be, O."
"It was my father that I killed,
      Mother, mother,
It was my father that I killed,
   Alas, and woe is me, O."

"What penance will ye do for that,
      Edward, Edward?
What penance will ye do for that,
   My dear son, now tell me, O?"
"I'll set my feet in yonder boat,
      Mother, mother,
I'll set my feet in yonder boat,
   And I'll fare over the sea, O."

"What will ye do with your towers and hall,
      Edward, Edward?
What will ye do with your towers and hall,
   That are so fair to see, O?"
"I'll let them stand till down they fall,
      Mother, mother,
I'll let them stand till down they fall,
   For here nevermore may I be, O."

"What will ye leave to your babes and your wife,
    Edward, Edward?
What will ye leave to your babes and your wife,
    When ye go over the sea, O?"
"The world's room—let them beg through life,
        Mother, mother,
The world's room—let them beg through life,
    For them nevermore will I see, O."

"And what will ye leave to your own mother dear,
        Edward, Edward?
And what will ye leave to your own mother dear,
    My dear son, now tell me, O?"
"The curse of Hell from me shall ye bear,
        Mother, mother,
The curse of Hell from me shall ye bear:
    Such counsel ye gave to me, O!"

AUTHOR UNKNOWN

Sir Patrick Spens

The king sits in Dunfermling town
    Drinking the blude-red wine;
"O where will I get a gude skipper
    To sail this ship o' mine?"

O up and spake an eldern knight,
    Sat at the king's right knee:
"Sir Patrick Spens is the best sailor
    That ever sail'd the sea."

Our king has written a letter,
    And seal'd it with his hand,
And sent it to Sir Patrick Spens,
    Was walking on the strand.

"To Noroway, to Noroway,
   To Noroway o'er the faem;
The king's daughter o' Noroway,
   'Tis thou must bring her hame."

The first word that Sir Patrick read,
   A loud laugh laughèd he;
The next word that Sir Patrick read,
   The tear blinded his e'e.

"O who is this has done this deed
   This ill deed unto me,
To send us out, at this time o' year,
   To sail upon the sea?

"Be it wind, be it weet, be it hail, be it sleet,
   Our ship must sail the faem;
The king's daughter o' Noroway,
   'Tis we must fetch her hame.

"Make haste, make haste, my merry men all;
   Our gude ship sails the morn."—
"Now ever alack, my master dear,
   I fear a deadly storm.

"Late, late yestreen I saw the new moone
   Wi' the auld moone in her arm;
And I fear, I fear, my master dear,
   That we will come to harm."

They hadna sail'd a league, a league,
   A league but barely three,
When the sky grew dark, and the wind blew loud,
   And angry grew the sea.

The anchors broke, the topmast split,
   It was sic a deadly storm:

And the waves came owre the broken ship
   Till a' her sides were torn.

O loath, loath, were our gude Scots lords
   To wet their cork-heel'd shoon;
But lang or a' the play was play'd
   Their hats they swam aboon.[1]

O lang, lang may the ladies sit,
   Wi' their fans into their hand,
Before they see Sir Patrick Spens
   Come sailing to the strand.

And lang, lang may the maidens sit
   Wi' their gold kames in their hair,
A-waiting for their ain dear loves,
   For them they'll see nae mair.

Half-owre, half-owre to Aberdour,
   'Tis fifty fathoms deep;
And there lies gude Sir Patrick Spens,
   Wi' the Scots lords at his feet.

AUTHOR UNKNOWN

"The Golden Vanity" is another ballad of betrayal which has accumulated many titles and countless changes since it was first printed in the seventeenth century. "Sir Walter Raleigh Sailing in the Lowlands," "The Lowlands Low," and "The Sweet Trinity" are three of the favored titles, while the enemy vessel varies from French to Spanish or even Turkish, as in the present version. Sailors used to sing it as a sea chanty.

[1] Their hats swam above their heads.

The Golden Vanity

There was a gallant ship, a gallant ship was she,
And the name of the ship was "The Golden Vanity,"
And they feared she would be taken by the Turkish enemy
   As she sailed upon the Lowland, Lowland, Lowland,
   As she sailed upon the Lowland sea.

Then up came a little cabin boy, and thus spoke he,
Speaking to the captain, "What will you give to me
If I swim alongside of the Turkish enemy
   And sink her in the Lowland, Lowland, Lowland,
   And sink her in the Lowland sea?"

"I'll give you an estate in the North Countrie,
And my one and only daughter your lovely bride shall be,
If you'll swim alongside of the Turkish enemy
   And sink her in the Lowland, Lowland, Lowland,
   And sink her in the Lowland sea."

Then the boy made ready and overboard sprang he,
And swam alongside of the Turkish enemy,
And with his auger sharp in her side he bored holes three,
   And he sunk her in the Lowland, Lowland, Lowland,
   He sunk her in the Lowland sea.

Then the boy swam around, and back again swam he,
And he called to the captain of "The Golden Vanity."
But the captain mocked, "You can drown for all of me!"
   And he left him in the Lowland, Lowland, Lowland,
   He left him in the Lowland sea.

The boy swam around, he came to the port side,
He looked up at his messmates, and bitterly he cried:
"Oh, messmates, take me up, for I'm drifting with the tide,
   And I'm sinking in the Lowland, Lowland, Lowland,
   I'm sinking in the Lowland sea."

His messmates took him up, but on the deck he died,
And they sewed him in a hammock that was so large and
    wide.
They lowered him overboard, but he drifted with the tide,
    And he sank beneath the Lowland, Lowland, Lowland,
    He sank beneath the Lowland sea.

AUTHOR UNKNOWN

The Douglas Tragedy

"Rise up, rise up, Lord Douglas!" she says,
    "And put on your armor so bright;
Let it ne'er be said that a daughter of ours
    Was married to a lord under night.

"Rise up, rise up, my seven bold sons,
    And put on your armor so bright;
And take better care of your youngest sister,
    For your eldest's away this night!"

Lady Margret was on a milk-white steed,
    Lord William was on a gray,
A buglet-horn hung down by his side,
    And swiftly they rode away.

Lord William looked over his left shoulder
    To see what he could see,
And there he spied her seven bold brothers
    Come riding over the lea.

"Light down, light down, Lady Margret," he said,
    "And hold my steed in your hand,
Until that against your seven bold brothers,
    And your father, I make a stand."

O, there she stood, and bitter she stood,
    And never shed one tear,

Until she saw her brothers fall,
  And her father who loved her so dear.

"O hold your hand, Lord William!" she said,
  "For your strokes are deep and sore;
Though lovers I can get many a one,
  A father I can never get more."

O she's taken off her handkerchief,
  It was of the holland so fine,
And aye she dressed her father's wounds;
  His blood ran down like wine.

"O choose, O choose, Lady Margret,
  Will ye go with me, or bide?"
"I'll go, I'll go, Lord William," she said.
  "Ye've left me no other guide."

He lifted her up on her milk-white steed,
  And mounted his dapple-gray,
With his buglet-horn hung down by his side,
  And slowly they rode away.

O they rode on, and on they rode,
  And all by the light of the moon,
Until they came to a wan water,
  And there they lighted down.

They lighted down to take a drink
  Of the spring that ran so clear,
But down the stream ran his red heart's blood,
  And she began to fear.

"Hold up, hold up, Lord William," she said,
  "I fear me you are slain!"
" 'Tis but the shadow of my scarlet cloak
  That shines in the water so plain."

O they rode on, and on they rode,
   And all by the light of the moon,
Until they saw his mother's hall,
   And there they lighted down.

"Get up, get up, lady mother," he says,
   "Get up, and let in your son!
Open the door, lady mother," he says,
   "For this night my fair lady I've won!

"Now make my bed, lady mother," he says,
   "O make it wide and deep,
And lay Lady Margret close at my back,
   And the sounder will I sleep!"

Lord William was dead long ere midnight,
   Lady Margret long ere day;
And all true lovers that go together
   May they have more luck than they!

Lord William was buried in Mary's Kirk,
   Lady Margret in Mary's Choir;
And out of her grave grew a bonny red rose,
   And out of the knight's a briar.

The briar twined about the rose,
   And the rose clung to the briar,
And so they grew ever closer together,
   As all true lovers desire.

AUTHOR UNKNOWN

The Demon Lover

"Oh, where have you been, my long, long love,
   This long seven years and more?"
"Oh, I've come to seek my former vows
   Ye granted me before."

"Oh, do not speak of your former vows,
   For they will breed sad strife;
Oh, do not speak of your former vows,
   For I have become a wife."

He turned him right and round about,
   And the tear blinded his ee:
"I would never have trodden on this ground
   If it had not been for thee."

"If I was to leave my husband dear,
   And my two babes also,
Oh, what have you to take me to,
   If with you I should go?"

"I have seven ships upon the sea—
   The eighth brought me to land—
With four-and-twenty bold mariners,
   And music on every hand."

She has taken up her two little babes,
   Kissed them on cheek and chin:
"Oh, fare ye well, my own two babes,
   For I'll never see you again."

She set her foot upon the ship—
   No mariners could she behold;
But the sails were of the taffeta,
   And the masts of the beaten gold.

She had not sailed a league, a league,
   A league but barely three,
When dismal grew his countenance,
   And drumlie[1] grew his ee.

They had not sailed a league, a league,
   A league but barely three,

---

[1] Drumlie: dark.

Until she espied his cloven foot,
    And she wept right bitterly.

"Oh, hold your tongue of your weeping," said he,
    "Of your weeping now let me be;
I will show you how the lilies grow
    On the banks of Italy."

"Oh, what hills are yon, yon pleasant hills,
    That the sun shines sweetly on?"
"Oh, yon are the hills of heaven," he said,
    "Where you will never win."

"Oh, whaten a mountain is yon," she said,
    "So dreary with frost and snow?"
"Oh, yon is the mountain of hell," he cried,
    "Where you and I will go."

He struck the top-mast with his hand,
    The fore-mast with his knee;
And he broke that gallant ship in twain,
    And sank her in the sea.

AUTHOR UNKNOWN

No hero has been celebrated more often in song than the fabulous Robin Hood. In Francis James Child's standard collection, *English and Scottish Popular Ballads,* almost forty ballads are devoted to the exploits of the reckless outlaw and his band of merry men. Many of the stories have been transplanted to America; the following has been heard in one form or another in almost every corner of the country.

Robin Hood and the Widow's Three Sons

There are twelve months in all the year,
  As I hear many men say,
But the merriest month in all the year
  Is the merry month of May.

Now Robin Hood is to Nottingham gone,
  With a link a down and a day,
And there he met a silly old woman,
  Was weeping on the way.

"What news? what news, thou silly old woman?
  What news hast thou for me?"
Said she, "There's three squires in Nottingham town
  To-day is condemn'd to die."

"O have they parishes burnt?" he said,
  "Or have they ministers slain?
Or have they robb'd any virgin,
  Or other men's wives have ta'en?"

"They have no parishes burnt, good sir,
  Nor yet have ministers slain,
Nor have they robbed any virgin,
  Nor other men's wives have ta'en."

"O what have they done?" said bold Robin Hood,
  "I pray thee tell to me."
"It's for slaying of the King's fallow deer,
  Bearing their long bows with thee."

Now Robin Hood is to Nottingham gone,
  With a link a down and a day,
And there he met with a silly old palmer,
  Was walking along the highway.

"What news? what news, thou silly old man?
　　What news, I do thee pray?"
Said he, "Three squires in Nottingham town
　　Are condemned to die this day."

"Come change thy apparel with me, old man,
　　Come change thy apparel for mine.
Here is forty shillings in good silver;
　　Go drink it in beer or wine."

"O thine apparel is good," he said,
　　"And mine is ragged and torn;
Wherever you go, wherever you ride,
　　Laugh ne'er an old man to scorn."

"Come change thy apparel with me, old churl,
　　Come change thy apparel with mine.
Here are twenty pieces of good broad gold;
　　Go feast thy brethren with wine."

Then he put on the old man's cloak,
　　Was patch'd black, blue, and red;
He thought no shame, all the day long,
　　To wear the bags of bread.

Then he put on the old man's hose,
　　Were patch'd from knee to wrist;
"By the truth of my body," said bold Robin Hood,
　　"I'd laugh if I had any list."[1]

Then he put on the old man's shoes,
　　Were patch'd both beneath and aboon;
Then Robin Hood swore a solemn oath,
　　"It's good habit that makes a man!"

Now Robin Hood is to Nottingham gone,
　　With a link a down and a down,

---

[1] List: desire for it.

And there he met with the proud Sheriff,
    Was walking along the town.

"O save, O save, O Sheriff," he said,
    "O save, and you may see!
And what will you give to a silly old man
    To-day will your hangman be?"

"Some suits, some suits," the Sheriff he said,
    "Some suits I'll give to thee;
Some suits, some suits, and pence thirteen
    To-day's a hangman's fee."

Then Robin he turns him round about,
    And jumps from stock to stone;
"By the truth of my body," the Sheriff he said,
    "That's well jumpt, thou nimble old man."

"I was ne'er a hangman in all my life,
    Nor yet intends to trade;
But curst be he," said bold Robin,
    "That first a hangman was made!"

"I've a bag for meal, and a bag for malt,
    And a bag for barley and corn;
A bag for bread, and a bag for beef,
    And a bag for my little small horn."

"I have a horn in my pocket,
    I got it from Robin Hood,
And still when I set it to my mouth,
    For thee it blows little good."

"O wind thy horn, thou proud fellow,
    Of thee I have no doubt;
I wish that thou give such a blast
    Till both thy eyes fall out."

The first loud blast that he did blow,
   He blew both loud and shrill;
A hundred and fifty of Robin Hood's men
   Came riding over the hill.

The next loud blast that he did give,
   He blew both loud and amain;
And quickly sixty of Robin Hood's men
   Came shining over the plain.

"O who are yon," the Sheriff he said,
   "Come tripping over the lea?"
"They're my attendants," brave Robin did say,
   "They'll pay a visit to thee."

They took the gallows from the dale,
   They set it in the glen,
They hang'd the proud Sheriff on that,
   And releas'd their own three men.

AUTHOR UNKNOWN

May Colvin

False Sir John a-wooing came,
   To a maid of beauty rare;
May Colvin was the lady's name,
   Her father's only heir.

He wooed her indoors, he wooed her out,
   He wooed her night and day;
Until he got the lady's consent
   To mount and ride away.

"Go fetch me some of your father's gold
   And some of your mother's fee,
And I'll carry you to the far Northland
   And there I'll marry thee."

She's gone to her father's coffers,
　　Where all his money lay;
And she's taken the red, and she's left the white,
　　And lightly she's tripped away.

She's gone down to her father's stable,
　　Where all his steeds did stand;
And she's taken the best and left the worst,
　　That was in her father's land.

He rode on, and she rode on,
　　They rode a long summer's day,
Until they came to a broad river,
　　An arm of a lonesome sea.

"Leap off the steed," says false Sir John;
　　"Your bridal bed you see;
For it's seven fair maids I have drownèd here,
　　And the eighth one you shall be.

"Cast off, cast off your silks so fine,
　　And lay them on a stone,
For they are too fine and costly
　　To rot in the salt sea foam."

"O turn about, thou false Sir John,
　　And look to the leaf o' the tree;
For it never became a gentleman
　　A naked woman to see."

He's turned himself straight round about
　　To look to the leaf o' the tree,
She's twined her arms about his waist,
　　And thrown him into the sea.

"O hold a grip of me, May Colvin,
　　For fear that I should drown;

I'll take you home to your father's gates,
 And safe I'll set you down."

"O safe enough I am, Sir John,
 And safer I will be;
For seven fair maids have you drownèd here,
 The eighth shall not be me.

"O lie you there, thou false Sir John,
 O lie you there," said she,
"For you lie not in a colder bed
 Than the one you intended for me."

So she went on her father's steed,
 As swift as she could away;
And she came home to her father's gates
 At the breaking of the day.

Up then spake the pretty parrot:
 "May Colvin, where have you been?
What has become of false Sir John,
 That wooed you yestere'en?"

"O hold your tongue, my pretty parrot,
 Nor tell no tales on me;
Your cage will be made of the beaten gold
 With spokes of ivory."

Up then spake her father dear,
 In the chamber where he lay:
"What ails you, pretty parrot,
 That you prattle so long ere day?"

"There came a cat to my door, master,
 I thought 'twould have worried me;
And I was calling on May Colvin
 To take the cat from me."

AUTHOR UNKNOWN

Bonnie George Campbell

High upon Highlands,
   And low upon Tay,
Bonnie George Campbell
   Rode out on a day;
Saddled and bridled,
   And gallant to see:
Home came his good horse,
   But home came not he.

Out ran his old mother,
   Wild with despair;
Out ran his bonnie bride,
   Tearing her hair.
He rode saddled and bridled,
   With boots to the knee:
Home came his good horse,
   But never came he.

"My meadow lies green,
   And my corn is unshorn,
My barn is unbuilt,
   And my babe is unborn."
He rode saddled and bridled,
   Careless and free:
Safe home came the saddle,
   But never came he.

AUTHOR UNKNOWN

Childe Maurice

Childe Maurice hunted the Silver Wood,
   He whistled and he sung:
"I think I see the woman yonder
   That I have loved so long."

He called to his little man John,
  "You do not see what I see;
For yonder I see the very first woman
  That ever lovèd me."

"Here is a glove, a glove," he says,
  "Lined all with fur it is;
Bid her to come to Silver Wood
  To speak with Childe Maurice.

"And here is a ring, a ring," he says,
  "A ring of the precious stone:
He prays her come to Silver Wood
  And ask the leave of none."

"Well do I love your errand, master,
  But better I love my life.
Would you have me go to John Steward's castle,
  To tryst away his wife?"

"Do not I give you meat?" he says,
  "Do not I give you fee?
How dare you stop my errand
  When that I bid you flee?"

When the lad came to John Steward's castle,
  He ran right through the gate
Until he came to the high, high hall
  Where the company sat at meat.

"Here is a glove, my lady," said he,
  "Lined all with fur it is;
It says you're to come to Silver Wood
  And speak with Childe Maurice."

"And here is a ring, a ring of gold,
  Set with the precious stone:
It prays you to come to Silver Wood
  And ask the leave of none."

Out then spake the wily nurse,
    A wily woman was she,
"If this be come from Childe Maurice
    It's dearly welcome to me."

"Thou liest, thou liest, thou wily nurse,
    So loud as I hear thee lie!
I brought it to John Steward's lady,
    And I trow thou be not she."

Then up and rose him John Steward,
    And an angry man was he:
"Did I think there was a lord in the world
    My lady loved but me!"

He dressed himself in his lady's gown,
    Her mantle and her hood;
But a little brown sword hung down by his knee,
    And he rode to Silver Wood.

Childe Maurice sat in Silver Wood,
    He whistled and he sung,
"I think I see the woman coming
    That I have loved so long."

But then stood up Childe Maurice
    His mother to help from horse:
"O alas, alas!" says Childe Maurice,
    "My mother was never so gross!"

"No wonder, no wonder," John Steward he said,
    "My lady loved thee well,
For the fairest part of my body
    Is blacker than thy heel."

John Steward took the little brown sword
    That hung low down by his knee;
He has cut the head off Childe Maurice
    And the body put on a tree.

And when he came to his lady—
  Looked over the castle-wall—
He threw the head into her lap,
  Saying, "Lady, take the ball!"

Says, "Dost thou know Childe Maurice' head,
  When that thou dost it see?
Now lap it soft, and kiss it oft,
  For thou loved'st him better than me."

But when she looked on Childe Maurice' head
  She ne'er spake words but three:
"I never bare no child but one,
  And you have slain him, trulye.

"I got him in my mother's bower
  With secret sin and shame;
I brought him up in the good greenwood
  Under the dew and rain."

And she has taken her Childe Maurice
  And kissed him, mouth and chin:
"O better I loved my Childe Maurice
  Than all my royal kin!"

"Woe be to thee!" John Steward he said,
  And a woe, woe man was he;
"For if you had told me he was your son
  He had never been slain by me."

Says, "Wicked be my merry men all,
  I gave meat, drink and cloth!
But could they not have holden me
  When I was in all that wrath?"

AUTHOR UNKNOWN

Fine Flowers in the Valley

She sat down below a thorn,
  Fine flowers in the valley;
And there she has her sweet babe born,
  And the green leaves they grow rarely.

"Smile na sae sweet, my bonny babe,
  Fine flowers in the valley,
And ye smile sae sweet, ye'll smile me dead,"
  And the green leaves they grow rarely.

She's ta'en out her little penknife,
  Fine flowers in the valley,
And robbed the sweet babe o' its life,
  And the green leaves they grow rarely.

She's dug a grave by the light o' the moon,
  Fine flowers in the valley,
And there she's buried her sweet babe in,
  And the green leaves they grow rarely.

As she was going to the church,
  Fine flowers in the valley,
She saw a sweet babe in the porch,
  And the green leaves they grow rarely.

"O sweet babe, and thou were mine,
  Fine flowers in the valley,
I wad clad thee in the silk so fine,"
  And the green leaves they grow rarely.

"O mother dear, when I was thine,
  Fine flowers in the valley,
Ye did na prove to me sae kind,"
  And the green leaves they grow rarely.

AUTHOR UNKNOWN

There are comparatively few humorous ballads, but the one about the beaten wife (originally called "The Wife Wrapped in the Wether's Skin") is still a favorite after several hundred years. The humbling of an arrogant woman has furnished the plot for many a play—notably Shakespeare's "The Taming of the Shrew"—and ballad-singers still make much of it today. The following, one of the later variations, dates from the nineteenth century.

Sweet William, His Wife, and the Sheepskin

Sweet William, he married a wife,
   Gentle Jenny called Rosemary,
To be the sweet comfort of his life,
   As the dew flies over the mulberry tree.

But Jenny would not in the kitchen go,
For fear of soiling her pretty white shoe.

She would not weave, and she would not spin,
For fear of hurting her gay gold ring.

One day sweet William came in from the plow,
Saying, "Dear wife, is dinner ready now?"

"There's a little cornbread that's left on the shelf,
If you want any more you can bake it yourself."

Sweet William went out to his sheep pen,
And stripped an old wether of its sheep skin.

He laid the skin around his wife's back,
And with a stout stick went whickety-whack!

"I'll tell my father and all my kin
How you hit me hard with a hickory limb."

"You can tell your father and all your kin,
I was only tanning my own sheep skin."

Next day when William came in from the plow
He said, "Dear wife, is dinner ready now?"

She covered the table and spread the board,
And, "Yes, my dear husband," was her every word.

Now they live free from all sorrow and strife,
And they say she makes William a very good wife.

AUTHOR UNKNOWN

Two other humorous ballads follow. Both had
their origins in the Orient. "Get Up and Bar the
Door" is actually an extended joke which had been
told by many story-tellers before it was put into
rhyme. The plot of "King John and the Abbot of
Canterbury" is said to have been popular in Egypt
as early as the seventh century. It is one of many
riddle stories in which a forfeit must be paid if the
wrong answer is given and which merits a reward
if the answer is correct.

Get Up and Bar the Door

It fell about the Martinmas time,
    And a gay time it was then,
When our goodwife got puddings to make,
    And she's boiled them in the pan.

The wind so cold blew south and north,
    And blew into the floor;

Quoth our goodman to our goodwife,
  "Get up and bar the door."

"My hand is in my household work,
  Goodman, as ye may see;
And it will not be barred for a hundred years,
  If it's to be barred by me!"

They made a pact between them both,
  They made it firm and sure,
That whosoe'er should speak the first,
  Should rise and bar the door.

Then by there came two gentlemen,
  At twelve o'clock at night,
And they could see neither house nor hall,
  Nor coal nor candlelight.

"Now whether is this a rich man's house,
  Or whether is it a poor?"
But never a word would one of them speak,
  For barring of the door.

The guests they ate the white puddings,
  And then they ate the black;
Tho' much the goodwife thought to herself,
  Yet never a word she spake.

Then said one stranger to the other,
  "Here, man, take ye my knife;
Do ye take off the old man's beard,
  And I'll kiss the goodwife."

"There's no hot water to scrape it off,
  And what shall we do then?"
"Then why not use the pudding broth,
  That boils into the pan?"

O up then started our goodman,
   An angry man was he;
"Will ye kiss my wife before my eyes!
   And with pudding broth scald me!"

Then up and started our goodwife,
   Gave three skips on the floor:
"Goodman, you've spoken the foremost word.
   Get up and bar the door!"

AUTHOR UNKNOWN

King John and the Abbot of Canterbury

An ancient story I'll tell you anon,
Of a notable prince, that was called King John;
He ruled over England with main and might,
But he did great wrong, and maintained little right.

And I'll tell you a story, a story so merry,
Concerning the Abbot of Canterbury;
How for his housekeeping and high renown,
They rode post to bring him to London town.

A hundred men, as the King heard say,
The Abbot kept in his house every day;
And fifty gold chains, without any doubt,
In velvet coats waited the Abbot about.

"How now, Father Abbot? I hear it of thee,
Thou keepest a far better house than me;
And for thy housekeeping and high renown,
I fear thou work'st treason against my crown."

"My liege," quoth the Abbot, "I would it were known,
I am spending nothing but what is my own;
And I trust your grace will not put me in fear,
For spending my own true-gotten gear."

"Yes, yes, Father Abbot, thy fault is high,
And now for the same thou needest must die;
And except thou canst answer me questions three,
Thy head struck off from thy body shall be.

"Now first," quo' the King, "as I sit here,
With my crown of gold on my head so fair,
Among all my liegemen of noble birth,
Thou must tell to one penny what I am worth.

"Secondly, tell me, beyond all doubt,
How quickly I may ride the whole world about;
And at the third question thou must not shrink,
But tell me here truly, what do I think?"

"O, these are deep questions for my shallow wit,
And I cannot answer your Grace as yet;
But if you will give me a fortnight's space,
I'll do my endeavor to answer your Grace."

"Now a fortnight's space to thee will I give,
And that is the longest thou hast to live;
For unless thou answer my questions three,
Thy life and thy lands are forfeit to me."

Away rode the Abbot all sad at this word;
He rode to Cambridge and Oxenford;
But never a doctor there was so wise,
That could by his learning an answer devise.

Then home rode the Abbot, with comfort so cold,
And he met his shepherd, a-going to fold:
"Now, good Lord Abbot, you are welcome home;
What news do you bring us from great King John?"

"Sad news, sad news, Shepherd, I must give;
That I have but three days more to live.

I must answer the King his questions three,
Or my head struck off from my body shall be.

"The first is to tell him, as he sits there,
With his crown of gold on his head so fair
Among all his liegemen of noble birth,
To within one penny, what he is worth.

"The second, to tell him, beyond all doubt,
How quickly he may ride this whole world about;
And at question the third, I must not shrink,
But tell him there truly, what does he think?"

"O, cheer up, my lord; did you never hear yet
That a fool may teach a wise man wit?
Lend me your serving-men, horse, and apparel,
And I'll ride to London to answer your quarrel.

"With your pardon, it oft has been told to me
That I'm like your lordship as ever can be:
And if you will but lend me your gown,
There is none shall know us at London town."

"Now horses and serving-men thou shalt have,
With sumptuous raiment gallant and brave;
With crosier, and mitre, and rochet, and cope,
Fit to draw near to our father, the pope."

"Now welcome, Sir Abbot," the King he did say,
" 'Tis well thou'rt come back to keep thy day;
For if thou canst answer my questions three,
Thy life and thy living both saved shall be.

"And first, as thou seest me sitting here,
With my crown of gold on my head so fair,
Among my liegemen of noble birth,
Tell to one penny what I am worth."

"For thirty pence our Saviour was sold
Among the false Jews as I have been told;
And twenty-nine is the worth of thee;
For I think thou are one penny worse than he."

The King, he laughed, and swore by St. Bittle,
"I did not think I was worth so little!
Now secondly tell me, beyond all doubt,
How quickly I may ride this world about."

"You must rise with the sun, and ride with the same,
Until the next morning he riseth again;
And then your Grace need never doubt
But in twenty-four hours you'll ride it about."

The King he laughed, and swore by St. Jone,
"I did not think I could do it so soon!
Now from question the third thou must not shrink,
But tell me truly, what do I think?"

"Yea, that I shall do, and make your Grace merry:
You think I'm the Abbot of Canterbury.
But I'm his poor shepherd, as plain you may see,
That am come to beg pardon for him and for me."

The King he laughed, and swore by the mass,
"I'll make thee Lord Abbot this day in his place!"
"Now nay, my Liege, be not in such speed;
For alas! I can neither write nor read."

"Four nobles a week, then I'll give to thee,
For this merry jest thou has shown to me;
And tell the old Abbot, when thou gettest home,
Thou has brought a free pardon from good King John."

AUTHOR UNKNOWN

"John Barleycorn" is another kind of joke in which the name gives the joke away. The burial of the hero, his resuscitation, his cutting-down and cudgelling are anything but tragic, for this is the way alcoholic liquor is made, and "John Barleycorn" is merely a personification of whisky.

John Barleycorn

There was three kings into the East,
    Three kings both great and high,
And they hae sworn a solemn oath
    John Barleycorn should die.

They took a plough and ploughed him down,
    Put clods upon his head,
And they hae sworn a solemn oath,
    John Barleycorn was dead.

But the cheerful spring came kindly on
    And showers began to fall;
John Barleycorn got up again,
    And sore surprised them all.

The sultry suns of summer came,
    And he grew thick and strong,
His head well armed wi' pointed spears,
    That no one should him wrong.

The sober autumn entered mild,
    When he grew wan and pale;
His bending joints and drooping head
    Showed he began to fail.

His color sickened more and more,
    He faded into age;

And then his enemies began
   To show their deadly rage.

They 've ta'en a weapon long and sharp,
   And cut him by the knee;
And tied him fast upon the cart,
   Like a rogue for forgerie.

They laid him down upon his back,
   And cudgelled him full sore;
They hung him up before the storm,
   And turned him o'er and o'er.

They filled up a darksome pit
   With water to the brim,
They heavèd in John Barleycorn,
   There let him sink or swim.

They laid him out upon the floor,
   To work him further woe,
And still, as signs of life appeared,
   They tossed him to and fro.

They wasted, o'er a scorching flame,
   The marrow of his bones;
But a miller used him worst of all,
   For he crushed him between two stones.

And they hae ta'en his very heart's blood,
   And drank it round and round;
And still the more and more they drank,
   Their joy did more abound.

John Barleycorn was a hero bold,
   Of noble enterprise;
For if you do but taste his blood,
   'T will make your courage rise.

Then let us toast John Barleycorn,
　　Each man a glass in hand;
And may his great posterity
　　Ne'er fail in old Scotland!

—OLD BALLAD REVISED BY ROBERT BURNS

PEOPLE

Here is a gallery of brilliant portraits, wide-ranging and sharply individualized. Out of the past leap such figures as Alfred Noyes's gallantly romantic "The Highwayman" and Thomas Hardy's grimly realistic "The Man He Killed." Further contrasts are revealed in Whittier's wistful "Maud Muller" and Keats's wild "Meg Merrilies," Meredith's aging "Juggling Jerry," Tennyson's scornful "Lady Clara Vere de Vere," and Southey's cruel "Bishop Hatto." The world of today is illuminated by William Butler Yeats's moving "Father Gilligan" and Robert Frost's stubbornly independent day-laborers in "The Death of the Hired Man" and "The Code." Holmes's "The Last Leaf" is a delicate but deeply felt expression of tenderness, while Cowper's "John Gilpin" is the hilarious record of a mad ride which became a farcical riot.

Different though they are, all these people have one thing in common: they are vividly unusual and, in their very singularity, unforgettable.

Father Gilligan

The old priest Peter Gilligan
  Was weary night and day,
For half his flock were in their beds,
  Or under green sods lay.

Once while he nodded on a chair,
  At the moth-hour of eve,
Another poor man sent for him,
  And he began to grieve.

"I have no rest, nor joy, nor peace,
  For people die and die;"
And after cried he, "God forgive!
  My body spake, not I!"

And then, half-lying on the chair,
  He knelt, prayed, fell asleep;
And the moth-hour went from the fields,
  And stars began to peep.

They slowly into millions grew,
  And leaves shook in the wind;
And God covered the world with shade,
  And whispered to mankind.

Upon the time of sparrow chirp
  When the moths came once more,
The old priest Peter Gilligan
  Stood upright on the floor.

"*Mavrone, mavrone!* the man has died,
  While I slept on the chair."
He roused his horse out of its sleep,
  And rode with little care.

He rode now as he never rode,
  By rocky lane and fen;
The sick man's wife opened the door:
  "Father! you come again!"

"And is the poor man dead?" he cried.
  "He died an hour ago."
The old priest Peter Gilligan
  In grief swayed to and fro.

"When you were gone he turned and died,
  As merry as a bird."
The old priest Peter Gilligan
  He knelt him at that word.

"He who hath made the night of stars
  For souls who tire and bleed,
Sent one of His great angels down
  To help me in my need.

"He who is wrapped in purple robes,
  With planets in his care,
Had pity on the least of things
  Asleep upon a chair."
                    —WILLIAM BUTLER YEATS

The Man He Killed

  "Had he and I but met
    By some old ancient inn,
  We should have sat us down to wet
    Right many a nipperkin!

  "But ranged as infantry,
    And staring face to face,
  I shot at him as he at me,
    And killed him in his place.

"I shot him dead because—
 Because he was my foe,
Just so: my foe of course he was;
 That's clear enough; although

"He thought he'd 'list, perhaps
 Off-hand like—just as I—
Was out of work—had sold his traps—
 No other reason why.

"Yes; quaint and curious war is!
 You shoot a fellow down
You'd treat if met where any bar is,
 Or help to half-a-crown."

       —THOMAS HARDY

The Code

There were three in the meadow by the brook
Gathering up windrows, piling cocks of hay,
With an eye always lifted toward the west
Where an irregular sun-bordered cloud
Darkly advanced with a perpetual dagger
Flickering across its bosom. Suddenly
One helper, thrusting pitchfork in the ground,
Marched himself off the field and home. One stayed.
The town-bred farmer failed to understand.

"What is there wrong?"
       "Something you just now said."
"What did I say?"
       "About our taking pains."

"To cock the hay?—because it's going to shower?
I said that more than half an hour ago.
I said it to myself as much as you."

"You didn't know. But James is one big fool.
He thought you meant to find fault with his work.
That's what the average farmer would have meant.
James would take time, of course, to chew it over
Before he acted: he's just got round to act."

"He is a fool if that's the way he takes me."

"Don't let it bother you. You've found out something.
The hand that knows his business won't be told
To do work better or faster—those two things.
I'm as particular as anyone:
Most likely I'd have served you just the same.
But I know you don't understand our ways.
You were just talking what was in your mind,
What was in all our minds, and you weren't hinting.
Tell you a story of what happened once:
I was up here in Salem at a man's
Named Sanders with a gang of four or five
Doing the haying. No one liked the boss.
He was one of the kind sports call a spider,
All wiry arms and legs that spread out wavy
From a humped body nigh as big's a biscuit
But work! that man could work, especially
If by so doing he could get more work
Out of his hired help. I'm not denying
He was hard on himself. I couldn't find
That he kept any hours—not for himself.
Daylight and lantern-light were one to him:
I've heard him pounding in the barn all night.
But what he liked was someone to encourage.
Them that he couldn't lead he'd get behind
And drive, the way you can, you know, in mowing—
Keep at their heels and threaten to mow their legs off
I'd seen about enough of his bulling tricks
(We call that bulling). I'd been watching him.
So when he paired off with me in the hayfield
To load the load, thinks I, Look out for trouble.

I built the load and topped it off; old Sanders
Combed it down with a rake and says, 'O.K.'
Everything went well till we reached the barn
With a big jag to empty in a bay.

You understand that meant the easy job
For the man up on top of throwing *down*
The hay and rolling it off wholesale,
Where on a mow it would have been slow lifting.
You wouldn't think a fellow'd need much urging
Under those circumstances, would you now?
But the old fool seizes his fork in both hands,
And looking up bewhiskered out of the pit,
Shouts like an army captain, 'Let her come!'
Thinks I, D'ye mean it? 'What was that you said?'
I asked out loud, so's there'd be no mistake,
'Did you say, Let her come?' 'Yes, let her come.'
He said it over, but he said it softer.
Never you say a thing like that to a man,
Not if he values what he is. God, I'd as soon
Murdered him as left out his middle name.
I'd built the load and knew right where to find it.
Two or three forkfuls I picked lightly round for
Like meditating, and then I just dug in
And dumped the rackful on him in ten lots.
I looked over the side once in the dust
And caught sight of him treading-water-like,
Keeping his head above. 'Damn ye,' I says,
'That gets ye!' He squeaked like a squeezed rat.
That was the last I saw or heard of him.
I cleaned the rack and drove out to cool off.
As I sat mopping hayseed from my neck,
And sort of waiting to be asked about it,
One of the boys sings out, 'Where's the old man?'
'I left him in the barn under the hay.
If ye want him, ye can go and dig him out.'
They realized from the way I swobbed my neck
More than was needed something must be up.

They headed for the barn; I stayed where I was.
They told me afterward. First they forked hay,
A lot of it, out into the barn floor.
Nothing! They listened for him. Not a rustle.
I guess they thought I'd spiked him in the temple
Before I buried him, or I couldn't have managed.
They excavated more. 'Go keep his wife
Out of the barn.' Someone looked in a window,
And curse me if he wasn't in the kitchen
Slumped way down in a chair, with both his feet
Against the stove, the hottest day that summer.
He looked so clean disgusted from behind
There was no one that dared to stir him up,
Or let him know that he was being looked at.
Apparently I hadn't buried him
(I may have knocked him down); but my just trying
To bury him had hurt his dignity.
He had gone to the house so's not to meet me.
He kept away from us all afternoon.
We tended to his hay. We saw him out
After a while picking peas in his garden:
He couldn't keep away from doing something."

"Weren't you relieved to find he wasn't dead?"

"No! and yet I don't know—it's hard to say.
I went about to kill him fair enough."

"You took an awkward way. Did he discharge you?"

"Discharge me? No! He knew I did just right."
                                        —ROBERT FROST

"The Death of the Hired Man" is many poems in
one: it is distinctly a story-poem, but it is also a study
of character, a dialogue, and a condensed drama, a

tense little one act play. Three people are involved:
a hard-working New England farmer, his understanding wife, and an elderly hired hand, incom-
petent but proud—and the third, the central character, the one who never appears in person, is the one
who is most fully revealed. Characterized by its con-
versational give-and-take, the poem is further distinguished by its simple but memorable disposals,
such as the two meanings of home—

"Home is the place where, when you have to go there,
They have to take you in."

                                    "I should have called it
Something you somehow haven't to deserve."

Written in low tones, almost in undertones, this is
a poem which the listener hears—or overhears—in
whispers.

The Death of the Hired Man

Mary sat musing on the lamp-flame at the table,
Waiting for Warren. When she heard his step,
She ran on tip-toe down the darkened passage
To meet him in the doorway with the news
And put him on his guard. "Silas is back."
She pushed him outward with her through the door
And shut it after her. "Be kind," she said.
She took the market things from Warren's arms
And set them on the porch, then drew him down
To sit beside her on the wooden steps.
"When was I ever anything but kind to him?
But I'll not have the fellow back," he said.
"I told him so last haying, didn't I?

'If he left then,' I said, 'that ended it.'
What good is he? Who else will harbor him
At his age for the little he can do?
What help he is there's no depending on.
Off he goes always when I need him most.
'He thinks he ought to earn a little pay,
Enough at least to buy tobacco with,
So he won't have to beg and be beholden.'
'All right,' I say, 'I can't afford to pay
Any fixed wages, though I wish I could.'
'Someone else can.' 'Then someone else will have to.'
I shouldn't mind his bettering himself
If that was what it was. You can be certain,
When he begins like that, there's someone at him
Trying to coax him off with pocket-money,—
In haying time, when any help is scarce.
In winter he comes back to us. I'm done."

"Sh! not so loud: he'll hear you," Mary said.

"I want him to: he'll have to soon or late."

"He's worn out. He's asleep beside the stove.
When I came up from Rowe's I found him here,
Huddled against the barn-door fast asleep,
A miserable sight, and frightening, too—
You needn't smile—I didn't recognize him—
I wasn't looking for him—and he's changed.
Wait till you see."

                    "Where did you say he'd been?"

"He didn't say. I dragged him to the house,
And gave him tea and tried to make him smoke.
I tried to make him talk about his travels,
Nothing would do: he just kept nodding off."

"What did he say? Did he say anything?"

"But little."

            "Anything? Mary, confess
He said he'd come to ditch the meadow for me."

"Warren!"

            "But did he? I just want to know."

"Of course he did. What would you have him say?
Surely you wouldn't grudge the poor old man
Some humble way to save his self-respect.
He added, if you really care to know,
He meant to clear the upper pasture, too.
That sounds like something you have heard before?
Warren, I wish you could have heard the way
He jumbled everything. I stopped to look
Two or three times—he made me feel so queer—
To see if he was talking in his sleep.
He ran on Harold Wilson—you remember—
The boy you had in haying four years since.
He's finished school, and teaching in his college.
Silas declares you'll have to get him back.
He says they two will make a team for work:
Between them they will lay this farm as smooth!
The way he mixed that in with other things.
He thinks young Wilson a likely lad, though daft
On education—you know how they fought
All through July under the blazing sun,
Silas up on the cart to build the load,
Harold along beside to pitch it on."

"Yes, I took care to keep well out of earshot."

"Well, those days trouble Silas like a dream.
You wouldn't think they would. How some things linger!
Harold's young college boy's assurance piqued him.
After so many years he still keeps finding

Good arguments he sees he might have used.
I sympathize. I know just how it feels
To think of the right thing to say too late.
Harold's associated in his mind with Latin.
He asked me what I thought of Harold's saying
He studied Latin like the violin
Because he liked it—that an argument!
He said he couldn't make the boy believe
He could find water with a hazel prong—
Which showed how much good school had ever done him.
He wanted to go over that. But most of all
He thinks if he could have another chance
To teach him how to build a load of hay—"

"I know, that's Silas' one accomplishment.
He bundles every forkful in its place,
And tags and numbers it for future reference,
So he can find and easily dislodge it
In the unloading. Silas does that well.
He takes it out in bunches like birds' nests.
You never see him standing on the hay
He's trying to lift, straining to lift himself."

"He thinks if he could teach him that, he'd be
Some good perhaps to someone in the world.
He hates to see a boy the fool of books.
Poor Silas, so concerned for other folk,
And nothing to look backward to with pride,
And nothing to look forward to with hope,
So now and never any different."

Part of a moon was falling down the west,
Dragging the whole sky with it to the hills.
Its light poured softly in her lap. She saw
And spread her apron to it. She put out her hand
Among the harp-like morning-glory strings,
Taut with the dew from garden bed to eaves,
As if she played unheard the tenderness

That wrought on him beside her in the night.
"Warren," she said, "he has come home to die:
You needn't be afraid he'll leave you this time."

"Home," he mocked gently.

                         "Yes, what else but home?
It all depends on what you mean by home.
Of course he's nothing to us, any more
Than was the hound that came a stranger to us
Out of the woods, worn out upon the trail."

"Home is the place where, when you have to go there,
They have to take you in."

                         "I should have called it
Something you somehow haven't to deserve."

Warren leaned out and took a step or two,
Picked up a little stick, and brought it back
And broke it in his hand and tossed it by.
"Silas has better claim on us, you think,
Than on his brother? Thirteen little miles
As the road winds would bring him to his door.
Silas has walked that far no doubt today.
Why didn't he go there? His brother's rich,
A somebody—director in the bank."

"He never told us that."

                         "We know it though."

"I think his brother ought to help, of course.
I'll see to that if there is need. He ought of right
To take him in, and might be willing to—
He may be better than appearances.
But have some pity on Silas. Do you think
If he'd had any pride in claiming kin

Or anything he looked for from his brother,
He'd keep so still about him all this time?"

"I wonder what's between them."

                              "I can tell you.
Silas is what he is—we wouldn't mind him—
But just the kind that kinsfolk can't abide.
He never did a thing so very bad.
He don't know why he isn't quite as good
As anyone. He won't be made ashamed
To please his brother, worthless though he is."

"I can't think Si ever hurt anyone."

"No, but he hurt my heart the way he lay
And rolled his old head on that sharp-edged chair-back.
He wouldn't let me put him on the lounge.
You must go in and see what you can do.
I made the bed up for him there tonight.
You'll be surprised at him—how much he's broken.
His working days are done; I'm sure of it."

"I'd not be in a hurry to say that."

"I haven't been. Go, look, see for yourself.
But, Warren, please remember how it is:
He's come to help you ditch the meadow.
He has a plan. You mustn't laugh at him.
He may not speak of it, and then he may.
I'll sit and see if that small sailing cloud
Will hit or miss the moon."

                              It hit the moon.
Then there were three there, making a dim row,
The moon, the little silver cloud, and she.

Warren returned—too soon, it seemed to her,

Slipped to her side, caught up her hand and waited.

"Warren?" she questioned.

                          "Dead," was all he answered.
                                   —ROBERT FROST

The Highwayman

Part One

The wind was a torrent of darkness among the gusty trees,
The moon was a ghostly galleon tossed upon cloudy seas,
The road was a ribbon of moonlight over the purple moor,
And the highwayman came riding—
        Riding—riding—
The highwayman came riding, up to the old inn-door.

He'd a French cocked-hat on his forehead, a bunch of lace at
    his chin,
A coat of the claret velvet, and breeches of brown doeskin:
They fitted with never a wrinkle; his boots were up to the
    thigh!
And he rode with a jewelled twinkle,
        His pistol butts a-twinkle,
His rapier hilt a-twinkle, under the jewelled sky.

Over the cobbles he clattered and clashed in the dark inn-
    yard,
And he tapped with his whip on the shutters, but all was
    locked and barred:
He whistled a tune to the window, and who should be waiting
    there
But the landlord's black-eyed daughter,
        Bess, the landlord's daughter,
Plaiting a dark red love-knot into her long black hair.

And dark in the dark old inn-yard a stable-wicket creaked
Where Tim, the ostler, listened; his face was white and
    peaked,
His eyes were hollows of madness, his hair like moldy hay;
But he loved the landlord's daughter,
       The landlord's red-lipped daughter:
Dumb as a dog he listened, and he heard the robber say—

"One kiss, my bonny sweetheart, I'm after a prize tonight,
But I shall be back with the yellow gold before the morning
    light.
Yet if they press me sharply, and harry me through the day,
Then look for me by moonlight,
       Watch for me by moonlight:
I'll come to thee by moonlight, though Hell should bar the
    way."

He rose upright in the stirrups, he scarce could reach her
    hand;
But she loosened her hair i' the casement! His face burnt like
    a brand
As the black cascade of perfume came tumbling over his
    breast;
And he kissed its waves in the moonlight,
       (Oh, sweet black waves in the moonlight)
Then he tugged at his reins in the moonlight, and galloped
    away to the West.

Part Two

He did not come in the dawning; he did not come at noon;
And out of the tawny sunset, before the rise o' the moon,
When the road was a gypsy's ribbon, looping the purple moor,
A red-coat troop came marching—
       Marching—marching—
King George's men came marching, up to the old inn-door.

They said no word to the landlord, they drank his ale instead;
But they gagged his daughter and bound her to the foot of her narrow bed.
Two of them knelt at her casement, with muskets at the side!
There was death at every window;
> And Hell at one dark window;
For Bess could see, through her casement, the road that *he* would ride.

They had tied her up to attention, with many a sniggering jest:
They had bound a musket beside her, with the barrel beneath her breast!
"Now keep good watch!" and they kissed her.
> She heard the dead man say—
Look for me by moonlight;
> *Watch for me by moonlight;*
I'll come to thee by moonlight, though Hell should bar the way!

She twisted her hands behind her; but all the knots held good!
She writhed her hands till her fingers were wet with sweat or blood!
They stretched and strained in the darkness, and the hours crawled by like years;
Till, now, on the stroke of midnight,
> Cold, on the stroke of midnight,
The tip of one finger touched it! The trigger at least was hers!

The tip of one finger touched it; she strove no more for the rest!
Up, she stood up to attention, with the barrel beneath her breast,
She would not risk their hearing: she would not strive again;
For the road lay bare in the moonlight,
> Blank and bare in the moonlight;
And the blood of her veins in the moonlight throbbed to her Love's refrain.

Tlot-tlot, tlot-tlot! Had they heard it? The horse-hoofs ringing
    clear—
Tlot-tlot, tlot-tlot, in the distance? Were they deaf that they
    did not hear?
Down the ribbon of moonlight, over the brow of the hill,
The highwayman came riding,
        Riding, riding!
The red-coats looked to their priming! She stood up straight
    and still!

Tlot-tlot, in the frosty silence! *Tlot-tlot* in the echoing night!
Nearer he came and nearer! Her face was like a light!
Her eyes grew wide for a moment; she drew one last deep
    breath,
Then her finger moved in the moonlight,
        Her musket shattered the moonlight,
Shattered her breast in the moonlight and warned him—with
    her death.

He turned; he spurred him Westward; he did not know who
    stood
Bowed with her head o'er the musket, drenched with her own
    red blood!
Not till the dawn he heard it, and slowly blanched to hear
How Bess, the landlord's daughter,
        The landlord's black-eyed daughter,
Had watched for her Love in the moonlight; and died in the
    darkness there.

Back, he spurred like a madman, shrieking a curse to the sky,
With the white road smoking behind him, and his rapier
    brandished high!
Blood-red were his spurs i' the golden noon; wine-red was his
    velvet coat;
When they shot him down on the highway,
        Down like a dog on the highway,
And he lay in his blood on the highway, with the bunch of
    lace at his throat.

      *   *   *   *   *

And still a winter's night, they say, when the wind is in the
    trees,
When the moon is a ghostly galleon tossed upon cloudy seas,
When the road is a ribbon of moonlight over the purple moor,
A highwayman comes riding—
      Riding—riding—
A highwayman comes riding, up to the old inn-door.

Over the cobbles he clatters and clangs in the dark inn-yard;
And he taps with his whip on the shutters, but all is locked
    and barred:
He whistles a tune to the window, and who should be waiting
    there
But the landlord's black-eyed daughter,
      Bess, the landlord's daughter,
Plaiting a dark red love-knot into her long black hair.

                    —ALFRED NOYES

The Last Leaf

I saw him once before,
As he pass'd by the door,
    And again
The pavement stones resound,
As he totters o'er the ground
    With his cane.

They say that in his prime,
Ere the pruning-knife of Time
    Cut him down,
Not a better man was found
By the Crier on his round
    Through the town.

But now he walks the streets,
And he looks at all he meets
    Sad and wan,

And he shakes his feeble head,
That it seems as if he said,
　　"They are gone."

The mossy marbles rest
On the lips that he has prest
　　In their bloom,
And the names he loved to hear
Have been carved for many a year
　　On the tomb.

My grandmamma has said—
Poor old lady, she is dead
　　Long ago—
That he had a Roman nose,
And his cheek was like a rose
　　In the snow.

But now his nose is thin,
And it rests upon his chin
　　Like a staff,
And a crook is in his back,
And a melancholy crack
　　In his laugh.

I know it is a sin
For me to sit and grin
　　At him here;
But the old three-corner'd hat,
And the breeches, and all that,
　　Are so queer!

And if I should live to be
The last leaf upon the tree
　　In the spring,
Let them smile, as I do now,
At the old forsaken bough
　　Where I cling.

　　　　　　　—OLIVER WENDELL HOLMES

Whittier's "Snow-Bound" is exactly what the sub-title calls it: "A Winter Idyl." It lovingly describes the protracted cold season in a lonely New England farm house a little more than a century ago, a time when, as the poet himself said in a prefatory note, "we had scanty sources of information—few books and only a small weekly newspaper . . . Under such circumstances story-telling was a necessary resource in the long winter evenings. My father when a young man had traversed the wilderness to Canada, and could tell us of his adventures with Indians and wild beasts, and of his sojourn in the French villages. My uncle was ready with his record of hunting and fishing and, it must be confessed, with stories, which he at least half believed, of witchcraft and apparitions. My mother, who was born in the Indian-haunted region of Somersworth, New Hampshire, told us of the inroads of the savages and the narrow escape of her ancestors."

The warm reality of a happy and wholesome life is reflected on every page of "Snow-Bound," intensi-fied by its rich characterizations. The four excerpts which follow are portraits done in the graphic man-ner of the Old Masters.

📖

From "Snow-Bound"

The Father

Our father rode again his ride
On Memphremagog's wooded side;
Sat down again to moose and samp[1]
In trapper's hut and Indian camp;
Lived o'er the old idyllic ease
Beneath St. François' hemlock-trees;

---

[1] Samp: porridge made of coarse Indian corn.

Again for him the moonlight shone
On Norman cap and bodiced zone;
Again he heard the violin play
Which led the village dance away,
And mingled in its merry whirl
The grandam and the laughing girl.
Or, nearer home, our steps he led
Where Salisbury's level marshes spread
   Mile-wide as flies the laden bee;
Where merry mowers, hale and strong,
Swept, scythe on scythe, their swaths along
   The low green prairies of the sea.
We shared the fishing off Boar's Head,
   And round the rocky Isles of Shoals
   The hake-broil on the drift-wood coals;
The chowder on the sand-beach made,
Dipped by the hungry, steaming hot,
With spoons of clam-shell from the pot.
We heard the tales of witchcraft old,
And dream and sign and marvel told
To sleepy listeners as they lay
Stretched idly on the salted hay,
Adrift along the winding shores,
When favoring breezes deigned to blow
The square sail of the gundelow
And idle lay the useless oars.

The Mother

Our mother, while she turned her wheel
Or run the new-knit stocking-heel,
Told how the Indian hordes came down
At midnight on Cochecho town,
And how her own great-uncle bore
His cruel scalp-mark to fourscore.
Recalling, in her fitting phrase,

So rich and picturesque and free,
(The common unrhymed poetry
Of simple life and country ways,)
The story of her early days,—
She made us welcome to her home;
Old hearths grew wide to give us room;
We stole with her a frightened look
At the gray wizard's conjuring-book,
The fame whereof went far and wide
Through all the simple country side;
We heard the hawks at twilight play,
The boat-horn on Piscataqua,
The loon's weird laughter far away;
We fished her little trout-brook, knew
What flowers in wood and meadow grew,
What sunny hillsides autumn-brown
She climbed to shake the ripe nuts down,
Saw where in sheltered cove and bay
The duck's black squadron anchored lay,
And heard the wild-geese calling loud
Beneath the gray November cloud.
Then, haply, with a look more grave,
And soberer tone, some tale she gave
From painful Sewell's ancient tome,
Beloved in every Quaker home,
Of faith fire-winged by martyrdom,
Or Chalkley's Journal, old and quaint,—
Gentlest of skippers, rare sea-saint!—
Who, when the dreary calms prevailed,
And water-butt and bread-cask failed,
And cruel, hungry eyes pursued
His portly presence mad for food,
With dark hints muttered under breath
Of casting lots for life or death,
Offered, if Heaven withheld supplies,
To be himself the sacrifice.
Then, suddenly, as if to save
The good man from his living grave,

A ripple on the water grew,
A school of porpoise flashed in view.
"Take, eat," he said, "and be content;
These fishes in my stead are sent
By Him who gave the tangled ram
To spare the child of Abraham."

The Uncle

Our uncle, innocent of books,
Was rich in lore of fields and brooks,
The ancient teachers never dumb
Of Nature's unhoused lyceum.
In moons and tides and weather wise,
He read the clouds as prophecies,
And foul or fair could well divine,
By many an occult hint and sign,
Holding the cunning-warded keys
To all the woodcraft mysteries;
Himself to Nature's heart so near
That all her voices in his ear
Of beast or bird had meanings clear,
Like Apollonius of old,
Who knew the tales the sparrows told,
Or Hermes who interpreted
What the sage cranes of Nilus said;
A simple, guileless, childlike man,
Content to live where life began;
Strong only on his native grounds,
The little world of sights and sounds
Whose girdle was the parish bounds,
Whereof his fondly partial pride
The common features magnified,
As Surrey hills to mountains grew
In White of Selborne's loving view,—
He told how teal and loon he shot,
And how the eagle's eggs he got,

The feats on pond and river done,
The prodigies of rod and gun;
Till, warming with the tales he told,
Forgotten was the outside cold,
The bitter wind unheeded blew,
From ripening corn the pigeons flew,
The partridge drummed i' the wood, the mink
Went fishing down the river-brink.
In fields with bean or clover gay,
The woodchuck, like a hermit gray,
 Peered from the doorway of his cell;
The muskrat plied the mason's trade,
And tier by tier his mud-walls laid;
And from the shagbark overhead
 The grizzled squirrel dropped his shell.

The Schoolmaster

Brisk wielder of the birch and rule,
The master of the district school
Held at the fire his favored place,
Its warm glow lit a laughing face
Fresh-hued and fair, where scarce appeared
The uncertain prophecy of beard.
He teased the mitten-blinded cat,
Played cross-pins on my uncle's hat,
Sang songs, and told us what befalls
In classic Dartmouth's college halls.
Born the wild Northern hills among,
From whence his yeoman father wrung
By patient toil subsistence scant,
Not competence and yet not want,
He early gained the power to pay
His cheerful, self-reliant way;
Could doff at ease his scholar's gown
To peddle wares from town to town;
Or through the long vacation's reach
In lonely lowland districts teach,

Where all the droll experience found
At stranger hearths in boarding round,
The moonlit skater's keen delight,
The sleigh-drive through the frosty night,
The rustic party, with its rough
Accompaniment of blind-man's-buff,
And whirling plate, and forfeits paid,
His winter task a pastime made.
Happy the snow-locked homes wherein
He tuned his merry violin,
Or played the athlete in the barn,
Or held the good dame's winding-yarn,
Or mirth-provoking versions told
Of classic legends rare and old,
Wherein the scenes of Greece and Rome
Had all the commonplace of home,
And little seemed at best the odds
'Twixt Yankee pedlers and old gods;
Where Pindus-born Araxes took
The guise of any grist-mill brook,
And dread Olympus at his will
Became a huckleberry hill.

A careless boy that night he seemed;
  But at his desk he had the look
And air of one who wisely schemed,
  And hostage from the future took
  In trainèd thought and lore of book.
Large-brained, clear-eyed,—of such as he
Shall Freedom's young apostles be,
Who, following in War's bloody trail,
Shall every lingering wrong assail;
All chains from limb and spirit strike,
Uplift the black and white alike;
Scatter before their swift advance
The darkness and the ignorance,
The pride, the lust, the squalid sloth,
Which nurtured Treason's monstrous growth,

Made murder pastime, and the hell
Of prison-torture possible;
The cruel lie of caste refute,
Old forms remould, and substitute
For Slavery's lash the freeman's will,
For blind routine, wise-handed skill;
A school-house plant on every hill,
Stretching in radiate nerve-lines thence
The quick wires of intelligence;
Till North and South together brought
Shall own the same electric thought,
In peace a common flag salute,
And, side by side in labor's free
And unresentful rivalry,
Harvest the fields wherein they fought.

—JOHN GREENLEAF WHITTIER

Meg Merrilies

Old Meg she was a gipsy;
   And lived upon the moors:
Her bed it was the brown heath turf,
   And her house was out of doors.
Her apples were swart blackberries,
   Her currants, pods o' broom;
Her wine was dew of the wild white rose,
   Her book a church-yard tomb.

Her brothers were the craggy hills,
   Her sisters larchen trees;
Alone with her great family
   She lived as she did please.
No breakfast had she many a morn,
   No dinner many a noon,
And, 'stead of supper, she would stare
   Full hard against the moon.

But every morn, of woodbine fresh
  She made her garlanding,
And, every night, the dark glen yew
  She wove, and she would sing.
And with her fingers, old and brown,
  She plaited mats of rushes,
And gave them to the cottagers
  She met among the bushes.

Old Meg was brave as Margaret Queen,
  And tall as Amazon;
An old red blanket cloak she wore,
  A chip-hat had she on.
God rest her aged bones somewhere!
  She died full long agone!

—JOHN KEATS

Juggling Jerry

Pitch here the tent, while the old horse grazes:
  By the old hedge-side we'll halt a stage.
It's nigh my last above the daisies:
  My next leaf'll be man's blank page.
Yes, my old girl! and it's no use crying:
  Juggler, constable, king, must bow.
One that outjuggles all's been spying
  Long to have me, and he has me now.

We've traveled times to this old common:
  Often we've hung our pots in the gorse.
We've had a stirring life, old woman,
  You, and I, and the old gray horse.
Races, and fairs, and royal occasions,
  Found us coming to their call:
Now they'll miss us at our stations:
  There's a Juggler outjuggles all!

Up goes the lark, as if all were jolly!
  Over the duck-pond the willow shakes.
Easy to think that grieving's folly,
  When the hand's firm as driven stakes!
Aye, when we're strong, and braced, and manful,
  Life's a sweet fiddle: but we're a batch
Born to become the Great Juggler's han'ful:
  Balls he shies up, and is safe to catch.

Here's where the lads of the village cricket:
  I was a lad not wide from here:
Couldn't I whip off the bail from the wicket!
  Like an old world those days appear!
Donkey, sheep, geese, and thatched ale-house—I know them!
  They are old friends of my halts, and seem,
Somehow, as if kind thanks I owe them:
  Juggling don't hinder the heart's esteem.

Juggling's no sin, for we must have victual:
  Nature allows us to bait for the fool.
Holding one's own makes us juggle no little;
  But, to increase it, hard juggling's the rule.
You that are sneering at my profession,
  Haven't you juggled a vast amount?
There's the Prime Minister, in one Session,
  Juggles more games than my sins'll count.

I've murdered insects with mock thunder:
  Conscience, for that, in men don't quail.
I've made bread from the bump of wonder:
  That's my business, and there's my tale.
Fashion and rank all praised the professor:
  Aye! and I've had my smile from the Queen:
Bravo, Jerry! she meant: God bless her!
  Ain't this a sermon on that scene?

I've studied men from my topsy-turvy
  Close, and, I reckon, rather true.

Some are fine fellows: some, right scurvy:
   Most, a dash between the two.
But it's a woman, old girl, that makes me
   Think more kindly of the race:
And it's a woman, old girl, that shakes me
   When the Great Juggler I must face.

We two were married, due and legal:
   Honest we've lived since we've been one.
Lord! I could then jump like an eagle:
   You danced bright as a bit o' the sun.
Birds in a May-bush we were! right merry!
   All night we kiss'd, we juggled all day.
Joy was the heart of Juggling Jerry!
   Now from his old girl he's juggled away.

It's past parsons to console us:
   No, nor no doctor fetch for me:
I can die without my bolus;
   Two of a trade, lass, never agree!
Parson and Doctor!—don't they love rarely
   Fighting the devil in other men's fields!
Stand up yourself and match him fairly:
   Then see how the rascal yields!

I, lass, have lived no gipsy, flaunting
   Finery while his poor helpmate grubs:
Coin I've stored, and you won't be wanting:
   You shan't beg from the troughs and tubs.
Nobly you've stuck to me, though in his kitchen
   Many a Marquis would hail you Cook!
Palaces you could have ruled and grown rich in,
   But your old Jerry you never forsook.

Hand up the chirper! ripe ale winks in it;
   Let's have comfort and be at peace.
Once a stout draught made me light as a linnet.
   Cheer up! the Lord must have his lease.

May be—for none see in that black hollow—
   It's just a place where we're held in pawn,
And, when the Great Juggler makes as to swallow,
   It's just the sword-trick—I ain't quite gone!

Yonder came smells of the gorse, so nutty,
   Gold-like and warm: it's the prime of May.
Better than mortar, brick and putty,
   Is God's house on a blowing day.
Lean me more up the mound; now I feel it:
   All the old heath-smells! Ain't it strange?
There's the world laughing, as if to conceal it,
   But He's by us, juggling the change.

I mind it well, by the sea-beach lying,
   Once—it's long gone—when two gulls we beheld,
Which, as the moon got up, were flying
   Down a big wave that sparked and swelled.
Crack, went a gun: one fell: the second
   Wheeled round him twice, and was off for new luck:
There in the dark her white wing beckoned:—
   Drop me a kiss—I'm the bird dead-struck!

               —GEORGE MEREDITH

Maud Muller

Maud Muller on a summer's day,
Raked the meadow sweet with hay.

Beneath her torn hat glowed the wealth
Of simple beauty and rustic health.

Singing, she wrought, and her merry glee
The mock-bird echoed from his tree.

But when she glanced to the far-off town,
White from its hill-slope looking down,

The sweet song died, and a vague unrest
And a nameless longing filled her breast,—

A wish that she hardly dared to own,
For something better than she had known.

The Judge rode slowly down the lane,
Smoothing his horse's chestnut mane.

He drew his bridle in the shade
Of the apple-trees, to greet the maid,

And asked a draught from the spring that flowed
Through the meadow across the road.

She stooped where the cool spring bubbled up,
And filled for him her small tin cup,

And blushed as she gave it, looking down
On her feet so bare, and her tattered gown.

"Thanks!" said the Judge; "a sweeter draught
From a fairer hand was never quaffed."

He spoke of the grass and flowers and trees,
Of the singing birds and humming bees;

Then talked of the haying and wondered whether
The cloud in the west would bring foul weather.

And Maud forgot her brier-torn gown,
And her graceful ankles bare and brown;

And listened, while a pleased surprise
Looked from her long-lashed hazel eyes.

At last, like one who for delay
Seeks a vain excuse, he rode away.

Maud Muller looked and sighed: "Ah me!
That I the Judge's bride might be!

"He would dress me up in silks so fine,
And praise and toast me at his wine.

"My father should wear a broadcloth coat;
My brother should sail a painted boat.

"I'd dress my mother so grand and gay,
And the baby should have a new toy each day.

"And I'd feed the hungry and clothe the poor,
And all should bless me who left our door."

The Judge looked back as he climbed the hill,
And saw Maud Muller standing still.

"A form more fair, a face more sweet,
Ne'er hath it been my lot to meet.

"And her modest answer and graceful air
Show her wise and good as she is fair.

"Would she were mine, and I to-day,
Like her, a harvester of hay;

"No doubtful balance of rights and wrongs,
Nor weary lawyers with endless tongues,

"But low of cattle and song of birds,
And health and quiet and loving words."

But he thought of his sisters, proud and cold,
And his mother, vain of her rank and gold,

So, closing his heart, the Judge rode on,
And Maud was left in the field alone.

But the lawyers smiled that afternoon,
When he hummed in court an old love-tune;

And the young girl mused beside the well
Till the rain on the unraked clover fell.

He wedded a wife of richest dower,
Who lived for fashion, as he for power.

Yet oft, in his marble hearth's bright glow,
He watched a picture come and go;

And sweet Maud Muller's hazel eyes
Looked out in their innocent surprise.

Oft, when the wine in his glass was red,
He longed for the wayside well instead;

And closed his eyes on his garnished rooms
To dream of meadows and clover-blooms.

And the proud man sighed, with a secret pain,
"Ah, that I were free again!

"Free as when I rode that day,
Where the barefoot maiden raked her hay."

She wedded a man unlearned and poor,
And many children played round her door.

But care and sorrow, and childbirth pain,
Left their traces on heart and brain.

And oft, when the summer sun shone hot
On the new-mown hay in the meadow lot,

And she heard the little spring brook fall
Over the roadside, through the wall,

In the shade of the apple-tree again
She saw a rider draw his rein;

And, gazing down with timid grace,
She felt his pleased eyes read her face.

Sometimes her narrow kitchen walls
Stretched away into stately halls;

The weary wheel to a spinnet turned,
The tallow candle an astral burned,

And for him who sat by the chimney lug,
Dozing and grumbling o'er pipe and mug,

A manly form at her side she saw,
And joy was duty and love was law.

Then she took up her burden of life again,
Saying only, "It might have been."

Alas for maiden, alas for Judge,
For rich repiner and household drudge!

God pity them both! and pity us all,
Who vainly the dreams of youth recall.

For of all sad words of tongue or pen,
The saddest are these: "It might have been!"

Ah, well! for us all some sweet hope lies
Deeply buried from human eyes;

And, in the hereafter, angels may
Roll the stone from its grave away!

—JOHN GREENLEAF WHITTIER

Telling the Bees

Here is the place; right over the hill
    Runs the path I took;
You can see the gap in the old wall still,
    And the stepping-stones in the shallow brook.

There is the house, with the gate red-barred,
    And the poplars tall;
And the barn's brown length, and the cattle-yard,
    And the white horns tossing above the wall.

There are the beehives ranged in the sun;
    And down by the brink
Of the brook are her poor flowers, weed-o'errun,
    Pansy and daffodil, rose and pink.

A year has gone, as the tortoise goes,
    Heavy and slow;
And the same rose blows, and the same sun glows,
    And the same brook sings of a year ago.

There's the same sweet clover-smell in the breeze;
    And the June sun warm
Tangles his wings of fire in the trees,
    Setting, as then, over Fernside Farm.

I mind me how with a lover's care
    From my Sunday coat
I brushed off the burrs, and smoothed my hair,
    And cooled at the brook-side my brow and throat.

Since we parted, a month had passed,—
    To love, a year;
Down through the beeches I looked at last
    On the little red gate and the well-sweep near.

I can see it all now,—the slantwise rain
  Of light through the leaves,
The sundown's blaze on her window-pane,
  The bloom of her roses under the eaves.

Just the same as a month before,—
  The house and the trees,
The barn's brown gable, the vine by the door,—
  Nothing changed but the hives of bees.

Before them, under the garden wall,
  Forward and back,
Went drearily singing the chore-girl small,
  Draping each hive with a shred of black.

Trembling, I listened: the summer sun
  Had the chill of snow;
For I knew she was telling the bees of one
  Gone on the journey we all must go!

Then I said to myself, "My Mary weeps
  For the dead to-day:
Haply her blind old grandsire sleeps
  The fret and the pain of his age away."

But her dog whined low; on the doorway sill,
  With his cane to his chin,
The old man sat; and the chore-girl still
  Sung to the bees stealing out and in.

And the song she was singing ever since
  In my ear sounds on:—
"Stay at home, pretty bees, fly not hence!
  Mistress Mary is dead and gone!"

                              —JOHN GREENLEAF WHITTIER

How's My Boy?

Ho, sailor of the sea!
How's my boy—my boy?
"What's your boy's name, good wife,
And in what good ship sail'd he?"

My boy John—
He that went to sea—
What care I for the ship, sailor?
My boy's my boy to me.

You come back from sea
And not know my John?
I might as well have asked some landsman
Yonder down in the town.
There's not an ass in all the parish
But he knows my John.

How's my boy—my boy?
And unless you let me know
I'll swear you are no sailor,
Blue jacket or no,
Brass button or no, sailor,
Anchor and crown or no!
Sure his ship was the *Jolly Briton*—

"Speak low, woman, speak low!"

And why should I speak low, sailor,
About my own boy John?
If I was loud as I am proud
I'd sing him over the town!
Why should I speak low, sailor?

"That good ship went down."

How's my boy—my boy?
What care I for the ship, sailor,
I never was aboard her.
Be she afloat, or be she aground,
Sinking or swimming, I'll be bound,
Her owners can afford her!
I say, how's my John?

"Every man on board went down,
Every man aboard her."

How's my boy—my boy?
What care I for the men, sailor?
I'm not their mother—
How's my boy—my boy?
Tell me of him and no other!
How's my boy—my boy?

—SYDNEY DOBELL

Lucy Gray

Or, Solitude

Oft I had heard of Lucy Gray:
And, when I crossed the wild,
I chanced to see at break of day
The solitary child.

No mate, no comrade Lucy knew;
She dwelt on a wide moor,
—The sweetest thing that ever grew
Beside a human door!

You yet may spy the fawn at play,
The hare upon the green;
But the sweet face of Lucy Gray
Will never more be seen.

"To-night will be a stormy night—
You to the town must go;
And take a lantern, child, to light
Your mother through the snow."

"That, Father, will I gladly do!
'Tis scarcely afternoon—
The minster-clock has just struck two,
And yonder is the moon!"

At this the Father raised his hook,
And snapped a faggot-band;
He plied his work;—and Lucy took
The lantern in her hand.

Not blither is the mountain roe:
With many a wanton stroke
Her feet disperse the powdery snow,
That rises up like smoke.

The storm came on before its time:
She wandered up and down;
And many a hill did Lucy climb;
But never reached the town.

The wretched parents all that night
Went shouting far and wide;
But there was neither sound nor sight
To serve them for a guide.

At day-break on a hill they stood
That overlooked the moor;
And thence they saw the bridge of wood,
A furlong from their door.

They wept, and, turning homeward, cried,
"In heaven we all shall meet!"

—When in the snow the mother spied
The print of Lucy's feet.

Then downward from the steep hill's edge
They tracked the footmarks small;
And through the broken hawthorn hedge,
And by the long stone wall;

And then an open field they crossed;
The marks were still the same;
They tracked them on, nor ever lost;
And to the bridge they came.

They followed from the snowy bank
Those footmarks, one by one,
Into the middle of the plank;
And further there were none!

—Yet some maintain that to this day
She is a living child;
That you may see sweet Lucy Gray
Upon the lonesome wild.

O'er rough and smooth she trips along,
And never looks behind;
And sings a solitary song
That whistles in the wind.

—WILLIAM WORDSWORTH

The Song of the Shirt

With fingers weary and worn,
    With eyelids heavy and red,
A woman sat, in unwomanly rags,
    Plying her needle and thread—
        Stitch—stitch—stitch!

In poverty, hunger, and dirt,
 And still with a voice of dolorous pitch
She sang the "Song of the Shirt!"

 "Work—work—work!
While the cock is crowing aloof;
 And work—work—work
Till the stars shine through the roof!
It's oh! to be a slave
 Along with the barbarous Turk,
Where woman has never a soul to save
 If this is Christian work!

 "Work—work—work
Till the brain begins to swim;
 Work—work—work
Till the eyes are heavy and dim!
Seam, and gusset, and band,—
 Band, and gusset, and seam,
Till over the buttons I fall asleep,
 And sew them on in a dream!

"O! men with Sisters dear!
 O! men with Mothers and Wives!
It is not linen you're wearing out,
 But human creatures' lives!
  Stitch—stitch—stitch,
 In poverty, hunger, and dirt,
Sewing at once, with a double thread,
 A Shroud as well as a Shirt.

 "But why do I talk of Death!
 That phantom of grisly bone,
I hardly fear his terrible shape,
 It seems so like my own—
 It seems so like my own,
 Because of the fasts I keep;
O God! that bread should be so dear,
 And flesh and blood so cheap!

"Work—work—work!
  My labour never flags;
And what are its wages? A bed of straw,
  A crust of bread—and rags.
That shattered roof,—and this naked floor,—
  A table,—a broken chair,—
And a wall so blank, my shadow I thank
  For sometimes falling there.

  "Work—work—work!
From weary chime to chime,
  Work—work—work—
As prisoners work for crime!
  Band, and gusset, and seam,
  Seam, and gusset, and band,
Till the heart is sick, and the brain benumbed,
  As well as the weary hand.

  "Work—work—work,
In the dull December light,
  And work—work—work,
When the weather is warm and bright—
  While underneath the eaves
  The brooding swallows cling,
As if to show me their sunny backs
  And twit me with the Spring.

  "Oh! but to breathe the breath
Of the cowslip and primrose sweet—
  With the sky above my head,
And the grass beneath my feet,
  For only one short hour
  To feel as I used to feel,
Before I knew the woes of want
  And the walk that costs a meal!

  "Oh! but for one short hour!
  A respite however brief!

No blessed leisure for Love or Hope,
　　But only time for Grief!
A little weeping would ease my heart,
　　But in their briny bed
My tears must stop, for every drop
　　Hinders needle and thread!"

With fingers weary and worn,
　　With eyelids heavy and red,
A woman sat, in unwomanly rags,
　　Plying her needle and thread—
　　　Stitch—stitch—stitch!
　　In poverty, hunger, and dirt,
And still with a voice of dolorous pitch,—
Would that its tone could reach the Rich!
　　She sang this "Song of the Shirt!"

　　　　　　　　　　　　　　—THOMAS HOOD

The incredible cruelty of Bishop Hatto has a distinct, if indefinite, historical background. Scholars are uncertain about the century, but they are positive about the place of origin. Bingen is the spot where the avaricious Hatto built his huge barns and warehouses; his fortress, the ill-famed Mouse Tower, stands on a small island in the river Rhine. It is said that his bones were buried there by the rats.

Bishop Hatto

The summer and autumn had been so wet
That in winter the corn was growing yet;
'Twas a piteous sight to see all around
The grain lie rotting on the ground.

Every day the starving poor
Crowded around Bishop Hatto's door,
For he had a plentiful last year's store,
And all the neighbourhood could tell
His granaries were furnish'd well.

At last Bishop Hatto appointed a day
To quiet the poor without delay;
He bade them to his great barn repair,
And they should have food for the winter there.

Rejoiced such tidings good to hear,
The poor folk flock'd from far and near;
The great barn was full as it could hold
Of women and children, and young and old.

Then when he saw it could hold no more,
Bishop Hatto he made fast the door;
And while for mercy on Christ they call,
He set fire to the barn and burnt them all.

"I' faith, 'tis an excellent bonfire!" quoth he,
"And the country is greatly obliged to me,
For ridding it in these times forlorn
Of rats, that only consume the corn."

So then to his palace returned he,
And he sat down to supper merrily,
And he slept that night like an innocent man
But Bishop Hatto never slept again.

In the morning as he enter'd the hall,
Where his picture hung against the wall,
A sweat like death all over him came,
For the rats had eaten it out of the frame.

As he look'd there came a man from the farm,
He had a countenance white with alarm;

"My lord, I open'd your granaries this morn,
And the rats had eaten all your corn."

Another came running presently,
And he was pale as pale could be,
"Fly! my Lord Bishop, fly," quoth he,
"Ten thousand rats are coming this way—
The Lord forgive you for yesterday!"

"I'll go to my tower on the Rhine," replied he,
" 'Tis the safest place in Germany;
The walls are high, and the shores are steep,
And the stream is strong, and the water deep."

Bishop Hatto fearfully hasten'd away,
And he cross'd the Rhine without delay,
And reach'd his tower, and barr'd with care
All the windows, doors, and loopholes there.

He laid him down and closed his eyes,
But soon a scream made him arise;
He started, and saw two eyes of flame
On his pillow from whence the screaming came.

He listen'd and look'd; it was only the cat;
But the Bishop he grew more fearful for that,
For she sat screaming, mad with fear,
At the army of rats that was drawing near.

For they have swum over the river so deep,
And they have climb'd the shores so steep,
And up the tower their way is bent
To do the work for which they were sent.

They are not to be told by the dozen or score,
By thousands they come, and by myriads and more;
Such numbers had never been heard of before,
Such a judgment had never been witness'd of yore.

Down on his knees the Bishop fell,
And faster and faster his beads did he tell,
As louder and louder drawing near
The gnawing of their teeth he could hear.

And in at the windows, and in at the door,
And through the walls helter-skelter they pour,
And down from the ceiling, and up through the floor,
From the right and the left, from behind and before,
From within and without, from above and below,
And all at once to the Bishop they go.

They have whetted their teeth against the stones,
And now they pick the Bishop's bones;
They gnaw'd the flesh from every limb,
For they were sent to do judgment on him.

—ROBERT SOUTHEY

☷

"Parson Gray" is not so much the portrait of a
character as a caricature. The serious author of "The
Deserted Village" allows himself a little diversion
and, instead of turning out a portrait, delights to
turn a few phrases inside out. Those who scorn puns
as "the lowest form of wit" will not approve of what
Oliver Goldsmith has done in the following light-
hearted lines.

☷

Parson Gray

A quiet home had Parson Gray,
  Secluded in a vale;
His daughters all were feminine,
  And all his sons were male.

How faithfully did Parson Gray
   The bread of life dispense—
Well "posted" in theology,
   And post and rail his fence.

'Gainst all the vices of the age
   He manfully did battle;
His chickens were a biped breed,
   And quadruped his cattle.

No clock more punctually went,
   He ne'er delayed a minute—
Nor ever empty was his purse,
   When he had money in it.

His piety was ne'er denied;
   His truths hit saint and sinner;
At morn he always breakfasted;
   He always dined at dinner.

He ne'er by any luck was grieved,
   By any care perplexed—
No filcher he, though when he preached,
   He always "took" a text.

As faithful characters he drew
   As mortal ever saw;
But ah! poor parson! when he died,
   His breath he could not draw!

—OLIVER GOLDSMITH

Alone

*Supposed to be written by Alexander Selkirk, during his
solitary abode in the island of Juan Fernandez*

I am monarch of all I survey,
   My right there is none to dispute;
From the centre all round to the sea,
   I am lord of the fowl and the brute.
O Solitude! where are the charms
   That sages have seen in thy face?
Better dwell in the midst of alarms
   Than reign in this horrible place.

I am out of humanity's reach,
   I must finish my journey alone,
Never hear the sweet music of speech,
   I start at the sound of my own.
The beasts that roam over the plain
   My form with indifference see;
They are so unacquainted with man,
   Their tameness is shocking to me.

Society, friendship and love,
   Divinely bestowed upon man,
O, had I the wings of a dove,
   How soon would I taste you again!
My sorrows I then might assuage,
   In the ways of religion and truth,
Might learn from the wisdom of age,
   And be cheer'd by the sallies of youth.

Religion! what treasure untold
   Lies hid in that heavenly word!
More precious than silver or gold,
   Or all that this earth can afford.
But the sound of the church-going bell,
   These valleys and rocks never heard,

Never sigh'd at the sound of a knell,
   Or smiled when a sabbath appear'd.

Ye winds that have made me your sport,
   Convey to this desolate shore
Some cordial, endearing report
   Of a land I shall visit no more.
My friends, do they now and then send
   A wish or a thought after me?
O, tell me I yet have a friend,
   Though a friend I am never to see.

How fleet is a glance of the mind!
   Compar'd with the speed of its flight,
The tempest himself lags behind
   And the swift-winged arrows of light.
When I think of my own native land,
   In a moment I seem to be there;
But, alas! recollection at hand
   Soon hurries me back to despair.

But the sea-fowl is gone to her nest,
   The beast is laid down in his lair;
Even here is a season of rest,
   And I to my cabin repair.
There's mercy in every place,
   And mercy, encouraging thought,
Gives even affliction a grace,
   And reconciles man to his lot.

—WILLIAM COWPER

The Outlaw

O Brignall banks are wild and fair,
   And Greta woods are green,
And you may gather garlands there,
   Would grace a summer queen:

And as I rode by Dalton Hall,
    Beneath the turrets high,
A Maiden on the castle wall
    Was singing merrily:—

"O, Brignall banks are fresh and fair,
    And Greta woods are green!
I'd rather rove with Edmund there
    Than reign our English Queen."

"If, Maiden, thou wouldst wend with me
    To leave both tower and town,
Thou first must guess what life lead we,
    That dwell by dale and down:
And if thou canst that riddle read,
    As read full well you may,
Then to the green-wood shalt thou speed
    As blithe as Queen of May."

Yet sung she, "Brignall banks are fair,
    And Greta woods are green!
I'd rather rove with Edmund there
    Than reign our English Queen.

"I read you by your bugle horn
    And by your palfrey good,
I read you for a Ranger sworn
    To keep the King's green-wood."
"A Ranger, Lady, winds his horn,
    And 'tis at peep of light;
His blast is heard at merry morn,
    And mine at dead of night."

Yet sung she, "Brignall banks are fair,
    And Greta woods are gay!
I would I were with Edmund there,
    To reign his Queen of May!

"With burnish'd brand and musketoon
  So gallantly you come,
I read you for a bold Dragoon,
  That lists the tuck of drum."
"I list no more the tuck of drum,
  No more the trumpet hear;
But when the beetle sounds his hum,
  My comrades take the spear.

"And O! though Brignall banks be fair,
  And Greta woods be gay,
Yet mickle must the maiden dare,
  Would reign my Queen of May!

"Maiden! a nameless life I lead,
  A nameless death I'll die;
The fiend whose lantern lights the mead
  Were better mate than I!
And when I'm with my comrades met
  Beneath the green-wood bough,
What once we were we all forget,
  Nor think what we are now."

Yet Brignall banks are fresh and fair,
  And Greta woods are green,
And you may gather flowers there
  Would grace a summer queen.
                              —SIR WALTER SCOTT

Proud Maisie

Proud Maisie is in the wood,
  Walking so early;
Sweet Robin sits on the bush
  Singing so rarely.

"Tell me, thou bonny bird,
    When shall I marry me?"
"When six braw gentlemen
    Kirkward shall carry ye."

"Who makes the bridal bed,
    Birdie, say truly?"
"The grey-headed sexton
    That delves the grave duly.

"The glow-worm o'er grave and stone
    Shall light thee steady;
The owl from the steeple sing
    Welcome, proud lady."

                —SIR WALTER SCOTT

Lady Clara Vere de Vere

Lady Clara Vere de Vere,
    Of me you shall not win renown:
You thought to break a country heart
    For pastime, ere you went to town.
At me you smiled, but unbeguiled
    I saw the snare, and I retired:
The daughter of a hundred Earls,
    You are not one to be desired.

Lady Clara Vere de Vere,
    I know you proud to bear your name,
Your pride is yet no mate for mine,
    Too proud to care from whence I came.
Nor would I break for your sweet sake
    A heart that doats on truer charms.
A simple maiden in her flower
    Is worth a hundred coats-of-arms.

Lady Clara Vere de Vere,
　　Some meeker pupil you must find,
For were you queen of all that is,
　　I could not stoop to such a mind.
You sought to prove how I could love,
　　And my disdain is my reply.
The lion on your old stone gates
　　Is not more cold to you than I.

Lady Clara Vere de Vere,
　　You put strange memories in my head.
Not thrice your branching limes have blown
　　Since I beheld young Laurence dead.
Oh your sweet eyes, your low replies:
　　A great enchantress you may be;
But there was that across his throat
　　Which you had hardly cared to see.

Lady Clara Vere de Vere,
　　When thus he met his mother's view,
She had the passions of her kind,
　　She spake some certain truths of you.
Indeed I heard one bitter word
　　That scarce is fit for you to hear;
Her manners had not that repose
　　Which stamps the caste of Vere de Vere.

Lady Clara Vere de Vere,
　　There stands a spectre in your hall:
The guilt of blood is at your door:
　　You changed a wholesome heart to gall.
You held your course without remorse,
　　To make him trust his modest worth,
And, last, you fix'd a vacant stare,
　　And slew him with your noble birth.

Trust me, Clara Vere de Vere,
　　From yon blue heavens above us bent

The grand old gardener and his wife
   Smile at the claims of long descent.
Howe'er it be, it seems to me,
   'Tis only noble to be good.
Kind hearts are more than coronets,
   And simple faith than Norman blood.

I know you, Clara Vere de Vere:
   You pine among your halls and towers:
The languid light of your proud eyes
   Is wearied of the rolling hours.
In glowing health, with boundless wealth,
   But sickening of a vague disease,
You know so ill to deal with time,
   You needs must play such pranks as these.

Clara, Clara Vere de Vere,
   If time be heavy on your hands,
Are there no beggars at your gate,
   Nor any poor about your lands?
Oh! teach the orphan-boy to read,
   Or teach the orphan-girl to sew,
Pray Heaven for a human heart,
   And let the foolish yeoman go.

          —ALFRED, LORD TENNYSON

John Gilpin

John Gilpin was a citizen
   Of credit and renown,
A train-band captain eke was he
   Of famous London Town.

John Gilpin's spouse said to her dear,
   "Though wedded we have been
These twice ten tedious years, yet we
   No holiday have seen.

"To-morrow is our wedding-day
  And we will then repair
Unto the Bell at Edmonton,
  All in a chaise and pair.

"My sister and my sister's child,
  Myself, and children three,
Will fill the chaise; so you must ride
  On horseback after we."

He soon replied, "I do admire
  Of womankind but one,
And you are she, my dearest dear,
  Therefore it shall be done.

"I am a linen-draper bold,
  As all the world doth know,
And my good friend, the Calender,
  Will lend his horse to go."

Quoth Mrs. Gilpin, "That's well said;
  And for that wine is dear,
We will be furnish'd with our own,
  Which is both bright and clear."

John Gilpin kiss'd his loving wife;
  O'erjoy'd was he to find
That, though on pleasure she was bent,
  She had a frugal mind.

The morning came, the chaise was brought,
  But yet was not allowed
To drive up to the door, lest all
  Should say that she was proud.

So three doors off the chaise was stay'd,
  Where they did all get in,

Six precious souls, and all agog
  To dash through thick and thin.

Smack went the whip, round went the wheels,
  Were never folk so glad;
The stones did rattle underneath,
  As if Cheapside were mad.

John Gilpin, at his horse's side,
  Seiz'd fast the flowing mane,
And up he got, in haste to ride,
  But soon came down again;

For saddle-tree scarce reach'd had he,
  His journey to begin,
When, turning round his head, he saw
  Three customers come in.

So down he came; for loss of time,
  Although it grieved him sore,
Yet loss of pence, full well he knew,
  Would trouble him much more.

'Twas long before the customers
  Were suited to their mind,
When Betty, screaming, came downstairs,
  "The wine is left behind!"

"Good lack!" quoth he, "yet bring it me,
  My leathern belt likewise,
In which I bear my trusty sword
  When I do exercise."

Now mistress Gilpin (careful soul!)
  Had two stone-bottles found,
To hold the liquor that she loved,
  And keep it safe and sound.

Each bottle had a curling ear,
  Through which the belt he drew,
And hung a bottle on each side,
  To make his balance true.

Then over all, that he might be
  Equipp'd from top to toe,
His long red cloak, well brush'd and neat,
  He manfully did throw.

Now see him mounted once again
  Upon his nimble steed,
Full slowly pacing o'er the stones,
  With caution and good heed.

But finding soon a smoother road
  Beneath his well-shod feet,
The snorting beast began to trot,
  Which gall'd him in his seat.

So, "Fair and softly," John he cried,
  But John he cried in vain;
That trot became a gallop soon,
  In spite of curb and rein.

So stooping down, as needs he must
  Who cannot sit upright,
He grasp'd the mane with both his hands,
  And eke, with all his might.

His horse, who never in that sort
  Had handled been before,
What thing upon his back had got
  Did wonder more and more.

Away went Gilpin, neck or nought;
  Away went hat and wig;

He little dreamt, when he set out,
   Of running such a rig.

The wind did blow, the cloak did fly,
   Like streamer long and gay,
Till loop and button failing both,
   At last it flew away.

Then might all people well discern
   The bottles he had slung;
A bottle swinging at each side,
   As hath been said or sung.

The dogs did bark, the children scream'd,
   Up flew the windows all;
And every soul cried out, Well done!
   As loud as he could bawl.

Away went Gilpin—who but he?
   His fame soon spread around,
"He carries weight! he rides a race!
   'Tis for a thousand pound!"

And still as fast as he drew near,
   'Twas wonderful to view
How in a trice the turnpike men
   Their gates wide open threw.

And now, as he went bowing down
   His reeking head full low,
The bottles twain behind his back
   Were shatter'd at a blow.

Down ran the wine into the road,
   Most piteous to be seen,
Which made his horse's flanks to smoke
   As they had basted been.

But still he seem'd to carry weight,
  With leathern girdle braced;
For all might see the bottle necks
  Still dangling at his waist.

Thus all through merry Islington
  These gambols he did play,
Until he came unto the Wash
  Of Edmonton so gay;

And there he threw the wash about
  On both sides of the way,
Just like unto a trundling mop,
  Or a wild goose at play.

At Edmonton his loving wife
  From the balcony spied
Her tender husband, wondering much
  To see how he did ride.

"Stop, stop, John Gilpin!—Here's the house"—
  They all aloud did cry;
"The dinner waits, and we are tired."
  Said Gilpin, "So am I!"

But yet his horse was not a whit
  Inclin'd to tarry there;
For why? his owner had a house
  Full ten miles off, at Ware.

So like an arrow swift he flew,
  Shot by an archer strong;
So did he fly—which brings me to
  The middle of my song.

Away went Gilpin, out of breath,
  And sore against his will,

Till, at his friend the Calender's,
   His horse at last stood still.

The Calender, amazed to see
   His neighbour in such trim,
Laid down his pipe, flew to the gate,
   And thus accosted him.

"What news? what news? your tidings tell,
   Tell me you must and shall—
Say, why bare-headed you are come,
   Or why you come at all?"

Now Gilpin had a pleasant wit,
   And loved a timely joke;
And thus, unto the Calender,
   In merry guise he spoke:

"I came because your horse would come,
   And, if I well forebode,
My hat and wig will soon be here,
   They are upon the road."

The Calender, right glad to find
   His friend in merry pin,
Return'd him not a single word,
   But to the house went in;

Whence straight he came, with hat and wig,
   A wig that flowed behind;
A hat not much the worse for wear,
   Each comely in its kind.

He held them up, and in his turn
   Thus show'd his ready wit;
"My head is twice as big as yours,
   They therefore needs must fit.

"But let me scrape the dust away,
      That hangs upon your face;
And stop and eat, for well you may
      Be in a hungry case."

Said John, "It is my wedding-day,
      And all the world would stare,
If wife should dine at Edmonton,
      And I should dine at Ware."

So, turning to his horse, he said,
      "I am in haste to dine;
'Twas for your pleasure you came here,
      You shall go back for mine."

Ah, luckless speech, and bootless boast!
      For which he paid full dear;
For, while he spake, a braying ass
      Did sing most loud and clear;

Whereat his horse did snort, as he
      Had heard a lion roar,
And gallop'd off with all his might,
      As he had done before.

Away went Gilpin, and away
      Went Gilpin's hat and wig;
He lost them sooner than at first,
      For why?—they were too big.

Now Mrs. Gilpin, when she saw
      Her husband posting down
Into the country far away,
      She pull'd out half-a-crown;

And thus unto the youth she said,
      That drove them to the Bell,

"This shall be yours, when you bring back
　　My husband safe and well."

The youth did ride, and soon did meet
　　John coming back amain;
Whom in a trice he tried to stop,
　　By catching at his rein;

But not performing what he meant,
　　And gladly would have done,
The frightened steed he frighted more,
　　And made him faster run.

Away went Gilpin, and away
　　Went postboy at his heels,
The postboy's horse right glad to miss
　　The rumbling of the wheels.

Six gentlemen upon the road
　　Thus seeing Gilpin fly,
With postboy scampering in the rear,
　　They rais'd a hue and cry:—

"Stop thief!—stop thief!—a highwayman!"
　　Not one of them was mute;
And all and each that passed that way
　　Did join in the pursuit.

And now the turnpike gates again
　　Flew open in short space:
The toll-men thinking as before
　　That Gilpin rode a race.

And so he did, and won it too,
　　For he got first to town;
Nor stopp'd till where he had got up
　　He did again get down.

Now let us sing, long live the king,
   And Gilpin, long live he;
And, when he next doth ride abroad,
   May I be there to see.

—WILLIAM COWPER

"My Last Duchess" is a graphic portrait which is also a miracle of condensation—a novel in fifty-six lines. The speaker is a highly cultured but domineering noble, a duke who is planning to marry the daughter of a count. Discussing the marriage settlement with the count's emissary, he shows off his art treasures and, at the same time, reveals his brutal character. Turning to a painting of his dead wife, the duke explains that she failed to value him as much as she should have done—a flattering phrase, a sunset, or a bough of cherries delighted her as much as the honor of his "nine-hundred-years-old name." Since the duke was clearly one who could not tolerate such lack of respect, he "gave commands"— what the orders were are not disclosed—whereupon she ceased to smile and, soon after, ceased to exist. The duke passes over her death as lightly as though he were not responsible for it, and returns blandly to the subject of a suitable dowry and his other objects of art.

With an uncanny gift for psychological portraiture, Browning has drawn not only the cruelly egotistical duke in all his hateful pride but also, by indirection, the young duchess in all her youth and innocence.

My Last Duchess

That's my last Duchess painted on the wall,
Looking as if she were alive. I call
That piece a wonder, now: Frà Pandolf's hands
Worked busily a day, and there she stands.
Will 't please you sit and look at her? I said
"Frà Pandolf" by design, for never read
Strangers like you that pictured countenance,
The depth and passion of its earnest glance,
But to myself they turned (since none puts by
The curtain I have drawn for you, but I)
And seemed as they would ask me, if they durst
How such a glance came there; so, not the first
Are you to turn and ask thus. Sir, 't was not
Her husband's presence only, called that spot
Of joy into the Duchess' cheek: perhaps
Frà Pandolf chanced to say, "Her mantle laps
Over my lady's wrist too much," or "Paint
Must never hope to reproduce the faint
Half-flush that dies along her throat:" such stuff
Was courtesy, she thought, and cause enough
For calling up that spot of joy. She had
A heart—how shall I say?—too soon made glad.
Too easily impressed: she liked whate'er
She looked on, and her looks went everywhere.
Sir, 't was all one! My favor at her breast,
The dropping of the daylight in the West,
The bough of cherries some officious fool
Broke in the orchard for her, the white mule
She rode with round the terrace—all and each
Would draw from her alike the approving speech,
Or blush, at least. She thanked men—good! but thanked
Somehow—I know not how—as if she ranked
My gift of a nine-hundred-years-old name
With anybody's gift. Who'd stoop to blame

This sort of trifling? Even had you skill
In speech—(which I have not)—to make your will
Quite clear to such an one, and say, "Just this
Or that in you disgusts me; here you miss,
Or there exceed the mark"—and if she let
Herself be lessoned so, nor plainly set
Her wits to yours, forsooth, and made excuse,
Even then would be some stooping; and I choose
Never to stoop. Oh sir, she smiled, no doubt,
Whenever I passed her; but who passed without
Much the same smile? This grew; I gave commands;
Then all smiles stopped together. There she stands
As if alive. Will 't please you rise? We'll meet
The company below, then. I repeat,
The Count your master's known munificence
Is ample warrant that no just pretence
Of mine for dowry will be disallowed;
Though his fair daughter's self, as I avowed
At starting, is my object. Nay, we'll go
Together down, sir. Notice Neptune, though,
Taming a sea-horse, thought a rarity,
Which Claus of Innsbruck cast in bronze for me!

—ROBERT BROWNING

THE HEART SPEAKS

As the title indicates, this section is devoted to beautifully worded—and sometimes unspoken—variations on the theme of love. Some of the poems are in the mood of an earlier and frankly more romantic time: gaily swaggering in the Scottish saga of "Lochinvar," from Sir Walter Scott's *Marmion;* unashamedly sentimental in Bret Harte's "Her Letter," with its reminders of the pioneering days of America's Far West. Here, too, is one of the greatest picture-and-story-poems in the English language, "The Eve of St. Agnes"—an old-world tapestry, a twilight tale, and a parable of young love triumphing over despair. Grief is here, also, its sorrow sounding in the grave music of A. E. Housman's "Bredon Hill" and Robert Browning's "Evelyn Hope." For the sake of contrast, a lighter note is expressed in Lowell's hesitant "The Courtin'" and Calverley's humorously turned (and brilliantly rhymed) "First Love."

As might be expected in a collection of story-poems, the ancient ballad form still persists; it takes on new life in modern adaptations. The spirit of the old ballad echoes strongly through Tennyson's surprising "Lady Clare" and Edna St. Vincent Millay's magic evocation of mother love in "Ballad of the Harp-Weaver."

Lady Clare

It was the time when lilies blow,
    And clouds are highest up in air,
Lord Ronald brought a lily-white doe
    To give his cousin, Lady Clare.

I trow they did not part in scorn:
    Lovers long-betrothed were they:
They two will wed the morrow morn,—
    God's blessing on the day!

"He does not love me for my birth,
    Nor for my lands so broad and fair;
He loves me for my own true worth,
    And that is well," said Lady Clare.

In there came old Alice the nurse,
    Said, "Who was this that went from thee?"
"It was my cousin," said Lady Clare,
    "To-morrow he weds with me."

"O God be thanked!" said Alice the nurse,
    "That all comes round so just and fair:
Lord Ronald is heir of all your lands,
    And you are *not* the Lady Clare."

"Are ye out of your mind, my nurse, my nurse,"
    Said Lady Clare, "that ye speak so wild?"
"As God's above," said Alice the nurse,
    "I speak the truth: you are my child.

"The old earl's daughter died at my breast;
    I speak the truth, as I live by bread!
I buried her like my own sweet child,
    And put my child in her stead."

"Falsely, falsely have ye done,
　O mother," she said, "if this be true,
To keep the best man under the sun
　So many years from his due."

"Nay now, my child," said Alice the nurse,
　"But keep the secret for your life,
And all you have will be Lord Ronald's,
　When you are man and wife."

"If I'm a beggar born," she said,
　"I will speak out, for I dare not lie.
Pull off, pull off, the brooch of gold,
　And fling the diamond necklace by."

"Nay now, my child," said Alice the nurse,
　"But keep the secret all you can."
She said, "Not so: but I will know
　If there be any faith in man."

"Nay now, what faith?" said Alice the nurse,
　"The man will cleave unto his right."
"And he shall have it," the lady replied,
　"Though I should die to-night."

"Yet give one kiss to your mother dear,
　Alas, my child, I sinned for thee."
"O mother, mother, mother," she said,
　"So strange it seems to me.

"Yet here's a kiss for my mother dear,
　My mother dear, if this be so,
And lay your hand upon my head,
　And bless me, mother, ere I go."

She clad herself in a russet gown,
　She was no longer Lady Clare:

She went by dale, and she went by down,
   With a single rose in her hair.

The lily-white doe Lord Ronald had brought
   Leaped up from where she lay,
Dropped her head in the maiden's hand,
   And followed her all the way.

Down stepped Lord Ronald from his tower:
   "O Lady Clare, you shame your worth!
Why come you dressed like a village maid,
   That are the flower of the earth?"

"If I come dressed like a village maid,
   I am but as my fortunes are:
I am a beggar born," she said,
   "And not the Lady Clare."

"Play me no tricks," said Lord Ronald,
   "For I am yours in word and in deed;
Play me no tricks," said Lord Ronald,
   "Your riddle is hard to read."

O, and proudly stood she up!
   Her heart within her did not fail;
She looked into Lord Ronald's eyes,
   And told him all her nurse's tale.

He laughed a laugh of merry scorn:
   He turned and kissed her where she stood:
"If you are not the heiress born,
   And I," said he, "the next in blood—

"If you are not the heiress born,
   And I," said he, "the lawful heir,
We two will wed to-morrow morn,
   And you shall still be Lady Clare."

            —ALFRED, LORD TENNYSON

Lochinvar

Oh, young Lochinvar is come out of the West,—
Through all the wide Border his steed was the best,
And save his good broadsword he weapons had none,—
He rode all unarm'd and he rode all alone.
So faithful in love, and so dauntless in war,
There never was knight like the young Lochinvar.

He stay'd not for brake, and he stopp'd not for stone,
He swam the Eske river where ford there was none,
But ere he alighted at Netherby gate,
The bride had consented, the gallant came late;
For a laggard in love and a dastard in war
Was to wed the fair Ellen of brave Lochinvar.

So boldly he enter'd the Netherby hall,
'Mong bridesmen and kinsmen and brothers and all.
Then spoke the bride's father, his hand on his sword
(For the poor craven bridegroom said never a word),
"Oh, come ye in peace here, or come ye in war,
Or to dance at our bridal, young Lord Lochinvar?"

"I long woo'd your daughter,—my suit you denied;
Love swells like the Solway, but ebbs like its tide;
And now am I come, with this lost love of mine
To lead but one measure, drink one cup of wine.
There are maidens in Scotland more lovely, by far,
That would gladly be bride to the young Lochinvar."

The bride kissed the goblet, the knight took it up,
He quaff'd off the wine and he threw down the cup.
She look'd down to blush, and she look'd up to sigh,
With a smile on her lips and a tear in her eye.
He took her soft hand ere her mother could bar:
"Now tread we a measure," said young Lochinvar.

So stately his form, and so lovely her face,
That never a hall such a galliard did grace,
While her mother did fret, and her father did fume,
And the bridegroom stood dangling his bonnet and plume,
And the bridesmaidens whisper'd, " 'Twere better by far
To have match'd our fair cousin with young Lochinvar."

One touch to her hand, and one word in her ear,
When they reach'd the hall-door, and the charger stood near;
So light to the croupe the fair lady he swung,
So light to the saddle before her he sprung!
"She is won! we are gone, over bank, bush, and scaur;
They'll have fleet steeds that follow," quoth young Lochinvar.

There was mounting 'mong Græmes of the Netherby clan;
Forsters, Fenwicks, and Musgraves, they rode and they ran;
There was racing and chasing on Cannobie Lee,
But the lost bride of Netherby ne'er did they see.
So daring in love, and so dauntless in war,
Have ye e'er heard of gallant like young Lochinvar?

—SIR WALTER SCOTT

Bredon Hill

In summertime on Bredon
    The bells they sound so clear;
Round both the shires they ring them
    In steeples far and near,
    A happy noise to hear.

Here of a Sunday morning
    My love and I would lie,
And see the colored counties,
    And hear the larks so high
    About us in the sky.

The bells would ring to call her
    In valleys miles away:
"Come all to church, good people,
    Good people, come and pray."
    But here my love would stay.

And I would turn and answer
    Among the springing thyme,
"Oh, peal upon our wedding,
    And we will hear the chime,
    And come to church in time."

But when the snows at Christmas
    On Bredon top were strown,
My love rose up so early
    And stole out unbeknown
    And went to church alone.

They tolled the one bell only,
    Groom there was none to see,
The mourners followed after,
    And so to church went she,
    And would not wait for me.

The bells they sound on Bredon,
    And still the steeples hum.
"Come all to church, good people"—
    Oh, noisy bells, be dumb;
    I hear you, I will come.

                              —A. E. HOUSMAN

Evelyn Hope

Beautiful Evelyn Hope is dead!
    Sit and watch by her side an hour.
That is her book-shelf, this her bed;
    She plucked that piece of geranium-flower,

Beginning to die too, in the glass.
  Little has yet been changed, I think;
The shutters are shut,—no light may pass
  Save two long rays through the hinge's chink.

Sixteen years old when she died!
  Perhaps she had scarcely heard my name,—
It was not her time to love; beside,
  Her life had many a hope and aim,
Duties enough and little cares;
  And now was quiet, now astir,—
Till God's hand beckoned unawares,
  And the sweet white brow is all of her.

Is it too late, then, Evelyn Hope?
  What! your soul was pure and true;
The good stars met in your horoscope,
  Made you of spirit, fire, and dew;
And just because I was thrice as old,
  And our paths in the world diverged so wide,
Each was naught to each, must I be told?
  We were fellow-mortals,—naught beside?

No, indeed! for God above
  Is great to grant as mighty to make,
And creates the love to reward the love;
  I claim you still, for my own love's sake!
Delayed, it may be, for more lives yet,
  Through worlds I shall traverse, not a few;
Much is to learn and much to forget
  Ere the time be come for taking you.

But the time will come—at last it will—
  When, Evelyn Hope, what meant, I shall say,
In the lower earth,—in the years long still,—
  That body and soul so pure and gay?
Why your hair was amber I shall divine,
  And your mouth of your own geranium's red,—

And what you would do with me, in fine,
   In the new life come in the old one's stead.

I have lived, I shall say, so much since then,
   Given up myself so many times,
Gained me the gains of various men,
   Ransacked the ages, spoiled the climes;
Yet one thing—one—in my soul's full scope,
   Either I missed or itself missed me,—
And I want and find you, Evelyn Hope!
   What is the issue? let us see!

I loved you, Evelyn, all the while;
   My heart seemed full as it could hold,—
There was place and to spare for the frank young smile,
   And the red young mouth, and the hair's young gold.
So, hush! I will give you this leaf to keep;
   See, I shut it inside the sweet, cold hand.
There, that is our secret! go to sleep;
   You will wake, and remember, and understand.

                    —ROBERT BROWNING

The Ballad of the Harp-Weaver

"Son," said my mother,
   When I was knee-high,
"You've need of clothes to cover you,
   And not a rag have I.

"There's nothing in the house
   To make a boy breeches,
Nor shears to cut a cloth with
   Nor thread to take stitches.

"There's nothing in the house
   But a loaf-end of rye,

And a harp with a woman's head
  Nobody will buy."
And she began to cry.

That was in the early fall.
  When came the late fall,
"Son," she said, "the sight of you
  Makes your mother's blood crawl,—

"Little skinny shoulder-blades
  Sticking through your clothes!
And where you'll get a jacket from
  God above knows!

"It's lucky for me, lad,
  Your daddy's in the ground,
And can't see the way I let
  His son go around!"
  And she made a queer sound.

That was in the late fall.
  When the winter came,
I'd not a pair of breeches
  Nor a shirt to my name.

I couldn't go to school,
  Or out of doors to play.
And all the other little boys
  Passed our way.

"Son," said my mother,
  "Come, climb into my lap,
And I'll chafe your little bones
  While you take a nap."

And, oh, but we were silly
  For half an hour or more,

Me with my long legs
    Dragging on the floor,

A-rock-rock-rocking
    To a mother-goose rhyme!
Oh, but we were happy
    For half an hour's time!

But there was I, a great boy,
    And what would folks say
To hear my mother singing me
    To sleep all day,
    In such a daft way?

Men say the winter
    Was bad that year;
Fuel was scarce,
    And food was dear.

A wind with a wolf's head
    Howled about our door,
And we burned up the chairs
    And sat upon the floor.

All that was left us
    Was a chair we couldn't break,
And the harp with a woman's head
    Nobody would take,
    For song or pity's sake.

The night before Christmas
    I cried with the cold,
I cried myself to sleep
    Like a two-year-old.

And in the deep night
    I felt my mother rise,

And stare down upon me
  With love in her eyes.

I saw my mother sitting
  On the one good chair,
A light falling on her
  From I couldn't tell where,

Looking nineteen,
  And not a day older,
And the harp with a woman's head
  Leaned against her shoulder.

Her thin fingers, moving
  In the thin, tall strings,
Were weav-weav-weaving
  Wonderful things.

Many bright threads,
  From where I couldn't see,
Were running through the harp-strings
  Rapidly,

And gold threads whistling
  Through my mother's hand.
I saw the web grow,
  And the pattern expand.

She wove a child's jacket,
  And when it was done
She laid it on the floor
  And wove another one.

She wove a red cloak
  So regal to see,
"She's made it for a king's son,"
  I said, "and not for me."
  But I knew it was for me.

She wove a pair of breeches
  Quicker than that!
She wove a pair of boots
  And a little cocked hat.

She wove a pair of mittens,
  She wove a little blouse,
She wove all night
  In the still, cold house.

She sang as she worked,
  And the harp-strings spoke;
Her voice never faltered,
  And the thread never broke.
  And when I awoke—

There sat my mother
  With the harp against her shoulder,
Looking nineteen
  And not a day older,

A smile about her lips,
  And a light about her head,
And her hands in the harp-strings
  Frozen dead.

And piled up beside her
  And toppling to the skies,
Were the clothes of a king's son,
  Just my size.

                           —EDNA ST. VINCENT MILLAY

     According to an old tradition, St. Agnes' Eve oc-
curs on January 20th and, since it is proverbially the
coldest day of the year, Keats begins his poem with
one of the coldest stanzas in all poetry. The bitter

chill of the first line is emphasized by the rest of the stanza: the owl hunched unhappily in spite of his feathers; the usually agile hare, trembling in his fur and limping through the icy grass; the closely huddled sheep; and the Beadsman telling his beads with frozen fingers, saying his prayers while his breath stands visibly suspended in the freezing air.

In contrast, the story itself is warm and opulent. It is based upon a legend that on St. Agnes' Eve girls are permitted a glimpse (or at least a vision) of their future husband. In this instance the lover wakes his beloved with "an ancient ditty, long since mute"—namely "La Belle Dame Sans Merci," one version of which may be found on page 358.

The Eve of St. Agnes

St. Agnes' Eve—Ah, bitter chill it was!
The owl, for all his feathers, was a-cold;
The hare limped trembling through the frozen grass,
And silent was the flock in woolly fold:
Numb were the Beadsman's fingers while he told
His rosary, and while his frosted breath,
Like pious incense from a censer old,
Seemed taking flight for heaven, without a death,
Past the sweet Virgin's picture, while his prayer he saith.

His prayer he saith, this patient, holy man;
Then takes his lamp, and riseth from his knees,
And back returneth, meager, barefoot, wan,
Along the chapel aisle by slow degrees:
The sculptured dead, on each side, seem to freeze,
Imprisoned in black, purgatorial rails:
Knights, ladies, praying in dumb orat'ries,
He passeth by, and his weak spirit fails
To think how they may ache in icy hoods and mails.

Northward he turneth through a little door,
And scarce three steps, ere Music's golden tongue
Flattered to tears this aged man and poor;
But no—already had his death-bell rung:
The joys of all his life were said and sung;
His was harsh penance on St. Agnes' Eve:
Another way he went, and soon among
Rough ashes sat he for his soul's reprieve,
And all night kept awake, for sinners' sake to grieve.

That ancient Beadsman heard the prelude soft;
And so it chanced, for many a door was wide,
From hurry to and fro. Soon, up aloft,
The silver, snarling trumpets 'gan to chide:
The level chambers, ready with their pride,
Were glowing to receive a thousand guests.
The carved angels, ever eager-eyed,
Stared, where upon their heads the cornice rests,
With hair blown back, and wings put crosswise on their
      breasts.

At length burst in the argent revelry,
With plume, tiara, and all rich array,
Numerous as shadows haunting faerily
The brain new-stuffed, in youth, with triumphs gay
Of old romance. These let us wish away,
And turn, sole-thoughted, to one Lady there,
Whose heart had brooded, all that wintry day,
On love, and winged St. Agnes' saintly care,
As she had heard old dames full many times declare.

They told her how, upon St. Agnes' Eve,
Young virgins might have visions of delight,
And soft adorings from their loves receive
Upon the honeyed middle of the night,
If ceremonies due they did aright;
As, supperless to bed they must retire,
And couch supine their beauties, lily white;

Nor look behind, nor sideways, but require
Of Heaven with upward eyes for all that they desire.

Full of this whim was thoughtful Madeline:
The music, yearning like a God in pain,
She scarcely heard: her maiden eyes divine,
Fixed on the floor, saw many a sweeping train
Pass by—she heeded not at all: in vain
Came many a tiptoe, amorous cavalier,
And back retired; not cooled by high disdain,
But she saw not: her heart was otherwhere;
She sighed for Agnes' dreams, the sweetest of the year.

She danced along with vague, regardless eyes,
Anxious her lips, her breathing quick and short:
The hallowed hour was near at hand: she sighs
Amid the timbrels, and the thronged resort
Of whisperers in anger or in sport;
'Mid looks of love, defiance, hate, and scorn,
Hoodwinked with faery fancy; all amort,
Save to St. Agnes and her lambs unshorn,
And all the bliss to be before tomorrow morn.

So, purposing each moment to retire,
She lingered still. Meantime, across the moors,
Had come young Porphyro, with heart on fire
For Madeline. Beside the portal doors,
Buttressed from moonlight, stands he, and implores
All saints to give him sight of Madeline,
But for one moment in the tedious hours,
That he might gaze and worship all unseen;
Perchance speak, kneel, touch, kiss—in sooth such things have
     been.

He ventures in: let no buzzed whisper tell,
All eyes be muffled, or a hundred swords
Will storm his heart, Love's feverous citadel:
For him, those chambers held barbarian hordes,

Hyena foemen, and hot-blooded lords,
Whose very dogs would execrations howl
Against his lineage; not one breast affords
Him any mercy in that mansion foul,
Save one old beldame, weak in body and in soul.

Ah, happy chance! the aged creature came,
Shuffling along with ivory-headed wand,
To where he stood, hid from the torch's flame,
Behind a broad hall pillar, far beyond
The sound of merriment and chorus bland.
He startled her: but soon she knew his face,
And grasped his fingers in her palsied hand,
Saying, "Mercy, Porphyro! hie thee from this place;
They are all here tonight, the whole bloody-thirsty race!

"Get hence! get hence! there's dwarfish Hildebrand:
He had a fever late, and in the fit
He cursed thee and thine, both house and land:
Then there's that old Lord Maurice, not a whit
More tame for his gray hairs—Alas me! flit!
Flit like a ghost away."—"Ah, Gossip dear,
We're safe enough; here in this arm-chair sit,
And tell me how—" "Good saints! not here, not here!
Follow me, child, or else these stones will be thy bier."

He followed through a lowly arched way,
Brushing the cobwebs with his lofty plume;
And as she muttered "Well-a—well-a-day!"
He found him in a little moonlight room,
Pale, latticed, chill, and silent as a tomb.
"Now tell me where is Madeline," said he,
"O tell me, Angela, by the holy loom
Which none but secret sisterhood may see,
When they St. Agnes' wool are weaving piously."

"St. Agnes! Ah! it is St. Agnes' Eve—
Yet men will murder upon holy days.

Thou must hold water in a witch's sieve,
And be liege-lord of all the Elves and Fays
To venture so: it fills me with amaze
To see thee, Porphyro!—St. Agnes' Eve!
God's help! my lady fair the conjurer plays
This very night: good angels her deceive!
But let me laugh awhile,—I've mickle time to grieve."

Feebly she laugheth in the languid moon,
While Porphyro upon her face doth look,
Like puzzled urchin on an aged crone
Who keepeth closed a wondrous riddle-book,
As spectacled she sits in chimney nook.
But soon his eyes grew brilliant, when she told
His lady's purpose; and he scarce could brook
Tears, at the thought of those enchantments cold,
And Madeline asleep in lap of legends old.

Sudden a thought came like a full-blown rose,
Flushing his brow, and in his pained heart
Made purple riot: then doth he propose
A stratagem, that makes the beldame start:
"A cruel man and impious thou art!
Sweet lady, let her pray, and sleep and dream
Alone with her good angels, far apart
From wicked men like thee. Go, go! I deem
Thou canst not surely be the same that thou didst seem."

"I will not harm her, by all saints I swear!"
Quoth Porphyro: "O may I ne'er find grace
When my weak voice shall whisper its last prayer,
If one of her soft ringlets I displace,
Or look with ruffian passion in her face.
Good Angela, believe me, by these tears;
Or I will, even in a moment's space,
Awake, with horrid shout, my foemen's ears,
And beard them, though they be more fanged than wolves
    and bears."

"Ah, why wilt thou affright a feeble soul?
A poor, weak, palsy-stricken, churchyard thing,
Whose passing-bell may ere the midnight toll;
Whose prayers for thee, each morn and evening,
Were never missed." Thus plaining, doth she bring
A gentler speech from burning Porphyro;
So woeful, and of such deep sorrowing,
That Angela gives promise she will do
Whatever he shall wish, betide her weal or woe.

Which was, to lead him, in close secrecy,
Even to Madeline's chamber, and there hide
Him in a closet, of such privacy
That he might see her beauty unespied,
And win perhaps that night a peerless bride,
While legioned fairies paced the coverlet,
And pale enchantment held her sleepy-eyed.
Never on such a night have lovers met,
Since Merlin paid his Demon all the monstrous debt.

"It shall be as thou wishest," said the Dame:
"All cates and dainties shall be stored there
Quickly on this feast-night: by the tambour frame
Her own lute thou wilt see: no time to spare,
For I am slow and feeble, and scarce dare
On such a catering trust my dizzy head.
Wait here, my child, with patience; kneel in prayer
The while. Ah! thou must needs the lady wed,
Or may I never leave my grave among the dead."

So saying she hobbled off with busy fear.
The lover's endless minutes slowly passed;
The dame returned, and whispered in his ear
To follow her; with aged eyes aghast
From fright of dim espial. Safe at last
Through many a dusky gallery, they gain
The maiden's chamber, silken, hushed and chaste;

'Where Porphyro took covert, pleased amain.
His poor guide hurried back with agues in her brain.

Her faltering hand upon the balustrade,
Old Angela was feeling for the stair,
When Madeline, St. Agnes' charmed maid,
Rose, like a missioned spirit, unaware:
With silver taper's light, and pious care,
She turned, and down the aged gossip led
To a safe level matting. Now prepare,
Young Porphyro, for gazing on that bed;
She comes, she comes again, like ring-dove frayed and fled.

Out went the taper as she hurried in;
Its little smoke, in pallid moonshine, died:
She closed the door, she panted, all akin
To spirits of the air, and visions wide:
No uttered syllable, or, woe betide!
But to her heart, her heart was voluble,
Paining with eloquence her balmy side;
As though a tongueless nightingale should swell
Her throat in vain, and die, heart-stifled, in her dell.

A casement high and triple-arched there was,
All garlanded with carven imageries,
Of fruits, and flowers, and bunches of knot-grass,
And diamonded with panes of quaint device,
Innumerable of stains and splendid dyes,
As are the tiger-moth's deep-damasked wings;
And in the midst, 'mong thousand heraldries,
And twilight saints, and dim emblazonings,
A shielded scutcheon blushed with blood of queens and kings.

Full on this casement shone the wintry moon,
And threw warm gules on Madeline's fair breast,
As down she knelt for Heaven's grace and boon;
Rose bloom fell on her hands, together prest,

And on her silver cross soft amethyst,
And on her hair a glory, like a saint:
She seemed a splendid angel, newly drest,
Save wings, for heaven:—Porphyro grew faint:
She knelt, so pure a thing, so free from mortal taint.

Anon his heart revives: her vespers done,
Of all its wreathed pearls her hair she frees;
Unclasps her warmed jewels one by one;
Loosens her fragrant bodice; by degrees
Her rich attire creeps rustling to her knees:
Half-hidden, like a mermaid in sea-weed,
Pensive awhile she dreams awake, and sees,
In fancy, fair St. Agnes in her bed,
But dares not look behind, or all the charm is fled.

Soon, trembling in her soft and chilly nest,
In sort of wakeful swoon, perplexed she lay,
Until the poppied warmth of sleep oppressed
Her soothed limbs, and soul fatigued away;
Flown, like a thought, until the morrow-day;
Blissfully havened both from joy and pain;
Clasped like a missal where swart Paynims pray;
Blinded alike from sunshine and from rain,
As though a rose should shut, and be a bud again.

Stolen to this paradise, and so entranced,
Porphyro gazed upon her empty dress,
And listened to her breathing, if it chanced
To wake into a slumberous tenderness;
Which when he heard, that minute did he bless,
And breathed himself: then from the closet crept,
Noiseless as fear in a wide wilderness,
And over the hushed carpet, silent, stept,
And 'tween the curtains peeped, where, lo!—how fast she
     slept.

Then by the bed-side, where the faded moon
Made a dim, silver twilight, soft he set
A table, and, half anguished, threw thereon
A cloth of woven crimson, gold, and jet:—
O for some drowsy Morphean amulet!
The boisterous, midnight, festive clarion,
The kettle-drum, and far-heard clarinet,
Affray his ears, though but in dying tone:—
The hall-door shuts again, and all the noise is gone.

And still she slept an azure-lidded sleep,
In blanched linen, smooth, and lavendered,
While he from forth the closet brought a heap
Of candied apple, quince, and plum, and gourd;
With jellies soother than the creamy curd,
And lucent syrops, tinct with cinnamon;
Manna and dates, in argosy transferred
From Fez; and spiced dainties, every one,
From silken Samarcand to cedared Lebanon.

These delicates he heaped with glowing hand
On golden dishes and in baskets bright
Of wreathed silver: sumptuous they stand
In the retired quiet of the night,
Filling the chilly room with perfume light.—
"And now, my love, my seraph fair, awake!
Thou art my heaven, and I thine eremite:
Open thine eyes, for meek St. Agnes' sake,
Or I shall drowse beside thee, so my soul doth ache."

Thus whispering, his warm, unnerved arm
Sank in her pillow. Shaded was her dream
By the dusk curtains:—'twas a midnight charm
Impossible to melt as iced stream:
The lustrous salvers in the moonlight gleam;
Broad golden fringe upon the carpet lies:
It seemed he never, never could redeem

From such a stedfast spell his lady's eyes
So mused awhile, entoiled in woofed phantasies.

Awakening up, he took her hollow lute,—
Tumultuous,—and, in chords that tenderest be,
He played an ancient ditty, long since mute,
In Provence called, "La belle dame sans mercy:"
Close to her ear touching the melody;—
Wherewith disturbed, she uttered a soft moan:
He ceased—she panted quick—and suddenly
Her blue affrayed eyes wide open shone:
Upon his knees he sank, pale as smooth-sculptured stone.

Her eyes were open, but she still beheld,
Now wide awake, the vision of her sleep:
There was a painful change, that nigh expelled
The blisses of her dream so pure and deep
At which fair Madeline began to weep,
And moan forth witless words with many a sigh,
While still her gaze on Porphyro would keep;
Who knelt, with joined hands and piteous eye,
Fearing to move or speak, she looked so dreamingly.

"Ah, Porphyro!" said she, "but even now
Thy voice was at sweet tremble in mine ear,
Made tuneable with every sweetest vow;
And those sad eyes were spiritual and clear:
How changed thou art! how pallid, chill, and drear!
Give me that voice again, my Porphyro,
Those looks immortal, those complainings dear!
Oh, leave me not in this eternal woe,
For if thou diest, my Love, I know not where to go."

Beyond a mortal man impassioned far
At these voluptuous accents, he arose,
Ethereal, flushed, and like a throbbing star
Seen 'mid the sapphire heaven's deep repose;

Into her dream he melted, as the rose
Blendeth its odor with the violet,—
Solution sweet: meantime the frost-wind blows
Like Love's alarum, pattering the sharp sleet
Against the window-panes; St. Agnes' moon hath set.

'Tis dark: quick pattereth the flaw-blown sleet.
"This is no dream, my bride, my Madeline!"
'Tis dark: the iced gusts still rave and beat:
"No dream, alas! alas! and woe is mine!
Porphyro will leave me here to fade and pine.
Cruel! what traitor could thee hither bring?
I curse not, for my heart is lost in thine,
Though thou forsakest a deceived thing;—
A dove forlorn and lost with sick unpruned wing."

"My Madeline! sweet dreamer! lovely bride!
Say, may I be for aye thy vassal blest?
Thy beauty's shield, heart-shaped and vermeil-dyed?
Ah, silver shrine, here will I take my rest
After so many hours of toil and quest,
A famished pilgrim,—saved by miracle.
Though I have found, I will not rob thy nest,
Saving of thy sweet self; if thou think'st well
To trust, fair Madeline, to no rude infidel.

"Hark! 'tis an elfin-storm from faery land,
Of haggard seeming, but a boon indeed:
Arise—arise! the morning is at hand;—
The bloated wassailers will never heed;—
Let us away, my love, with happy speed;
There are no ears to hear, or eyes to see,—
Drowned all in Rhenish and the sleepy mead:
Awake! arise! my love, and fearless be,
For o'er the southern moors I have a home for thee."

She hurried at his words, beset with fears,
For there were sleeping dragons all around,

At glaring watch, perhaps, with ready spears—
Down the wide stairs a darkling way they found;
In all the house was heard no human sound.
A chain-drooped lamp was flickering by each door;
The arras, rich with horseman, hawk, and hound,
Fluttered in the besieging wind's uproar;
And the long carpets rose along the gusty floor.

They glide, like phantoms, into the wide hall;
Like phantoms, to the iron porch they glide,
Where lay the Porter, in uneasy sprawl,
With a huge empty flagon by his side:
The wakeful bloodhound rose, and shook his hide,
But his sagacious eye an inmate owns:—
By one, and one, the bolts full easy slide:—
The chains lie silent on the footworn stones;
The key turns, and the door upon its hinges groans.

And they are gone; aye, ages long ago
These lovers fled away into the storm.
That night the Baron dreamt of many a woe,
And all his warrior-guests with shade and form
Of witch, and demon, and large coffin-worm,
Were long be-nightmared. Angela the old
Died palsy-twitched, with meager face deform;
The Beadsman, after thousand aves told,
For aye unsought-for slept among his ashes cold.

—JOHN KEATS

The Glove and the Lions

King Francis was a hearty king, and loved a royal sport,
And one day, as his lions fought, sat looking on the court.
The nobles fill'd the benches, with the ladies in their pride,
And 'mongst them sat the Count de Lorge, with one for whom
    he sigh'd:

And truly 'twas a gallant thing to see that crowning show,
Valor and love, and a king above, and the royal beasts below.

Ramp'd and roar'd the lions, with horrid laughing jaws;
They bit, they glared, gave blows like beams, a wind went
    with their paws,
With wallowing might and stifled roar they roll'd on one an-
    other,
Till all the pit with sand and mane was in a thunderous
    smother;
The bloody foam above the bars came whisking through the
    air;
Said Francis then, "Faith, gentlemen, we're better here than
    there."
De Lorge's love o'erheard the king, a beauteous, lively dame,
With smiling lips and sharp bright eyes, which always seem'd
    the same;
She thought, The Count my lover is brave as brave can be;
He surely would do wondrous things to show his love of me;
King, ladies, lovers, all look on; the occasion is divine;
I'll drop my glove, to prove his love; great glory will be mine.

She dropp'd her glove, to prove his love, then look'd at him
    and smiled;
He bow'd, and in a moment leap'd among the lions wild:
The leap was quick, return was quick, he has regain'd his
    place,
Then threw the glove, but not with love, right in the lady's
    face.
"By heaven," said Francis, "rightly done!" and he rose from
    where he sat;
"No love," quoth he, "but vanity, sets love a task like that."

                                        —LEIGH HUNT

The Romance of the Swan's Nest

Little Ellie sits alone
Mid the beeches of a meadow,
　By a stream-side on the grass,
　And the trees are showering down
Doubles of their leaves in shadow,
　On her shining hair and face.

She has thrown her bonnet by,
And her feet she has been dipping
　In the shallow water's flow.
　Now she holds them nakedly
In her hands all sleek and dripping,
　While she rocketh to and fro.

Little Ellie sits alone,
And the smile she softly uses
　Fills the silence like a speech,
　While she thinks what shall be done,—
And the sweetest pleasure chooses
　For her future within reach.

Little Ellie in her smile
Chooses . . . "I will have a lover,
　Riding on a steed of steeds!
　He shall love me without guile,
And to *him* I will discover
　The swan's nest among the reeds.

"And the steed shall be red-roan,
And the lover shall be noble,
　With an eye that takes the breath.
　And the lute he plays upon
Shall strike ladies into trouble,
　And his sword strikes men to death.

"And the steed it shall be shod
All in silver, housed in azure,
  And the mane shall swim the wind;
  And the hoofs along the sod
Shall flash onward and keep measure,
  Till the shepherds look behind.

"But my lover will not prize
All the glory that he rides in,
  When he gazes in my face.
  He will say, 'O Love, thine eyes
Build the shrine my soul abides in,
  And I kneel here for thy grace.'

"Then, ay then—he shall kneel low
With the red-roan steed anear him,
  Which shall seem to understand—
  Till I answer, 'Rise and go!
For the world must love and fear him,
  Whom I gift with heart and hand.'

"Then he will arise so pale,
I shall feel my own lips tremble
  With a *yes* I must not say;
  Nathless maiden-brave, 'Farewell,'
I will utter, and dissemble;—
  'Light to-morrow with to-day.'

"Then he'll ride among the hills
To the wide world past the river,
  There to put away all wrong;
  To make straight distorted wills,
And to empty the broad quiver
  Which the wicked bear along.

"Three times shall a young foot-page
Swim the stream and climb the mountain

And kneel down beside my feet;—
'Lo, my master sends this gage,
Lady, for thy pity's counting!
    What wilt thou exchange for it?'

"And the first time, I will send
A white rosebud for a guerdon,—
    And the second time, a glove;
But the third time, I may bend
From my pride, and answer, 'Pardon,
    If he comes to take my love.'

"Then the young foot-page will run,—
Then my lover will ride faster,
    Till he kneeleth at my knee:
'I am a duke's oldest son!
Thousand serfs do call me master,—
    But, O Love, I love but *thee!*'

"He will kiss me on the mouth
Then, and lead me as a lover
    Through the crowds that praise his deeds;
And, when soul-tied by one troth,
Unto *him* I will discover
    That swan's nest among the reeds."

Little Ellie, with her smile
Not yet ended, rose up gayly,
    Tied the bonnet, donned the shoe,
And went homeward, round a mile,
Just to see, as she did daily,
    What more eggs were with the two.

Pushing through the elm-tree copse,
Winding up the stream, light-hearted,
    Where the osier pathway leads,—
Past the boughs she stoops—and stops.

Lo, the wild swan had deserted,
   And a rat had gnawed the reeds.

Ellie went home sad and slow.
If she found the lover ever,
   With his red-roan steed of steeds,
   Sooth I know not! but I know
She could never show him—never,
   That swan's nest among the reeds!

                    —ELIZABETH BARRETT BROWNING

Before Sedan

"The dead hand clasped a letter."—Special Correspondent

Here in this leafy place,
   Quiet he lies,
Cold, with his sightless face
   Turned to the skies;
'Tis but another dead;—
All you can say is said.

Carry his body hence,—
   Kings must have slaves;
Kings climb to eminence
   Over men's graves.
So this man's eye is dim;—
Throw the earth over him.

What was the white you touched,
   There at his side?
Paper his hand had clutched
   Tight ere he died;
Message or wish, may be:—
Smooth out the folds and see.

Hardly the worst of us
    Here could have smiled!—
Only the tremulous
    Words of a child:—
Prattle, that had for stops
Just a few ruddy drops.

Look. She is sad to miss,
    Morning and night,
His—her dead father's—kiss,
    Tries to be bright,
Good to mamma, and sweet
That is all. *"Marguerite."*

Ah, if beside the dead
    Slumbered the pain!
Ah, if the hearts that bled
    Slept with the slain!
If the grief died!—But no.
Death will not have it so.

                                    —AUSTIN DOBSON

The Courtin'

God makes sech nights, all white an' still
    Fur'z you can look or listen,
Moonshine an' snow on field an' hill,
    All silence an' all glisten.

Zekle crep' up quite unbeknown
    An' peeked in thru' the winder,
An' there sot Huldy all alone,
    'Ith no one nigh to hender.

A fireplace filled the room's one side
    With half a cord o' wood in—
There warn't no stoves (tell comfort died)
    To bake ye to a puddin'.

The wa'nut logs shot sparkles out
  Towards the pootiest, bless her,
An' leetle flames danced all about
  The chiny on the dresser.

Agin the chimbley crook-necks hung,
  An' in amongst 'em rusted
The ole queen's arm thet gran'ther Young
  Fetched back from Concord busted.

The very room, coz she was in,
  Seemed warm from floor to ceilin',
An' she looked full ez rosy agin
  Ez the apples she was peelin'.

'Twas kin' o' kingdom-come to look
  On sech a blessed cretur,
A dogrose blushin' to a brook
  Ain't modester nor sweeter.

He was six foot o' man, A 1,
  Clear grit an' human natur';
None couldn't quicker pitch a ton
  Nor dror a furrer straighter.

He'd sparked it with full twenty gals,
  He'd squired 'em, danced 'em, druv 'em,
Fust this one, an' then thet, by spells—
  All is, he couldn't love 'em.

But long o' her his veins 'ould run
  All crinkly like curled maple,
The side she breshed felt full o' sun
  Ez a south slope in Ap'il.

She thought no v'ice hed sech a swing
  Ez hisn in the choir;

My! when he made Ole Hunderd ring
    She *knowed* the Lord was nigher.

An' she'd blush scarlit, right in prayer,
    When her new meetin'-bunnet
Felt somehow thru' its crown a pair
    O' blue eyes sot upun it.

Thet night, I tell ye, she looked *some!*
    She seemed to've gut a new soul,
For she felt sartin-sure he'd come,
    Down to her very shoe-sole.

She heered a foot, an' knowed it tu,
    A-raspin' on the scraper,—
All ways to once her feelin's flew
    Like sparks in burnt-up paper.

He kin' o' l'itered on the mat
    Some doubtfle o' the sekle,
His heart kep' goin' pity-pat,
    But hern went pity Zekle.

An' yit she gin her cheer a jerk
    Ez though she wished him furder,
An' on her apples kep' to work,
    Parin' away like murder.

"You want to see my Pa, I s'pose!"
    "Wal . . . no . . . I come designin'"—
"To see my Ma? She's sprinklin' clo'es
    Agin to-morrer's i'nin'."

To say why gals act so or so,
    Or don't, 'ould be presumin';
Mebby to mean *yes* an' say *no*
    Comes nateral to women.

He stood a spell on one foot fust,
  Then stood a spell on t'other,
An' on which one he felt the wust
  He couldn't ha' told ye nuther.

Says he, "I'd better call agin";
  Says she, "Think likely, Mister":
Thet last word pricked him like a pin,
  An' . . . Wal, he up an' kist her.

When Ma bimeby upon 'em slips,
  Huldy sot pale ez ashes,
All kin' o' smily roun' the lips
  An' teary roun' the lashes.

For she was jes' the quiet kind
  Whose naturs never vary,
Like streams that keep a summer mind
  Snowhid in Jenooary.

The blood clost roun' her heart felt glued
  Too tight for all expressin',
Tell mother see how metters stood,
  An' gin 'em both her blessin'.

Then her red come back like the tide
  Down to the Bay o' Fundy,
An' all I know is they was cried
  In meetin' come nex' Sunday.

                    —JAMES RUSSELL LOWELL

Her Letter

I'm sitting alone by the fire,
  Dressed just as I came from the dance,
In a robe even *you* would admire,—
  It cost a cool thousand in France;

I'm be-diamonded out of all reason,
 My hair is done up in a cue:
In short, sir, "the belle of the season"
 Is wasting an hour upon you.

A dozen engagements I've broken;
 I left in the midst of a set;
Likewise a proposal, half spoken,
 That waits—on the stairs—for me yet.
They say he'll be rich,—when he grows up,—
 And then he adores me indeed;
And you, sir, are turning your nose up,
 Three thousand miles off, as you read.

"And how do I like my position?"
 "And what do I think of New York?"
"And now, in my higher ambition,
 With whom do I waltz, flirt, or talk?"
"And isn't it nice to have riches,
 And diamonds and silks, and all that?"
"And aren't they a change to the ditches
 And tunnels of Poverty Flat?"

Well, yes,—if you saw us out driving
 Each day in the Park, four-in-hand,
If you saw poor dear mamma contriving
 To look supernaturally grand,—
If you saw papa's picture, as taken
 By Brady, and tinted at that,—
You'd never suspect he sold bacon
 And flour at Poverty Flat.

And yet, just this moment, when sitting
 In the glare of the grand chandelier,—
In the bustle and glitter befitting
 The "finest *soirée* of the year,"—
In the midst of a *gaze de Chambéry*,
 And the hum of the smallest of talk,—

Somehow, Joe, I thought of the "Ferry,"
  And the dance that we had on "The Fork";

Of Harrison's barn, with its muster
  Of flags festooned over the wall;
Of candles that shed their soft lustre
  And tallow on head-dress and shawl;
Of the steps that we took to one fiddle,
  Of the dress of my queer *vis-à-vis;*
And how I once went down the middle
  With the man that shot Sandy McGee;

Of the moon that was quietly sleeping
  On the hill, when the time came to go;
Of the few baby peaks that were peeping
  From under their bedclothes of snow;
Of that ride,—that to me was the rarest;
  Of—the something you said at the gate.
Ah! Joe, then I wasn't an heiress
  To "the best-paying lead in the State."

Well, well, it's all past; yet it's funny
  To think, as I stood in the glare
Of fashion and beauty and money,
  That I should be thinking, right there,
Of some one who breasted high water,
  And swam the North Fork, and all that,
Just to dance with old Folinsbee's daughter,
  The Lily of Poverty Flat.

But goodness! what nonsense I'm writing!
  (Mamma says my taste still is low),
Instead of my triumphs reciting,
  I'm spooning on Joseph,—heigh-ho!
And I'm to be "finished" by travel,—
  Whatever's the meaning of that.
Oh, why did papa strike pay gravel
  In drifting on Poverty Flat?

Good-night!—here's the end of my paper;
    Good-night!—if the longitude please,—
For maybe, while wasting my taper,
    Your sun's climbing over the trees.
But know, if you haven't got riches,
    And are poor, dearest Joe, and all that,
That my heart's somewhere there in the ditches,
    And you've struck it,—on Poverty Flat.

                                    —BRET HARTE

First Love

O my earliest love, who, ere I number'd
    Ten sweet summers, made my bosom thrill!
Will a swallow—or a swift, or some bird—
    Fly to her and say, I love her still?

Say my life's a desert drear and arid,
    To its one green spot I aye recur:
Never, never—although three times married—
    Have I cared a jot for aught but her.

No, mine own! though early forced to leave you,
    Still my heart was there where first we met;
In those "Lodgings with an ample sea-view,"
    Which were, forty years ago, "To Let."

There I saw her first, our landlord's oldest
    Little daughter. On a thing so fair
Thou, O Sun,—who (so they say) beholdest
    Everything,—hast gazed, I tell thee, ne'er.

There she sat—so near me, yet remoter
    Than a star—a blue-eyed, bashful imp:
On her lap she held a happy bloater.
    'Twixt her lips a yet more happy shrimp.

And I loved her, and our troth we plighted
  On the morrow by the shingly shore:
In a fortnight to be disunited
  By a bitter fate forevermore.

O my own, my beautiful, my blue-eyed!
  To be young once more, and bite my thumb
At the world and all its cares with you, I'd
  Give no inconsiderable sum.

Hand in hand we tramp'd the golden seaweed,
  Soon as o'er the gray cliff peep'd the dawn:
Side by side, when came the hour for tea, we'd
  Crunch the mottled shrimp and hairy prawn:—

Has she wedded some gigantic shrimper,
  That sweet mite with whom I loved to play?
Is she girt with babes that whine and whimper,
  That bright being who was always gay?

Yes—she has at least a dozen wee things!
  Yes—I see her darning corduroys,
Scouring floors, and setting out the tea-things,
  For a howling herd of hungry boys,

In a home that reeks of tar and sperm-oil!
  But at intervals she thinks, I know,
Of those days which we, afar from turmoil,
  Spent together forty years ago.

O my earliest love, still unforgotten,
  With your downcast eyes of dreamy blue!
Never, somehow, could I seem to cotton
  To another as I did to you!

                    —CHARLES STUART CALVERLEY

Candor

"I know what you're going to say," she said,
 And she stood up, looking uncommonly tall:
 "You are going to speak of the hectic fall,
And say you're sorry the summer's dead,
 And no other summer was like it, you know,
 And can I imagine what made it so.
Now aren't you, honestly?" "Yes," I said.

"I know what you're going to say," she said:
 "You are going to ask if I forget
 That day in June when the woods were wet,
And you carried me"—here she drooped her head—
 "Over the creek; you are going to say,
 Do I remember that horrid day.
Now aren't you, honestly?" "Yes," I said.

"I know what you're going to say," she said:
 "You are going to say that since that time
 You have rather tended to run to rhyme,
And"—her clear glance fell, and her cheek grew red—
 "And have I noticed your tone was queer?
 Why, everybody has seen it here!
Now aren't you, honestly?" "Yes," I said.

"I know what you're going to say," I said:
 "You're going to say you've been much annoyed;
 And I'm short of tact—you will say, devoid—
And I'm clumsy and awkward; and call me Ted;
 And I bear abuse like a dear old lamb;
 And you'll have me, anyway, just as I am.
Now aren't you, honestly?" "Ye-es," she said.

                                —HENRY CUYLER BUNNER

The Ideal Husband to His Wife

We've lived for forty years, dear wife,
   And walked together side by side,
And you to-day are just as dear
   As when you were my bride.
I've tried to make life glad for you,
   One long, sweet honeymoon of joy,
A dream of marital content,
   Without the least alloy.
I've smoothed all boulders from our path,
   That we in peace might toil along,
By always hastening to admit
   That I was right and you were wrong.

No mad diversity of creed
   Has ever sundered me from thee;
For I permit you evermore
   To borrow your ideas of me.
And thus it is, through weal or woe,
   Our love forevermore endures;
For I permit that you should take
   My views and creeds and make them yours.
And thus I let you have my way,
   And thus in peace we toil along,
For I am willing to admit
   That I am right and you are wrong.

And when our matrimonial skiff
   Strikes snags in love's meandering stream,
I lift our shallop from the rocks,
   And float as in a placid dream.
And well I know our marriage bliss
   While life shall last will never cease;
For I shall always let thee do,
   In generous love, just what I please.

Peace comes, and discord flies away,
   Love's bright day follows hatred's night;
For I am ready to admit
   That you are wrong and I am right.

—SAM WALTER FOSS

PRAISE AND PATRIOTISM

The poems in this section are on many different
levels, personal, historical, and symbolical, but all
have the power to stir the mind and touch the heart.
They take the reader through many lives as well as
many crises. Some, like Leigh Hunt's "Abou Ben
Adhem" and John Hay's "Banty Tim," attest man's
essential dignity, his combination of communal faith
and individual courage. Others, such as Thomas
Moore's lyrical cry, "The Minstrel Boy," James Montgomery's tragic "The Patriot's Password," and Lord
Byron's dramatic monolog, "The Prisoner of Chillon," palpitate with the fervor of man's great dream:
a deathless longing for liberty. The poems by Tennyson, Whitman, and Holmes disclose further aspects of
heroic humanity—quiet courage, universal love of
justice, and a devotion to duty which is "the way
to glory."

Abou Ben Adhem

Abou Ben Adhem (may his tribe increase!)
Awoke one night from a deep dream of peace,
And saw within the moonlight in his room,
Making it rich, and like a lily in bloom,
An Angel, writing in a book of gold;
Exceeding peace had made Ben Adhem bold,
And to the presence in the room he said,
"What writest thou?"—The vision raised its head,
And with a look made of all sweet accord,
Answer'd, "The names of those who love the Lord."
"And is mine one?" said Abou. "Nay, not so,"
Replied the angel. Abou spoke more low,
But cheerily still; and said, "I pray thee, then,
Write me as one that loves his fellowmen."
The angel wrote and vanish'd. The next night
It came again, with a great wakening light,
And show'd the names whom love of God had bless'd,
And, lo! Ben Adhem's name led all the rest.

—LEIGH HUNT

Banty Tim

I reckon I git your drift, gents—
    You 'low the boy shan't stay;
This is a white man's country;
    You're dimocrats, you say;
And whereas, and seein', and wherefore
    The times bein' all out o' j'int,
The nigger has got to mosey
    From the limits o' Spunky P'int.

Le's reason the thing a minut.
    I'm an old-fashioned dimocrat, too.
Though I laid my politics out o' the way
    For to keep till the war was through.

But I come back here, allowin'
  To vote as I used to do,
Though it gravels me like the devil to train
  Along o' sich fools as you.

Now, dog my cats if I kin see
  In all the light of day,
What you've got to do with the question
  Ef Tim shall go or stay.
And furder than that I give notice,
  Ef one of you tetches the boy,
He kin check his trunks to a warmer clime
  Than he'll find in Illanoy.

Why, blame your hearts, jest hear me.
  You know that ungodly day
When our left struck Vicksburg Heights,
  How ripped and torn and tattered we lay.
When the rest retreated I stayed behind,
  Fur reasons sufficient to me—
With a rib caved in and a leg on a strike,
  I sprawled on that cursed glacee.[1]

Lord! how the hot sun went for us,
  And br'iled and blistered and burned!
How the rebel bullets whizzed round us
  When a cuss in his death grip turned!
Till long toward dusk I seen a thing
  I couldn't believe for a spell;
That nigger—that Tim—was a crawlin' to me
  Through that fireproof, gilt-edged hell!

The rebels seen him as quick as me,
  And the bullets buzzed like bees;
But he jumped for me and shouldered me,
  Though a shot brought him once to his knees.

---

[1] Glacee: an exposed surface.

But he staggered up and packed me off,
  With a dozen stumbles and falls,
Till safe in our line he drapped us both,
  His black hide riddled with balls.

So, my gentle gazelles, thar's my answer,
  And here stands Banty Tim;
He trumped death's ace for me that day,
  And I'm not going back on him!
You may rezoloot till the cows come home
  But ef one of you tetches the boy,
He'll wrastle his hash tonight in hell,
  Or my name's not Tilmon Joy!

—JOHN HAY

John Burns of Gettysburg

Have you heard the story that gossips tell
Of Burns of Gettysburg? No? Ah, well:
Briefer the story of poor John Burns:
He was the fellow who won renown,—
The only man who didn't back down
When the rebels rode through his native town;
But held his own in the fight next day,
When all his townsfolk ran away.
That was in July, sixty-three,—
The very day that General Lee,
Flower of Southern chivalry,
Baffled and beaten, backward reeled
From a stubborn Meade and a barren field.

I might tell how, but the day before,
John Burns stood at his cottage door,
Looking down the village street,
Where, in the shade of his peaceful vine,
He heard the low of his gathered kine,
And felt their breath with incense sweet;

Or I might say, when the sunset burned
The old farm gable, he thought it turned
The milk that fell like a babbling flood
Into the milk-pail, red as blood!
Or how he fancied the hum of bees
Were bullets buzzing among the trees.
But all such fanciful thoughts as these
Were strange to a practical man like Burns,
Who minded only his own concerns,
Troubled no more by fancies fine
Than one of his calm-eyed, long-tailed kine,—
Quite old-fashioned and matter-of-fact,
Slow to argue, but quick to act.
That was the reason, as some folks say,
He fought so well on that terrible day.

And it was terrible. On the right
Raged for hours the heady fight,
Thundered the battery's double bass,—
Difficult music for men to face;
While on the left—where now the graves
Undulate like the living waves
That all that day unceasing swept
Up to the pits the rebels kept—
Round-shot ploughed the upland glades,
Sown with bullets, reaped with blades;
Shattered fences here and there
Tossed their splinters in the air;
The very trees were stripped and bare;
The barns that once held yellow grain
Were heaped with harvests of the slain;
The cattle bellowed on the plain,
The turkeys screamed with might and main,
The brooding barn-fowl left their rest
With strange shells bursting in each nest.

Just where the tide of battle turns,
Erect and lonely, stood old John Burns.

How do you think the man was dressed?
He wore an ancient long buff vest,
Yellow as saffron,—but his best;
And, buttoned over his manly breast,
Was a bright blue coat, with a rolling collar,
And large gilt buttons,—size of a dollar,—
With tails that the country-folk called "swaller."
He wore a broad-brimmed, bell-crowned hat,
White as the locks on which it sat.
Never had such a sight been seen
For forty years on the village green,
Since old John Burns was a country beau,
And went to the "quiltings" long ago.

Close at his elbows all that day,
Veterans of the Peninsula,
Sunburnt and bearded, charged away;
And striplings, downy of lip and chin,—
Clerks that the Home-Guard mustered in,—
Glanced, as they passed, at the hat he wore,
Then at the rifle his right hand bore;
And hailed him, from out their youthful lore,
With scraps of a slangy repertoire:
"How are you, White Hat?" "Put her through!"
"Your head's level!" and "Bully for you!"
Called him "Daddy,"—begged he'd disclose
The name of the tailor who made his clothes,
And what was the value he set on those;
While Burns, unmindful of jeer or scoff,
Stood there picking the rebels off,—
With his long brown rifle, and bell-crowned hat,
And the swallow-tails they were laughing at.

'Twas but a moment, for that respect
Which clothes all courage their voices checked;
And something the wildest could understand
Spoke in the old man's strong right hand,

And his corded throat, and the lurking frown
Of his eyebrows under his old bell-crown;
Until, as they gazed, there crept an awe
Through the ranks in whispers, and some men saw,
In the antique vestments and long white hair,
The Past of the Nation in battle there;
And some of the soldiers since declare
That the gleam of his old white hat afar,
Like the crested plume of the brave Navarre,
That day was their oriflamme of war.

So raged the battle. You know the rest:
How the rebels, beaten and backward pressed,
Broke at the final charge and ran.
At which John Burns—a practical man—
Shouldered his rifle, unbent his brows,
And then went back to his bees and cows.

That is the story of old John Burns;
This is the moral the reader learns:
In fighting the battle, the question's whether
You'll show a hat that's white, or a feather!

—BRET HARTE

The Minstrel Boy

The Minstrel Boy to the war is gone
    In the ranks of death you'll find him,
His father's sword he has girded on,
    And his wild harp slung behind him.
"Land of song!" said the warrior bard,
    "Tho' all the world betrays thee,
One sword, at least, thy rights shall guard,
    One faithful harp shall praise thee."

The minstrel fell! but the foeman's chain
    Could not bring that proud soul under;

The harp he loved ne'er spoke again,
 For he tore its chords asunder;
And said, "No chain shall sully thee,
 Thou soul of love and bravery.
Thy songs were made for the pure and free,
 They shall never sound in slavery."

        —THOMAS MOORE

Unstable in his personal emotions, Lord Byron
was constant in his passion for freedom. This passion
cost him his life. He joined the Greek insurgents in
their struggle for independence and died at thirty-
six, opposing the tyrannical Turks. Eight years before his death Byron had put his love for humanity
and his hatred of injustice in an impassioned sonnet.
On a visit to Lake Geneva in Switzerland, Byron
had inspected the rocky castle of Chillon where
Bonnivard, a Swiss patriot, had been imprisoned and
persecuted for trying to free his countrymen from
foreign oppression. The sonnet begins:

 Eternal Spirit of the chainless Mind!
 Brightest in dungeons, Liberty, thou art!

With this as his theme, Byron elaborated and per-
sonified the sentiment in the narrative which follows.

The Prisoner of Chillon

My hair is gray, but not with years,
  Nor grew it white
  In a single night,
As men's have grown from sudden fears;
My limbs are bowed, though not with toil,
 But rusted with a vile repose;

For they have been a dungeon's spoil,
   And mine has been the fate of those
To whom the goodly earth and air
Are banned and barred—forbidden fare.
But this was for my father's faith
I suffered chains and courted death
That father perished at the stake
For tenets he would not forsake;
And for the same his lineal race
In darkness found a dwelling-place.
We were seven, who now are one—
   Six in youth, and one in age,
Finished as they had begun,
   Proud of Persecution's rage;
One in fire, and two in field,
Their belief with blood have sealed:
Dying, as their father died,
For the God their foes denied.
Three were in a dungeon cast,
Of whom this wreck is left the last.

II.

There are seven pillars, of Gothic mould,
In Chillon's dungeons deep and old;
There are seven columns, massy and gray,
Dim with a dull imprisoned ray,
A sunbeam which hath lost its way,
And through the crevice and the cleft
Of the thick wall is fallen and left;
Creeping o'er the floor so damp,
Like a marsh's meteor lamp:
And in each pillar there is a ring,
   And in each ring there is a chain;
That iron is a cankering thing,
   For in these limbs its teeth remain,
With marks that will not wear away
Till I have done with this new day,

Which now is painful to these eyes,
Which have not seen the sun so rise
For years—I cannot count them o'er;
I lost their long and heavy score
When my last brother drooped and died,
And I lay living by his side.

III.

They chained us each to a column stone
And we were three—yet each alone.
We could not move a single pace;
We could not see each other's face,
But with that pale and livid light
That made us strangers in our sight;
And thus together, yet apart—
Fettered in hand, but joined in heart;
'Twas still some solace, in the dearth
Of the pure elements of earth,
To hearken to each other's speech,
And each turn comforter to each
With some new hope, or legend old,
Or song heroically bold;
But even these at length grew cold.
Our voices took a dreary tone,
An echo of the dungeon-stone,
　A grating sound—not full and free,
　As they of yore were wont to be;
　It might be fancy—but to me
They never sounded like our own.

IV.

I was the eldest of the three;
　And to uphold and cheer the rest
　I ought to do, and did, my best—
And each did well in his degree.

    The youngest, whom my father loved,
Because our mother's brow was given
To him—with eyes as blue as heaven—
    For him my soul was sorely moved;
And truly might it be distressed
To see such bird in such a nest;
For he was beautiful as day
    (When day was beautiful to me
    As to young eagles, being free),
    A polar day, which will not see
A sunset till its summer's gone,
    Its sleepless summer of long light,
The snow-clad offspring of the sun:
    And thus he was as pure and bright,
And in his natural spirit gay,
With tears for naught but other's ills,
And then they flowed like mountain-rills,
Unless he could assuage the woe
Which he abhorred to view below.

v.

The other was as pure of mind,
But formed to combat with his kind;
Strong in his frame, and of a mood
Which 'gainst the world in war had stood,
And perished in the foremost rank
    With joy; but not in chains to pine.
His spirit withered with their clank;
    I saw it silently decline—
    And so, perchance, in sooth, did mine;
But yet I forced it on to cheer
Those relics of a home so dear.
He was a hunter of the hills,
    Had followed there the deer and wolf;
    To him this dungeon was a gulf,
And fettered feet the worst of ills.

VI.

Lake Leman lies by Chillon's walls.
A thousand feet in depth below
Its massy waters meet and flow;
Thus much the fathom-line was sent
From Chillon's snow-white battlement,
Which round about the wave inthrals:
A double dungeon wall and wave
Have made—and like a living grave.
Below the surface of the lake
The dark vault lies wherein we lay,
We heard it ripple night and day;
Sounding o'er our heads it knocked
And I have felt the winter's spray
Wash through the bars when winds were high
And wanton in the happy sky;
And then the very rock hath rocked,
And I have felt it shake, unshocked,
Because I could have smiled to see
The death that would have set me free.

VII.

I said my nearer brother pined,
I said his mighty heart declined,
He loathed and put away his food;
It was not that 'twas coarse and rude,
For we were used to hunter's fare,
And for the like had little care:
The milk drawn from the mountain goat
Was changed for water from the moat,
Our bread was such as captive's tears
Have moistened many a thousand years,
Since man first pent his fellow men
Like brutes within an iron den;
But what were these to us or him?
These wasted not his heart or limb;

My brother's soul was of that mould
Which in a palace had grown cold,
Had his free breathing been denied
The range of the steep mountain's side.
But why delay the truth?—he died.
I saw, and could not hold his head,
Nor reach his dying hand—nor dead,
Though hard I strove, but strove in vain,
To rend and gnash my bonds in twain.
He died—and they unlocked his chain,
And scooped for him a shallow grave
Even from the cold earth of our cave.
I begged them, as a boon, to lay
His corse in dust whereon the day
Might shine—it was a foolish thought;
But then within my brain it wrought,
That even in death his freeborn breast
In such a dungeon could not rest.
I might have spared my idle prayer—
They coldly laughed, and laid him there,
The flat and turfless earth above
The being we so much did love;
His empty chain above it leant—
Such murder's fitting monument!

VIII.

But he, the favorite and the flower,
Most cherished since his natal hour,
His mother's image in fair face,
The infant love of all his race,
His martyred father's dearest thought,
My latest care—for whom I sought
To hoard my life, that his might be
Less wretched now, and one day free—
He, too, who yet had held untired
A spirit natural or inspired—

He, too, was struck, and day by day
Was withered on the stalk away.
O God! it is a fearful thing
To see the human soul take wing
In any shape, in any mood:
I've seen it rushing forth in blood;
I've seen it on the breaking ocean
Strive with a swoln, convulsive motion;
I've seen the sick and ghastly bed
Of sin, delirious with its dread;
But these were horrors—this was woe
Unmixed with such—but sure and slow.
He faded, and so calm and meek,
So softly worn, so sweetly weak,
So tearless, yet so tender—kind,
And grieved for those he left behind;
With all the while a cheek whose bloom
Was as a mockery of the tomb,
Whose tints as gently sunk away
As a departing rainbow's ray—
An eye of most transparent light,
That almost made the dungeon bright,
And not a word of murmur—not
A groan o'er his untimely lot,—
A little talk of better days,
A little hope my own to raise,
For I was sunk in silence—lost
In this last loss, of all the most;
And then the sighs he would suppress
Of fainting nature's feebleness,
More slowly drawn, grew less and less:
I listened, but I could not hear—
I called, for I was wild with fear;
I knew 'twas hopeless, but my dread
Would not be thus admonished;
I called, and thought I heard a sound—
I burst my chain with one strong bound,

And rushed to him:—I found him not,
I only stirred in this black spot,
I only lived—*I* only drew
The accursed breath of dungeon-dew;
The last—the sole—the dearest link
Between me and the eternal brink,
Which bound me to my failing race,
Was broken in this fatal place.
One on the earth, and one beneath—
My brothers—both had ceased to breathe:
I took that hand which lay so still,
Alas! my own was full as chill;
I had not strength to stir, or strive,
But felt that I was still alive—
A frantic feeling, when we know
That what we love shall ne'er be so.
  I know not why
  I could not die,
I had no earthly hope—but faith,
And that forbade a selfish death.

IX.

What next befell me then and there
 I know not well—I never knew—
First came the loss of light, and air,
 And then of darkness too:
I had no thought, no feeling—none—
Among the stones I stood a stone,
And was, scarce conscious what I wist,
As shrubless crags within the mist;
For all was blank, and bleak, and gray,
It was not night—it was not day,
It was not even the dungeon-light,
So hateful to my heavy sight,
But vacancy absorbing space,
And fixedness—without a place;

There were no stars—no earth—no time—
No check—no change—no good—no crime—
But silence, and a stirless breath,
Which neither was of life nor death;
A sea of stagnant idleness,
Blind, boundless, mute, and motionless!

X.

A light broke in upon my brain—
　　It was the carol of a bird;
It ceased, and then it came again—
　　The sweetest song ear ever heard;
And mine was thankful till my eyes
Ran over with the glad surprise
And they that moment could not see
I was the mate of misery;
But then by dull degrees came back
My senses to their wonted track:
I saw the dungeon walls and floor
Close slowly round me as before;
I saw the glimmer of the sun
Creeping as it before had done;
But through the crevice where it came
That bird was perched as fond and tame,
　　And tamer than upon the tree—
A lovely bird with azure wings,
And song that said a thousand things,
　　And seemed to say them all for me!
I never saw its like before—
I ne'er shall see its likeness more.
It seemed, like me, to want a mate,
But was not half so desolate;
And it was come to love me when
None lived to love me so again,
And, cheering from my dungeon's brink,
Had brought me back to feel and think.

I know not if it late were free,
   Or broke its cage to perch on mine;
But knowing well captivity,
   Sweet bird! I could not wish for thine—
Or if it were, in winged guise,
A visitant from Paradise;
For—Heaven forgive that thought! the while
Which made me both to weep and smile;
I sometimes deemed that it might be
My brother's soul come down to me;
But then at last away it flew,
And then 'twas mortal well I knew;
For he would never thus have flown,
And left me twice so doubly lone—
Lone as the corse within its shroud,
Lone as a solitary cloud,
   A single cloud on a sunny day,
While all the rest of heaven is clear,
A frown upon the atmosphere,
That hath no business to appear
   When skies are blue, and earth is gay.

XI.

A kind of change came in my fate—
My keepers grew compassionate.
I know not what had made them so—
They were inured to sights of woe;
But so it was—my broken chain
With links unfastened did remain;
And it was liberty to stride
Along my cell from side to side,
And up and down, and then athwart,
And tread it over every part;
And round the pillars one by one,
Returning where my walk begun—
Avoiding only as I trod,
My brothers' graves without a sod;

For if I thought with heedless tread
My step profaned their lowly bed,
My breath came gaspingly and thick,
And my crushed heart fell blind and sick.

XII.

I made a footing in the wall,
    It was not therefrom to escape,
For I had buried one and all
    Who loved me in a human shape;
And the whole earth would henceforth be
A wider prison unto me:
No child—no sire—no kin had I,
No partner in my misery;
I thought of this, and I was glad,
For thought of them had made me mad;
But I was curious to ascend
To my barred windows, and to bend
Once more, upon the mountains high
The quiet of a loving eye.

XIII.

I saw them—and they were the same,
They were not changed like me in frame;
I saw their thousand years of snow
On high—their wide long lake below,
And the blue Rhone in fullest flow;
I heard the torrents leap and gush
O'er channelled rock and broken bush;
I saw the white-walled distant town,
And whiter sails go skimming down;
And then there was a little isle,
Which in my very face did smile,
    The only one in view;
A small green isle, it seemed no more,
Scarce broader than my dungeon floor,

But in it there were three tall trees,
And o'er it blew the mountain breeze,
And by it there were waters flowing,
And on it there were young flowers growing,
    Of gentle breath and hue.
The fish swam by the castle-wall,
And they seemed joyous, each and all;
The eagle rode the rising blast—
Methought he never flew so fast
As then to me he seemed to fly;
And then new tears came in my eye,
And I felt troubled, and would fain
I had not left my recent chain;
And when I did descend again
The darkness of my dim abode
Fell on me as a heavy load;
It was as is a new-dug grave,
Closing o'er one we sought to save;
And yet my glance, too much oppressed,
Had almost need of such a rest.

                    XIV.

It might be months, or years, or days—
    I kept no count, I took no note—
I had no hope my eyes to raise,
    And clear them of their dreary mote;
At last men came to set me free,
    I asked not why, and recked not where;
It was at length the same to me,
Fettered or fetterless to be;
    I learned to love despair.
And thus, when they appeared at last,
And all my bonds aside were cast,
These heavy walls to me had grown
A hermitage—and all my own!
And half I felt as they were come
To tear me from a second home.

With spiders I had friendship made,
And watched them in their sullen trade;
Had seen the mice by moonlight play;
And why should I feel less than they?
We were all inmates of one place,
And I, the monarch of each race,
Had power to kill; yet, strange to tell!
In quiet we had learned to dwell.
My very chains and I grew friends,
So much a long communion tends
To make us what we are:—even I
Regained my freedom with a sigh.

—GEORGE GORDON, LORD BYRON

One of the smaller but most spectacular of all
sea fights occurred in 1591 when a single ship
fought off an entire fleet. Sir Richard Grenville was
the English naval commander of the "Revenge,"
isolated off Flores, in the Azores, when the Spanish
battle-ships—variously estimated from fifty to fifty-
three—came in sight. The "Revenge" fought them
for fifteen hours. Although Grenville was fatally
wounded, his battle-cry—"Fight on! Fight on!"—won
the admiration of the enemy and continued to echo
through history.

The "Revenge"

At Flores in the Azores Sir Richard Grenville lay,
And a pinnace, like a flutter'd bird, came flying from far
    away:
"Spanish ships of war at sea! we have sighted fifty-three!"
Then sware Lord Thomas Howard: " 'Fore God I am no
    coward;

But I cannot meet them here, for my ships are out of gear,
And the half my men are sick. I must fly, but follow quick.
We are six ships of the line; can we fight with fifty-three?"

Then spake Sir Richard Grenville; "I know you are no
     coward;
You fly them for a moment to fight with them again.
But I've ninety men and more that are lying sick ashore.
I should count myself the coward if I left them, my Lord
     Howard,
To these Inquisition dogs and the devildoms of Spain."

So Lord Howard past away with five ships of war that day,
Till he melted like a cloud in the silent summer heaven;
But Sir Richard bore in hand all his sick men from the land
Very carefully and slow,
Men of Bideford in Devon,
And we laid them on the ballast down below;
For we brought them all aboard,
And they blest him in their pain, that they were not left to
     Spain,
To the thumbscrew and the stake, for the glory of the Lord.

He had only a hundred seamen to work the ship and to fight,
And he sailed away from Flores till the Spaniard came in
     sight,
With his huge sea-castles heaving upon the weather bow.
"Shall we fight or shall we fly?
Good Sir Richard, tell us now,
For to fight is but to die!
There'll be little of us left by the time this sun be set,"
And Sir Richard said again: "We be all good English men.
Let us bang these dogs of Seville, the children of the devil,
For I never turn'd my back upon Don or devil yet."

Sir Richard spoke and he laugh'd, and we roar'd a hurrah,
     and so
The little Revenge ran on sheer into the heart of the foe,

With her hundred fighters on deck, and her ninety sick below;
For half of their fleet to the right and half to the left were
seen,
And the little Revenge ran on thro' the long sea-lane between.

Thousands of their soldiers look'd down from their decks
and laugh'd,
Thousands of their seamen made mock at the mad little
craft
Running on and on, till delay'd
By their mountain-like San Philip that, of fifteen hundred
tons,
And up-shadowing high above us with her yawning tiers
of guns,
Took the breath from our sails, and we stay'd.

And while now the great San Philip hung above us like a
cloud
Whence the thunderbolt will fall
Long and loud,
Four galleons drew away
From the Spanish fleet that day,
And two upon the larboard and two upon the starboard lay,
And the battle-thunder broke from them all.

But anon the great San Philip, she bethought herself and
went
Having that within her womb that had left her ill content;
And the rest they came aboard us, and they fought us hand
to hand,
For a dozen times they came with their pikes and musquet-
eers,
And a dozen times we shook 'em off as a dog that shakes
his ears
When he leaps from the water to the land.

And the sun went down, and the stars came out far over
    the summer sea,
But never a moment ceased the fight of the one and the
    fifty-three.
Ship after ship, the whole night long, their high built gal-
    leons came,
Ship after ship, the whole night long, with her battle-thun-
    der and flame;
Ship after ship, the whole night long, drew back with her
    dead and her shame.
For more were sunk and many were shatter'd, and so could
    fight us no more—
God of battles, was ever a battle like this in the world be-
    fore?

For he said "Fight on! fight on!"
Tho' his vessel was all but a wreck;
And it chanced that, when half of the short summer night
    was gone,
With a grisly wound to be drest he had left the deck,
But a bullet struck him that was dressing it suddenly dead,
And himself he was wounded again in the side and the
    head,
And he said "Fight on! fight on!"

And the night went down, and the sun smiled out far over
    the summer sea,
And the Spanish fleet with broken sides lay round us all in
    a ring;
But they dared not touch us again, for they fear'd that we
    still could sting,
So they watch'd what the end would be.
And we had not fought them in vain,
But in perilous plight were we,
Seeing forty of our poor hundred were slain,
And half of the rest of us maim'd for life
In the crash of the cannonades and the desperate strife;

And the sick men down in the hold were most of them
    stark and cold,
And the pikes were all broken or bent, and the powder was
    all of it spent;
And the masts and the rigging were lying over the side;
But Sir Richard cried in his English pride,
"We have fought such a fight for a day and a night
As may never be fought again!
We have won great glory, my men!
And a day less or more
At sea or ashore,
We die—does it matter when?
Sink me the ship, Master Gunner—sink her, split her in
    twain!
Fall into the hands of God, not into the hands of Spain!"
And the gunner said "Ay, ay," but the seamen made reply:
"We have children, we have wives,
And the Lord hath spared our lives.
We will make the Spaniard promise, if we yield, to let us go;
We shall live to fight again and to strike another blow."
And the lion there lay dying, and they yielded to the foe.

And the stately Spanish men to their flagship bore him then,
Where they laid him by the mast, old Sir Richard caught at
    last,
And they praised him to his face with their courtly foreign
    grace;
But he rose upon their decks, and he cried:
"I have fought for Queen and Faith like a valiant man and
    true;
I have only done my duty as a man is bound to do:
With a joyful spirit I Sir Richard Grenville die!"
And he fell upon their decks, and he died.

And they stared at the dead that had been so valiant and
    true,
And had holden the power and glory of Spain so cheap

That he dared her with one little ship and his English few;
Was he devil or man? He was devil for aught they knew,
But they sank his body with honor down into the deep,
And they mann'd the Revenge with a swarthier alien crew,
And away she sail'd with her loss and long'd for her own;
When a wind from the lands they had ruin'd awoke from
    sleep,
And the water began to heave and the weather to moan,
And or ever that evening ended a great gale blew,
And a wave like the wave that is raised by an earthquake
    grew,
Till it smote on their hulls and their sails and their masts
    and their flags,
And the whole sea plunged and fell on the shot-shatter'd
    navy of Spain,
And the little Revenge herself went down by the island crags
To be lost evermore in the main.

—ALFRED, LORD TENNYSON

Walt Whitman's "An Old-Time Sea-Fight" furnishes a series of contrasts to Tennyson's "The 'Revenge.'" Although both are accounts of famous
naval battles and both were written in the middle of
the nineteenth century, one is by an English poet
laureate, the other by the American "poet of de-
mocracy." Both stories are told in loosely rhythmical
lines, but one is tightly rhymed throughout while
the other dispenses with rhyme altogether. The
event celebrated in "The 'Revenge'" took place
more than three and a half centuries ago; "An Old-
Time Sea-Fight" tells of a famous encounter during
the Revolutionary War, on September 23, 1779,
when John Paul Jones' "Bon Homme Richard" was
attacked by the greatly superior British warship
"Serapis." Both poems have not only a subject in

common but a common feeling: the spirit of dauntless determination.

Another war, the War Between the States, is the background for the graphic and deeply touching "Come Up from the Fields Father," also by Walt Whitman.

From "Song of Myself"

An Old-Time Sea-Fight

Would you hear of an old-time sea-fight?
Would you learn who won by the light of the moon and stars?
List to the yarn, as my grandmother's father the sailor told it
    to me.

Our foe was no skulk in his ship I tell you (said he),
His was the surly English pluck, and there is no tougher or
    truer, and never was and never will be;
Along the lower'd eve he came horribly raking us.

We closed with him, the yards entangled, the cannon touch'd,
My captain lash'd fast with his own hands.

We had receiv'd some eighteen pound shots under the water,
On our lower-gun-deck two large pieces had burst at the first
    fire, killing all around and blowing up overhead.

Fighting at sun-down, fighting at dark,
Ten o'clock at night, the full moon well up, our leaks on the
    gain, and five feet of water reported,
The master-at-arms loosing the prisoners confined in the after-
    hold to give them a chance for themselves.

The transit to and from the magazine is now stopt by the sen-
    tinels,

They see so many strange faces they do not know whom to
    trust.

Our frigate takes fire,
The other asks if we demand quarter?
If our colours are struck and the fighting done?

Now I laugh content, for I hear the voice of my little
    captain,
We have not struck, he composedly cries, *we have just begun
    our part of the fighting.*

Only three guns are in use,
One is directed by the captain himself against the enemy's
    main-mast,
Two well serv'd with grape and canister silence his musketry
    and clear his decks.

The tops alone second the fire of this little battery, especially
    the main-top,
They hold out bravely during the whole of the action.

Not a moment's cease,
The leaks gain fast on the pumps, the fire eats toward the
    powder-magazine.

One of the pumps has been shot away, it is generally
    thought we are sinking.

Serene stands the little captain,
He is not hurried, his voice is neither high nor low,
His eyes give more light to us than our battle-lanterns.

Toward twelve there in the beams of the moon they
    surrender to us.

                          —WALT WHITMAN

Come Up from the Fields Father

Come up from the fields father, here's a letter from our Pete,
And come to the front door mother, here's a letter from thy
        dear son.

Lo, 'tis autumn,
Lo, where the trees, deeper green, yellower and redder,
Cool and sweeten Ohio's villages with leaves fluttering in
        the moderate wind,
Where apples ripe in the orchards hang and grapes on the
        trellis'd vines,
(Smell you the smell of the grapes on the vines?
Smell you the buckwheat where the bees were lately buzz-
        ing?)
Above all, lo, the sky so calm, so transparent after the rain,
        and with wondrous clouds,
Below too, all calm, all vital and beautiful, and the farm
        prospers well.

Down in the fields all prospers well,
But now from the fields come father, come at the daughter's
        call,
And come to the entry mother, to the front door come right
        away.
Fast as she can she hurries, something ominous, her steps
        trembling,
She does not tarry to smooth her hair nor adjust her cap.

Open the envelope quickly,
O this is not our son's writing, yet his name is sign'd,
O a strange hand writes for our dear son, O stricken mother's
        soul!

All swims before her eyes, flashes with black, she catches
        the main words only,

Sentences broken, *gunshot wound in the breast, cavalry
     skirmish, taken to hospital,*
At present low, but will soon be better.

Ah now the single figure to me,
Amid all teeming and wealthy Ohio with all its cities and
     farms,
Sickly white in the face and dull in the head, very faint,
By the jamb of a door leans.

Grieve not so, dear mother, (the just-grown daughter speaks
     through her sobs,
The little sisters huddle around speechless and dismay'd,)
See, dearest mother, the letter says Pete will soon be better.

Alas poor boy, he will never be better, (nor may-be needs to
     be better that brave and simple soul,)
While they stand at home at the door he is dead already,
The only son is dead.

But the mother needs to be better,
She with thin form presently drest in black,
By day her meals untouch'd, then at night fitfully sleeping,
     often waking,
In the midnight waking, weeping, longing with one deep
     longing,
O that she might withdraw unnoticed, silent from life es-
     cape and withdraw,
To follow, to seek, to be with her dear dead son.

                                        —WALT WHITMAN

     The "Constitution" was a small warship (tech-
nically a frigate) that had fought so well and so
often in the War of 1812 that it had been nick-
named "Old Ironsides." In 1830 the Secretary of the

Navy considered she had outlived her usefulness, and recommended that the vessel be disposed of or demolished. When he heard of this, Oliver Wendell Holmes, the New England poet, editor, and essayist, wrote a sad and ironic poem about the old "eagle of the sea." The poem was reprinted everywhere, and there was so much public resentment that "Old Ironsides" was saved from "the harpies of the shore," those who would have profited from its destruction. Instead of being sold or broken up, "Old Ironsides" was rebuilt and remained afloat, a symbol of glorious achievement.

Old Ironsides

September 14, 1830

Ay, tear her tattered ensign down!
  Long has it waved on high,
And many an eye has danced to see
  That banner in the sky;
Beneath it rung the battle shout,
  And burst the cannon's roar—
The meteor of the ocean air
  Shall sweep the clouds no more.

Her deck, once red with heroes' blood,
  Where knelt the vanquished foe,
When winds were hurrying o'er the flood,
  And waves were white below,
No more shall feel the victor's tread,
  Or know the conquered knee—
The harpies of the shore shall pluck
  The eagle of the sea!

Oh, better that her shattered hulk
  Should sink beneath the wave;

Her thunders shook the mighty deep,
  And there should be her grave;
Nail to the mast her holy flag,
  Set every threadbare sail,
And give her to the god of storms,
  The lightning and the gale!

—OLIVER WENDELL HOLMES

Bannockburn

At Bannockburn the English lay,—
The Scots they were na far away,
But waited for the break o' day
    That glinted in the east.

But soon the sun broke through the heath
And lighted up that field o' death,
When Bruce, wi' soul-inspiring breath,
    His heralds thus addressed:—

Scots, wha hae wi' Wallace bled,
Scots, wham Bruce has aften led;
Welcome to your gory bed,
    Or to victorie.

Now's the day, and now's the hour
See the front o' battle lour:
See approach proud Edward's power,—
    Chains and slaverie!

Wha will be a traitor knave?
Wha can fill a coward's grave?
Wha sae base as be a slave?
    Let him turn and flee!

Wha for Scotland's king and law
Freedom's sword will strongly draw,

Freeman stand, or freeman fa'?
    Let him follow me!

By Oppression's woes and pains!
By your sons in servile chains,
We will drain our dearest veins,
    But they shall be free!

Lay the proud usurpers low!
Tyrants fall in every foe!
Liberty's in every blow!
    Let us do, or die!

—ROBERT BURNS

Boadicea

When the British warrior queen,
    Bleeding from the Roman rods,
Sought, with an indignant mien,
    Counsel of her country's gods,

Sage beneath the spreading oak
    Sat the Druid, hoary chief;
Every burning word he spoke
    Full of rage and full of grief.

"Princess! if our agèd eyes
    Weep upon thy matchless wrongs,
'Tis because resentment ties
    All the terrors of our tongues.

"Rome shall perish—write that word
    In the blood that she has spilt,—
Perish, hopeless and abhorred,
    Deep in ruin as in guilt.

"Rome, for empire far renowned,
    Tramples on a thousand states;
Soon her pride shall kiss the ground,—
    Hark! the Gaul is at her gates!

"Other Romans shall arise,
    Heedless of a soldier's name;
Sounds, not arms, shall win the prize,
    Harmony the path to fame.

"Then the progeny that springs
    From the forests of our land,
Armed with thunder, clad with wings,
    Shall a wider world command.

"Regions Cæsar never knew
    Thy posterity shall sway;
Where his eagles never flew,
    None invincible as they."

Such the bard's prophetic words,
    Pregnant with celestial fire,
Bending as he swept the chords
    Of his sweet but awful lyre.

She, with all a monarch's pride,
    Felt them in her bosom glow;
Rushed to battle, fought, and died,—
    Dying, hurled them at the foe.

"Ruffians, pitiless as proud,
    Heaven awards the vengeance due;
Empire is on us bestowed,
    Shame and ruin wait for you!"

                              —WILLIAM COWPER

The Patriot's Password

Arnold Winkelried: Switzerland, 1386

"Make way for Liberty!" he cried,
Made way for Liberty—and died.

In arms the Austrian phalanx stood,
A living wall, a human wood;
A wall,—where every conscious stone
Seemed to its kindred thousands grown;
A rampart all assaults to bear,
Till time to dust their frames should wear:
A wood,—like that enchanted grove
In which with fiends Rinaldo strove,
Where every silent tree possessed
A spirit prisoned in its breast,
Which the first stroke of coming strife
Might startle into hideous life:
So still, so dense, the Austrians stood,
A living wall, a human wood.
Impregnable their front appears,
All-horrent with projected spears,
Whose polished points before them shine,
From flank to flank, one brilliant line,
Bright as the breakers' splendors run
Along the billows to the sun.

Opposed to these, a hovering band
Contended for their father-land:
Peasants, whose new-found strength had broke
From manly necks the ignoble yoke,
And forged their fetters into swords,
On equal terms to fight their lords,
And what insurgent rage had gained
In many a mortal fray maintained.
Marshalled once more, at Freedom's call,
They came to conquer or to fall,

Where he who conquered, he who fell,
Was deemed a dead, or living, Tell;
Such virtue had that patriot breathed,
So to the soil his soul bequeathed,
That wheresoe'er his arrows flew,
Heroes in his own likeness grew,
And warriors sprang from every sod,
Which his awakening footstep trod.

And now the work of life and death
Hung on the passing of a breath;
The fire of conflict burned within,
The battle trembled to begin;
Yet, while the Austrians held their ground,
Point for assault was nowhere found;
Where'er the impatient Switzers gazed,
The unbroken line of lances blazed;
That line 'twas suicide to meet,
And perish at their tyrants' feet:
How could they rest within their graves,
And leave their homes the haunts of slaves?
Would they not feel their children tread
With clanging chains, above their head?

It must not be: this day, this hour,
Annihilates the invader's power:
All Switzerland is in the field,
She will not fly, she cannot yield,
She must not fall; her better fate
Here gives her an immortal date.
Few were the number she could boast,
Yet every freeman was a host,
And felt as 'twere a secret known
That one should turn the scale alone,
While each unto himself were he
On whose sole arm hung victory.

It did depend on *one* indeed;
Behold him,—Arnold Winkelried!
There sounds not to the trump of fame
The echo of a nobler name.
Unmarked he stood amid the throng,
In rumination deep and long,
Till you might see, with sudden grace,
The very thought come o'er his face,
And by the motion of his form
Anticipate the bursting storm,
And by the uplifting of his brow
Tell where the bolt would strike, and how.

But 'twas no sooner thought than done,
The field was in a moment won;
"Make way for Liberty!" he cried,
Then ran, with arms extended wide,
As if his dearest friend to clasp;
Ten spears he swept within his grasp;
"Make way for Liberty!" he cried;
Their keen points met from side to side;
He bowed amidst them, like a tree,
And thus made way for Liberty.

Swift to the breach his comrades fly;
"Make way for Liberty!" they cry,
And through the Austrian phalanx dart,
As rushed the spears through Arnold's heart;
While, instantaneous, as his fall,
Rout, ruin, panic seized them all;
An earthquake could not overthrow
A city with a surer blow.

Thus Switzerland again was free;
Thus Death made way for Liberty!

—JAMES MONTGOMERY

Burial of Sir John Moore

Not a drum was heard, not a funeral note,
  As his corse to the rampart we hurried;
Not a soldier discharged his farewell shot
  O'er the grave where our hero we buried.

We buried him darkly, at dead of night,
  The sods with our bayonets turning;
By the struggling moonbeams' misty light,
  And the lantern dimly burning.

No useless coffin enclosed his breast,
  Not in sheet or in shroud we wound him;
But he lay, like a warrior taking his rest,
  With his martial cloak around him.

Few and short were the prayers we said,
  And we spoke not a word of sorrow;
But we steadfastly gazed on the face of the dead,
  And we bitterly thought of the morrow.

We thought, as we hollowed his narrow bed,
  And smoothed down his lonely pillow,
That the foe and the stranger would tread o'er
    his head,
And we far away on the billow!

Lightly they'll talk of the spirit that's gone,
  And o'er his cold ashes upbraid him;
But little he'll reck, if they let him sleep on
  In the grave where a Briton has laid him!

But half of our heavy task was done,
  When the clock struck the hour for retiring;
And we heard the distant and random gun
  That the foe was suddenly firing.

Slowly and sadly we laid him down,
  From the field of his fame fresh and gory!
We carved not a line, and we raised not a stone,
  But we left him alone with his glory.

—CHARLES WOLFE

FABLE AND FANTASY

A fable is a kind of myth, a legend that has been told and retold until it acquires new meaning. Frequently it has an added purpose and is used (in the words of Samuel Johnson) "to point a moral and adorn a tale." But, though a fable usually teaches a lesson, it is often enjoyed as a fantasy for its own sake.

This section blends serious fable and smiling fantasy. "King Robert of Sicily" and "The Vision of Sir Launfal" are stirring as poems and impressive as sermons. "The Battle of Blenheim" is a quietly ironic but grim protest against the murderous folly of war. On the other hand, "The Pied Piper of Hamelin" is a moral preachment wrapped in fantastic fable, a verbal scherzo which mingles whimsicality and wisdom. "The Enchanted Shirt" is a satire with a light twist and a happy ending, while "The Deacon's Masterpiece" is a piece of straight-faced, humorous, and completely native folklore.

The Enchanted Shirt

The King was sick. His cheek was red,
  And his eye was clear and bright;
He ate and drank with a kingly zest,
  And peacefully snored at night.

But he said he was sick, and a king should know,
  And doctors came by the score.
They did not cure him. He cut off their heads,
  And sent to the schools for more.

At last two famous doctors came,
  And one was as poor as a rat,—
He had passed his life in studious toil,
  And never found time to grow fat.

The other had never looked in a book;
  His patients gave him no trouble:
If they recovered, they paid him well;
  If they died, their heirs paid double.

Together they looked at the royal tongue,
  As the King on his couch reclined;
In succession they thumped his august chest,
  But no trace of disease could find.

The old sage said, "You're as sound as a nut."
  "Hang him up," roared the King in a gale—
In a ten-knot gale of royal rage;
  The other leech grew a shade pale;

But he pensively rubbed his sagacious nose,
  And thus his prescription ran—
The King will be well, if he sleeps one night
  In the Shirt of a Happy Man.

Wide o'er the realm the couriers rode,
    And fast their horses ran,
And many they saw, and to many they spoke,
    But they found no Happy Man.

They found poor men who would fain be rich,
    And rich who thought they were poor;
And men who twisted their waist in stays,
    And women that shorthose wore.

They saw two men by the roadside sit,
    And both bemoaned their lot;
For one had buried his wife, he said,
    And the other one had not.

At last they came to a village gate,
    A beggar lay whistling there;
He whistled, and sang, and laughed, and rolled
    On the grass in the soft June air.

The weary courtiers paused and looked
    At the scamp so blithe and gay;
And one of them said, "Heaven save you, friend!
    You seem to be happy to-day."

"Oh yes, fair sirs," the rascal laughed,
    And his voice rang free and glad;
"An idle man has so much to do
    That he never has time to be sad."

"This is our man," the courier said;
    "Our luck has led us aright.
I will give you a hundred ducats, friend,
    For the loan of your shirt to-night."

The merry blackguard lay back on the grass,
    And laughed till his face was black;

"I would do it, God wot," and he roared with the fun,
    "But I haven't a shirt to my back."

Each day to the King the reports came in
    Of his unsuccessful spies,
And the sad panorama of human woes
    Passed daily under his eyes.

And he grew ashamed of his useless life,
    And his maladies hatched in gloom;
He opened his windows and let the air
    Of the free heaven into his room.

And out he went in the world, and toiled
    In his own appointed way;
And the people blessed him, the land was glad,
    And the King was well and gay.

                    —JOHN HAY

The Battle of Blenheim

It was a summer evening;
    Old Kaspar's work was done,
And he before his cottage door
    Was sitting in the sun;
And by him sported on the green
His little grandchild Wilhelmine.

She saw her brother Peterkin
    Roll something large and round,
Which he beside the rivulet
    In playing there had found.
He came to ask what he had found,
That was so large, and smooth, and round.

Old Kaspar took it from the boy,
    Who stood expectant by;

And then the old man shook his head,
    And with a natural sigh,
" 'Tis some poor fellow's skull," said he,
"Who fell in the great victory.

"I find them in the garden,
    For there's many here about;
And often, when I go to plow,
    The plowshare turns them out;
For many thousand men," said he,
"Were slain in that great victory."

"Now tell us what 'twas all about,"
    Young Peterkin, he cries;
And little Wilhelmine looks up
    With wonder-waiting eyes;
"Now tell us all about the war,
And what they fought each other for."

"It was the English," Kaspar cried,
    "Who put the French to rout;
But what they fought each other for,
    I could not well make out;
But everybody said," quoth he,
"That 'twas a famous victory.

"My father lived at Blenheim then,
    Yon little stream hard by;
They burnt his dwelling to the ground,
    And he was forced to fly;
So with his wife and child he fled,
Nor had he where to rest his head.

"With fire and sword the country round
    Was wasted far and wide,
And many a childing mother then,
    And new-born baby, died;

But things like that, you know, must be
At every famous victory.

"They say it was a shocking sight
    After the field was won;
For many thousand bodies here
    Lay rotting in the sun;
But things like that, you know, must be
After a famous victory.

"Great praise the Duke of Marlboro' won,
    And our good Prince Eugene."
"Why, 'twas a very wicked thing!"
    Said little Wilhelmine.
"Nay, nay, my little girl," quoth he;
"It was a famous victory.

"And everybody praised the Duke
    Who this great fight did win."
"But what good came of it at last?"
    Quoth little Peterkin.
"Why, that I cannot tell," said he;
"But 'twas a famous victory."

—ROBERT SOUTHEY

Fable

The mountain and the squirrel
Had a quarrel,
And the former called the latter "Little Prig";
Bun replied,
"You are doubtless very big;
But all sorts of things and weather
Must be taken in together,
To make up a year
And a sphere.

And I think it no disgrace
To occupy my place.
If I'm not so large as you,
You are not so small as I,
And not half so spry.
I'll not deny you make
A very pretty squirrel track;
Talents differ; all is well and wisely put;
If I cannot carry forests on my back,
Neither can you crack a nut."

—RALPH WALDO EMERSON

Although written in entirely different styles, "The Fool's Prayer," "King Robert of Sicily," and "The Vision of Sir Launfal" have much in common. All three were written by New England poets who lived during the middle of the nineteenth century. Each is a parable, a story that points a moral and teaches a lesson: the kings of the first two poems and the knight of the second learn that "pride must have a fall" and that the haughtiest spirit can be touched and uplifted by humility.

"King Robert of Sicily" is founded on an Eastern legend which spread through Europe in many languages and different forms. The idea of "The Vision of Sir Launfal" was suggested by Malory's tales of King Arthur's Round Table, but the working out of the plot was Lowell's own concept. It centers about the fabulous search for the Holy Grail, the cup from which Jesus drank at the Last Supper with his disciples.

The Fool's Prayer

The royal feast was done; the King
   Sought some new sport to banish care,
And to his jester cried: "Sir Fool,
   Kneel now, and make for us a prayer!"

The jester doffed his cap and bells,
   And stood the mocking court before;
They could not see the bitter smile
   Behind the painted grin he wore.

He bowed his head, and bent his knee
   Upon the monarch's silken stool;
His pleading voice arose: "O Lord,
   Be merciful to me, a fool!

"No pity, Lord, could change the heart
   From red with wrong to white as wool;
The rod must heal the sin: but, Lord,
   Be merciful to me, a fool!

" 'Tis not by guilt the onward sweep
   Of truth and right, O Lord, we stay;
'Tis by our follies that so long
   We hold the earth from heaven away.

"These clumsy feet, still in the mire,
   Go crushing blossoms without end;
These hard, well-meaning hands we thrust
   Among the heart-strings of a friend.

"The ill-timed truth we might have kept—
   Who knows how sharp it pierced and stung?
The word we had not sense to say—
   Who knows how grandly it had rung?

"Our faults no tenderness should ask,
    The chastening stripes must cleanse them all;
But for our blunders—oh, in shame
    Before the eyes of heaven we fall.

"Earth bears no balsam for mistakes.
    Men crown the knave, and scourge the tool
That did his will; but Thou, O Lord,
    Be merciful to me, a fool!"

The room was hushed; in silence rose
    The King, and sought his gardens cool,
And walked apart, and murmured low,
    "Be merciful to me, a fool!"

—EDWARD ROWLAND SILL

King Robert of Sicily

Robert of Sicily, brother of Pope Urbane
And Valmond, Emperor of Allemaine,
Appareled in magnificent attire,
With retinue of many a knight and squire,
On St. John's eve, at vespers, proudly sat
And heard the priests chant the Magnificat.
And as he listened, o'er and o'er again
Repeated, like a burden or refrain,
He caught the words, *"Deposuit potentes
De sede, et exaltavit humiles"*;
And slowly lifting up his kingly head
He to a learned clerk beside him said,
"What mean these words?" The clerk made answer meet,
"He has put down the mighty from their seat,
And has exalted them of low degree."
Thereat King Robert muttered scornfully,
" 'Tis well that such seditious words are sung
Only by priests and in the Latin tongue;

For unto priests and people be it known,
There is no power can push me from my throne!"
And leaning back, he yawned and fell asleep,
Lulled by the chant monotonous and deep.

When he awoke, it was already night;
The church was empty, and there was no light,
Save where the lamps, that glimmered few and faint,
Lighted a little space before some saint.
He started from his seat and gazed around,
But saw no living thing and heard no sound.
He groped towards the door, but it was locked;
He cried aloud, and listened, and then knocked,
And uttered awful threatenings and complaints,
And imprecations upon men and saints.
The sounds re-echoed from the roof and walls
As if dead priests were laughing in their stalls!

At length the sexton, hearing from without
The tumult of the knocking and the shout,
And thinking thieves were in the house of prayer,
Came with his lantern, asking, "Who is there?"
Half choked with rage, King Robert fiercely said,
"Open: 'tis I, the King! Art thou afraid?"
The frightened sexton, muttering, with a curse,
"This is some drunken vagabond, or worse!"
Turned the great key and flung the portal wide;
A man rushed by him at a single stride,
Haggard, half naked, without hat or cloak,
Who neither turned, nor looked at him, nor spoke,
But leaped into the blackness of the night,
And vanished like a specter from his sight.

Robert of Sicily, brother of Pope Urbane
And Valmond, Emperor of Allemaine,
Despoiled of his magnificent attire,
Bare-headed, breathless, and besprent with mire,

With sense of wrong and outrage desperate,
Strode on and thundered at the palace gate;
Rushed through the court-yard, thrusting in his rage
To right and left each seneschal and page,
And hurried up the broad and sounding stair,
His white face ghastly in the torches' glare.
From hall to hall he passed with breathless speed;
Voices and cries he heard, but did not heed,
Until at last he reached the banquet-room,
Blazing with light, and breathing with perfume.

There on the dais sat another king,
Wearing his robes, his crown, his signet-ring,
King Robert's self in features, form, and height
But all transfigured with angelic light!
It was an Angel; and his presence there
With a divine effulgence filled the air,
An exultation, piercing the disguise,
Though none the hidden Angel recognize.

A moment speechless, motionless, amazed,
The throneless monarch on the Angel gazed,
Who met his looks of anger and surprise
With the divine compassion of his eyes;
Then said, "Who art thou? and why com'st thou here?"
To which King Robert answered, with a sneer,
"I am the King, and come to claim my own
From an impostor, who usurps my throne!"
And suddenly, at these audacious words,
Up sprang the angry guests, and drew their swords;
The Angel answered, with unruffled brow,
"Nay, not the King, but the King's Jester, thou
Henceforth shalt wear the bells and scalloped cape,
And for thy counsellor shalt lead an ape:
Thou shalt obey my servants when they call,
And wait upon my henchmen in the hall!"

Deaf to King Robert's threats and cries and prayers,
They thrust him from the hall and down the stairs;
A group of tittering pages ran before,
And as they opened wide the folding-door,
His heart failed, for he heard, with strange alarms,
The boisterous laughter of the men-at-arms,
And all the vaulted chamber roar and ring
With the mock plaudits of "Long live the King!"
Next morning, waking with the day's first beam,
He said within himself, "It was a dream!"
But the straw rustled as he turned his head,
There were the cap and bells beside his bed,
Around him rose the bare, discolored walls,
Close by, the steeds were champing in their stalls,
And in the corner, a revolting shape,
Shivering and chattering sat the wretched ape.
It was no dream; the world he loved so much
Had turned to dust and ashes at his touch!

Days came and went; and now returned again
To Sicily the old Saturnian reign;
Under the Angel's governance benign
The happy island danced with corn and wine,
And deep within the mountain's burning breast
Enceladus, the giant, was at rest.
Meanwhile King Robert yielded to his fate,
Sullen and silent and disconsolate.
Dressed in the motley garb that Jesters wear,
With looks bewildered and a vacant stare,
Close shaven above the ears, as monks are shorn,
By courtiers mocked, by pages laughed to scorn,
His only friend the ape, his only food
What others left,—he still was unsubdued.
And when the Angel met him on his way,
And half in earnest, half in jest, would say,
Sternly, though tenderly, that he might feel
The velvet scabbard held a sword of steel,

"Art thou the King?" the passion of his woe
Burst from him in resistless overflow,
And, lifting high his forehead, he would fling
The haughty answer back, "I am, I am the King!"

Almost three years were ended; when there came
Ambassadors of great repute and name
From Valmond, Emperor of Allemaine,
Unto King Robert, saying that Pope Urbane
By letter summoned them forthwith to come
On Holy Thursday to his city of Rome.
The Angel with great joy received his guests,
And gave them presents of embroidered vests,
And velvet mantles with rich ermine lined,
And rings and jewels of the rarest kind.
Then he departed with them o'er the sea
Into the lovely land of Italy,
Whose loveliness was more resplendent made
By the mere passing of that cavalcade,
With plumes, and cloaks, and housings, and the stir
Of jeweled bridle and of golden spur.
And lo! among the menials, in mock state,
Upon a piebald steed, with shambling gait,
His cloak of fox-tails flapping in the wind,
The solemn ape demurely perched behind,
King Robert rode, making huge merriment
In all the country towns through which they went.

The Pope received them with great pomp, and blare
Of bannered trumpets, on Saint Peter's square,
Giving his benediction and embrace,
Fervent, and full of apostolic grace.
While with congratulations and with prayers
He entertained the Angel unawares,
Robert, the Jester, bursting through the crowd,
Into their presence rushed, and cried aloud,
"I am the King! Look, and behold in me
Robert, your brother, King of Sicily!

This man, who wears my semblance to your eyes,
Is an impostor in a King's disguise.
Do you not know me? Does no voice within
Answer my cry, and say we are akin?"
The Pope in silence, but with troubled mien,
Gazed at the Angel's countenance serene;
The Emperor, laughing, said, "It is strange sport
To keep a madman for thy Fool at court!"
And the poor, baffled Jester in disgrace
Was hustled back among the populace.

In solemn state the Holy Week went by,
And Easter Sunday gleamed upon the sky;
The presence of the Angel, with its light,
Before the sun rose, made the city bright,
And with new fervor filled the hearts of men,
Who felt that Christ indeed had risen again.
Even the Jester, on his bed of straw,
With haggard eyes the unwonted splendor saw,
He felt within a power unfelt before,
And, kneeling humbly on his chamber floor,
He heard the rushing garments of the Lord
Sweep through the silent air, ascending heavenward.

And now the visit ending, and once more
Valmond returning to the Danube's shore,
Homeward the Angel journeyed, and again
The land was made resplendent with his train,
Flashing along the towns of Italy
Unto Salerno, and from there by sea.
And when once more within Palermo's wall,
And, seated on the throne in his great hall,
He heard the Angelus from convent towers,
As if the better world conversed with ours,
He beckoned to King Robert to draw nigher,
And with a gesture bade the rest retire;
And when they were alone, the Angel said,
"Art thou the King?" Then bowing down his head

King Robert crossed both hands upon his breast,
And meekly answered him: "Thou knowest best!
My sins as scarlet are; let me go hence,
And in some cloister's school of penitence,
Across those stones, that pave the way to heaven,
Walk barefoot, till my guilty soul is shriven!"

The Angel smiled, and from his radiant face
A holy light illumined all the place,
And through the open window, loud and clear,
They heard the monks chant in the chapel near,
Above the stir and tumult of the street:
"He has put down the mighty from their seat,
And has exalted them of low degree!"
And through the chant a second melody
Rose like the throbbing of a single string:
"I am an Angel, and thou art the King!"

King Robert, who was standing near the throne,
Lifted his eyes, and lo! he was alone!
But all appareled as in days of old,
With ermined mantle and with cloth of gold;
And when his courtiers came, they found him there
Kneeling upon the floor, absorbed in silent prayer.

—HENRY WADSWORTH LONGFELLOW

The Vision of Sir Launfal

Prelude To Part First

Over his keys the musing organist,
    Beginning doubtfully and far away,
First lets his fingers wander as they list,
    And builds a bridge from Dreamland for his lay:
Then, as the touch of his loved instrument
    Gives hope and fervor, nearer draws his theme,

First guessed by faint auroral flushes sent
   Along the wavering vista of his dream.

———

Not only around our infancy
Doth heaven with all its splendors lie;
Daily, with souls that cringe and plot,
We Sinais climb and know it not.

Over our manhood bend the skies;
   Against our fallen and traitor lives
The great winds utter prophecies;
   With our faint hearts the mountain strives;
Its arms outstretched, the druid wood
   Waits with its benedicite;
And to our age's drowsy blood
   Still shouts the inspiring sea.

Earth gets its price for what Earth gives us;
   The beggar is taxed for a corner to die in,
The priest hath his fee who comes and shrives us,
   We bargain for the graves we lie in;
At the devil's booth are all things sold,
Each ounce of dross costs its ounce of gold;
   For a cap and bells our lives we pay,
Bubbles we buy with a whole soul's tasking:
'T is heaven alone that is given away,
'T is only God may be had for the asking;
No price is set on the lavish summer;
June may be had by the poorest comer.

And what is so rare as a day in June?
   Then, if ever, come perfect days;
Then Heaven tries earth if it be in tune,
   And over it softly her warm ear lays:
Whether we look, or whether we listen,
We hear life murmur, or see it glisten;

Every clod feels a stir of might,
   An instinct within it that reaches and towers,
And, groping blindly above it for light,
   Climbs to a soul in grass and flowers;
The flush of life may well be seen
   Thrilling back over hills and valleys;
The cowslip startles in meadows green,
   The buttercup catches the sun in its chalice,
And there's never a leaf nor a blade too mean
   To be some happy creature's palace;
The little bird sits at his door in the sun,
   Atilt like a blossom among the leaves,
And lets his illumined being o'errun
   With the deluge of summer it receives;
His mate feels the eggs beneath her wings,
And the heart in her dumb breast flutters and sings;
He sings to the wide world, and she to her nest,—
In the nice ear of Nature which song is the best?

Now is the high-tide of the year,
   And whatever of life hath ebbed away
Comes flooding back with a ripply cheer,
   Into every bare inlet and creek and bay;
Now the heart is so full that a drop overfills it,
We are happy now because God wills it;
No matter how barren the past may have been,
'T is enough for us now that the leaves are green;
We sit in the warm shade and feel right well
How the sap creeps up and the blossoms swell;
We may shut our eyes, but we cannot help knowing
That skies are clear and grass is growing;
The breeze comes whispering in our ear,
That dandelions are blossoming near,
   That maize has sprouted, that streams are flowing,
That the river is bluer than the sky,
That the robin is plastering his house hard by;
And if the breeze kept the good news back,
For other couriers we should not lack;

We could guess it all by yon heifer's lowing,—
And hark! how clear bold chanticleer,
Warmed with the new wine of the year,
 Tells all in his lusty crowing!

Joy comes, grief goes, we know not how;
Everything is happy now,
 Everything is upward striving;
'T is as easy now for the heart to be true
As for grass to be green or skies to be blue,—
 'T is the natural way of living:
Who knows whither the clouds have fled?
 In the unscarred heaven they leave no wake;
And the eyes forget the tears they have shed,
 The heart forgets its sorrow and ache;
The soul partakes the season's youth,
 And the sulphurous rifts of passion and woe
Lie deep 'neath a silence pure and smooth,
 Like burnt-out craters healed with snow.
What wonder if Sir Launfal now
Remembered the keeping of his vow?

Part First

I.

"My golden spurs now bring to me,
 And bring to me my richest mail,
For to-morrow I go over land and sea
 In search of the Holy Grail;
Shall never a bed for me be spread,
Nor shall a pillow be under my head,
Till I begin my vow to keep;
Here on the rushes will I sleep,
And perchance there may come a vision true
Ere day create the world anew."
 Slowly Sir Launfal's eyes grew dim,
 Slumber fell like a cloud on him,
And into his soul the vision flew.

II.

The crows flapped over by twos and threes,
In the pool drowsed the cattle up to their knees,
   The little birds sang as if it were
   The one day of summer in all the year,
And the very leaves seemed to sing on the trees:
The castle alone in the landscape lay
Like an outpost of winter, dull and gray:
'T was the proudest hall in the North Countree,
And never its gates might opened be,
Save to lord or lady of high degree;
Summer besieged it on every side,
But the churlish stone her assaults defied;
She could not scale the chilly wall,
Though around it for leagues her pavilions tall
Stretched left and right,
Over the hills and out of sight;
   Green and broad was every tent,
   And out of each a murmur went
Till the breeze fell off at night.

III.

The drawbridge dropped with a surly clang,
And through the dark arch a charger sprang,
Bearing Sir Launfal, the maiden knight,
In his gilded mail, that flamed so bright
It seemed the dark castle had gathered all
Those shafts the fierce sun had shot over its wall
   In his siege of three hundred summers long,
And, binding them all in one blazing sheaf,
   Had cast them forth: so, young and strong,
And lightsome as a locust-leaf,
Sir Launfal flashed forth in his maiden mail,
To seek in all climes for the Holy Grail.

IV.

It was morning on hill and stream and tree,
    And morning in the young knight's heart;
Only the castle moodily
Rebuffed the gifts of the sunshine free,
    And gloomed by itself apart;
The season brimmed all other things up
Full as the rain fills the pitcher-plant's cup.

V.

As Sir Launfal made morn through the darksome gate,
    He was 'ware of a leper, crouched by the same,
Who begged with his hand and moaned as he sate;
    And a loathing over Sir Launfal came;
The sunshine went out of his soul with a thrill,
    The flesh 'neath his armor 'gan to shrink and crawl,
And midway its leap his heart stood still
    Like a frozen waterfall;
For this man, so foul and bent of stature,
Rasped harshly against his dainty nature,
And seemed the one blot on the summer morn,—
So he tossed him a piece of gold in scorn.

VI.

The leper raised not the gold from the dust:
"Better to me the poor man's crust,
Better the blessing of the poor,
Though I turn me empty from his door;
That is no true alms which the hand can hold;
He gives only the worthless gold
    Who gives from a sense of duty;
But he who gives but a slender mite,
And gives to that which is out of sight,
    That thread of the all-sustaining Beauty
Which runs through all and doth all unite,—
The hand cannot clasp the whole of his alms,
The heart outstretches its eager palms,

For a god goes with it and makes it store
To the soul that was starving in darkness before."

Prelude To Part Second

Down swept the chill wind from the mountain peak,
    From the snow five thousand summers old;
On open wold and hill-top bleak
    It had gathered all the cold,
And whirled it like sleet on the wanderer's cheek;
It carried a shiver everywhere
From the unleafed boughs and pastures bare;
The little brook heard it and built a roof
'Neath which he could house him, winter-proof;
All night by the white stars' frosty gleams
He groined his arches and matched his beams;
Slender and clear were his crystal spars
As the lashes of light that trim the stars:
He sculptured every summer delight
In his halls and chambers out of sight;
Sometimes his tinkling waters slipt
Down through a frost-leaved forest-crypt,
Long, sparkling aisles of steel-stemmed trees
Bending to counterfeit a breeze;
Sometimes the roof no fretwork knew
But silvery mosses that downward grew;
Sometimes it was carved in sharp relief
With quaint arabesques of ice-fern leaf;
Sometimes it was simply smooth and clear
For the gladness of heaven to shine through, and here
He had caught the nodding bulrush-tops
And hung them thickly with diamond drops,
That crystalled the beams of moon and sun,
And made a star of every one:
No mortal builder's most rare device
Could match this winter-palace of ice;

'T was as if every image that mirrored lay
In his depths serene through the summer day,
Each fleeting shadow of earth and sky,
    Lest the happy model should be lost,
Had been mimicked in fairy masonry
    By the elfin builders of the frost.

Within the hall are song and laughter,
    The cheeks of Christmas glow red and jolly,
And sprouting is every corbel and rafter
    With lightsome green of ivy and holly;
Through the deep gulf of the chimney wide
Wallows the Yule-log's roaring tide;
The broad flame-pennons droop and flap
    And belly and tug as a flag in the wind;
Like a locust shrills the imprisoned sap,
    Hunted to death in its galleries blind;
And swift little troops of silent sparks,
    Now pausing, now scattering away as in fear,
Go threading the soot-forest's tangled darks
    Like herds of startled deer.

But the wind without was eager and sharp,
Of Sir Launfal's gray hair it makes a harp,
    And rattles and wrings
    The icy strings,
Singing, in dreary monotone,
A Christmas carol of its own,
    Whose burden still, as he might guess,
    Was—"Shelterless, shelterless, shelterless!"
The voice of the seneschal flared like a torch
As he shouted the wanderer away from the porch,
And he sat in the gateway and saw all night
    The great hall-fire, so cheery and bold,
    Through the window-slits of the castle old,
Build out its piers of ruddy light
Against the drift of the cold.

Part Second

I.

There was never a leaf on bush or tree,
The bare boughs rattled shudderingly;
The river was dumb and could not speak,
   For the weaver Winter its shroud had spun;
A single crow on the tree-top bleak
   From his shining feathers shed off the cold sun;
Again it was morning, but shrunk and cold,
As if her veins were sapless and old,
And she rose up decrepitly
For a last dim look at earth and sea.

II.

Sir Launfal turned from his own hard gate,
For another heir in his earldom sate;
An old, bent man, worn out and frail,
He came back from seeking the Holy Grail;
Little he recked of his earldom's loss,
No more on his surcoat was blazoned the cross,
But deep in his soul the sign he wore,
The badge of the suffering and the poor.

III.

Sir Launfal's raiment thin and spare
Was idle mail 'gainst the barbed air,
For it was just at the Christmas time;
So he mused, as he sat, of a sunnier clime,
And sought for a shelter from cold and snow
In the light and warmth of long-ago;
He sees the snake-like caravan crawl
O'er the edge of the desert, black and small,

Then nearer and nearer, till, one by one,
He can count the camels in the sun,
As over the red-hot sands they pass
To where, in its slender necklace of grass,
The little spring laughed and leapt in the shade,
And with its own self like an infant played,
And waved its signal of palms.

IV.

"For Christ's sweet sake, I beg an alms";—
The happy camels may reach the spring,
But Sir Launfal sees only the grewsome thing,
The leper, lank as the rain-blanched bone,
That cowers beside him, a thing as lone
And white as the ice-isles of Northern seas
In the desolate horror of his disease.

V.

And Sir Launfal said,—"I behold in thee
An image of Him who died on the tree;
Thou also hast had thy crown of thorns,—
Thou also hast had the world's buffets and scorns,—
And to thy life were not denied
The wounds in the hands and feet and side:
Mild Mary's Son, acknowledge me;
Behold, through him, I give to thee!"

VI.

Then the soul of the leper stood up in his eyes
    And looked at Sir Launfal, and straightway he
Remembered in what a haughtier guise
    He had flung an alms to leprosie,
When he girt his young life up in gilded mail
And set forth in search of the Holy Grail.
The heart within him was ashes and dust;
He parted in twain his single crust,

He broke the ice on the streamlet's brink,
And gave the leper to eat and drink,
'T was a mouldy crust of coarse brown bread,
  'T was water out of a wooden bowl,—
Yet with fine wheaten bread was the leper fed,
  And 't was red wine he drank with his thirsty soul.

VII.

As Sir Launfal mused with a downcast face,
A light shone round about the place;
The leper no longer crouched at his side,
But stood before him glorified,
Shining and tall and fair and straight
As the pillar that stood by the Beautiful Gate,—
Himself the Gate whereby men can
Enter the temple of God in Man.

VIII.

His words were shed softer than leaves from the pine,
And they fell on Sir Launfal as snows on the brine,
That mingle their softness and quiet in one
With the shaggy unrest they float down upon;
And the voice that was softer than silence said,
"Lo it is I, be not afraid!
In many climes, without avail,
Thou hast spent thy life for the Holy Grail;
Behold, it is here,—this cup which thou
Didst fill at the streamlet for me but now;
This crust is my body broken for thee,
This water his blood that died on the tree;
The Holy Supper is kept, indeed,
In whatso we share with another's need;
Not what we give, but what we share,
For the gift without the giver is bare;
Who gives himself with his alms feeds three,
Himself, his hungering neighbor, and me."

IX.

Sir Launfal awoke as from a swound:
"The Grail in my castle here is found!
Hang my idle armor up on the wall,
Let it be the spider's banquet-hall;
He must be fenced with stronger mail
Who would seek and find the Holy Grail."

X.

The castle gate stands open now,
  And the wanderer is welcome to the hall
As the hangbird is to the elm-tree bough;
  No longer scowl the turrets tall,
The Summer's long siege at last is o'er;
When the first poor outcast went in at the door,
She entered with him in disguise,
And mastered the fortress by surprise;
There is no spot she loves so well on ground,
She lingers and smiles there the whole year round;
The meanest serf on Sir Launfal's land
Has hall and bower at his command;
And there's no poor man in the North Countree
But is lord of the earldom as much as he.

                  —JAMES RUSSELL LOWELL

In common with "King Robert of Sicily"—and also
"Paul Revere's Ride" (see page 409)—"The Birds of
Killingworth" is one of the memorable stories in
Longfellow's "Tales of a Wayside Inn." Killingworth,
in Connecticut, was named (inaccurately) after the
English town of Kenilworth, and there is a slight
foundation for the legend that the town leaders
made war upon the birds. Appropriately enough, it

is the Poet in the "Tales of a Wayside Inn" who tells
how the birds—and the people—were saved.

The Birds of Killingworth

It was the season, when through all the land
    The merle and mavis build, and building sing
Those lovely lyrics, written by His hand,
    Whom Saxon Cædmon calls the Blithe-heart King;
When on the boughs the purple buds expand,
    The banners of the vanguard of the Spring,
And rivulets, rejoicing, rush and leap,
And wave their fluttering signals from the steep.

The robin and the blue-bird, piping loud,
    Filled all the blossoming orchards with their glee;
The sparrows chirped as if they still were proud
    Their race in Holy Writ should mentioned be;
And hungry crows assembled in a crowd,
    Clamored their piteous prayer incessantly,
Knowing who hears the ravens cry, and said:
"Give us, O Lord, this day our daily bread!"

Across the Sound the birds of passage sailed,
    Speaking some unknown language strange and sweet
Of tropic isle remote, and passing hailed
    The village with the cheers of all their fleet;
Or quarrelling together, laughed and railed
    Like foreign sailors, landed in the street
Of seaport town, and with outlandish noise
Of oaths and gibberish frightening girls and boys.

Thus came the jocund Spring in Killingworth,
    In fabulous days, some hundred years ago;
And thrifty farmers, as they tilled the earth,
    Heard with alarm the cawing of the crow,

That mingled with the universal mirth,
    Cassandra-like, prognosticating woe;
They shook their heads, and doomed with dreadful words
To swift destruction the whole race of birds.

And a town-meeting was convened straightway
    To set a price upon the guilty heads
Of these marauders, who, in lieu of pay,
    Levied blackmail upon the garden beds
And cornfields, and beheld without dismay
    The awful scarecrow, with his fluttering shreds;
The skeleton that waited at their feast,
Whereby their sinful pleasure was increased.

Then from his house, a temple painted white,
    With fluted columns, and a roof of red,
The Squire came forth, august and splendid sight!
    Slowly descending, with majestic tread,
Three flights of steps, nor looking left nor right,
    Down the long street he walked, as one who said,
"A town that boasts inhabitants like me
Can have no lack of good society!"

The Parson, too, appeared, a man austere,
    The instinct of whose nature was to kill;
The wrath of God he preached from year to year,
    And read, with fervor, Edwards on the Will;
His favorite pastime was to slay the deer
    In Summer on some Adirondack hill;
E'en now, while walking down the rural lane,
He lopped the wayside lilies with his cane.

From the Academy, whose belfry crowned
    The hill of Science with its vane of brass,
Came the Preceptor, gazing idly round,
    Now at the clouds, and now at the green grass,
And all absorbed in reveries profound
    Of fair Almira in the upper class,

Who was, as in a sonnet he had said,
As pure as water, and as good as bread.

And next the Deacon issued from his door,
　In his voluminous neck-cloth, white as snow;
A suit of sable bombazine he wore;
　His form was ponderous, and his step was slow;
There never was so wise a man before;
　He seemed the incarnate "Well, I told you so!"
And to perpetuate his great renown
There was a street named after him in town.

These came together in the new townhall,
　With sundry farmers from the region round.
The Squire presided, dignified and tall,
　His air impressive and his reasoning sound;
Ill fared it with the birds, both great and small;
　Hardly a friend in all that crowd they found,
But enemies enough, who every one
Charged them with all the crimes beneath the sun.

When they had ended, from his place apart,
　Rose the Preceptor, to redress the wrong,
And, trembling like a steed before the start,
　Looked round bewildered on the expectant throng;
Then thought of fair Almira, and took heart
　To speak out what was in him, clear and strong,
Alike regardless of their smile or frown,
And quite determined not to be laughed down.

"Plato, anticipating the Reviewers,
　From his republic banished without pity
The Poets; in this little town of yours,
　You put to death, by means of a Committee,
The ballad-singers and the Troubadours,
　The street-musicians of the heavenly city,
The birds, who make sweet music for us all
In our dark hours, as David did for Saul.

"The thrush that carols at the dawn of day
  From the green steeples of the piny wood;
The oriole in the elm; the noisy jay,
  Jargoning like a foreigner at his food;
The blue-bird balanced on some topmost spray,
  Flooding with melody the neighborhood;
Linnet and meadow-lark, and all the throng
That dwell in nests, and have the gift of song.

"You slay them all! and wherefore? for the gain
  Of a scant handful more or less of wheat,
Or rye, or barley, or some other grain,
  Scratched up at random by industrious feet,
Searching for worm or weevil after rain!
  Of a few cherries, that are not so sweet
As are the songs these uninvited guests
Sing at their feast with comfortable breasts.

"Do you ne'er think what wondrous beings these?
  Do you ne'er think who made them, and who taught
The dialect they speak, where melodies
  Alone are the interpreters of thought?
Whose household words are songs in many keys,
  Sweeter than instrument of man e'er caught!
Whose habitations in the tree-tops even
Are half-way houses on the road to heaven!

"Think, every morning when the sun peeps through
  The dim, leaf-latticed windows of the grove,
How jubilant the happy birds renew
  Their old, melodious madrigals of love!
And when you think of this, remember too
  'T is always morning somewhere, and above
The awakening continents, from shore to shore,
Somewhere the birds are singing evermore.

"Think of your woods and orchards without birds!
  Of empty nests that cling to boughs and beams

As in an idiot's brain remembered words
    Hang empty 'mid the cobwebs of his dreams!
Will bleat of flocks or bellowing of herds
    Make up for the lost music, when your teams
Drag home the stingy harvest, and no more
The feathered gleaners follow to your door?

"What! would you rather see the incessant stir
    Of insects in the windrows of the hay,
And hear the locust and the grasshopper
    Their melancholy hurdy-gurdies play?
Is this more pleasant to you than the whir
    Of meadow-lark, and her sweet roundelay,
Or twitter of little field-fares, as you take
Your nooning in the shade of bush and brake?

"You call them thieves and pillagers; but know,
    They are the winged wardens of your farms,
Who from the cornfields drive the insidious foe,
    And from your harvests keep a hundred harms;
Even the blackest of them all, the crow,
    Renders good service as your man-at-arms,
Crushing the beetle in his coat of mail,
And crying havoc on the slug and snail.

"How can I teach your children gentleness,
    And mercy to the weak, and reverence
For life which, in its weakness or excess,
    Is still a gleam of God's omnipotence,
Or Death which, seeming darkness, is no less
    The selfsame light, although averted hence,
When by your laws, your actions, and your speech,
You contradict the very things I teach?"

With this he closed; and through the audience went
    A murmur, like the rustle of dead leaves;
The farmers laughed and nodded and some bent
    Their yellow heads together like their sheaves;

Men have no faith in fine-spun sentiment
   Who put their trust in bullocks and in beeves.
The birds were doomed; and, as the record shows,
A bounty offered for the heads of crows.

There was another audience out of reach,
   Who had no voice nor vote in making laws,
But in the papers read his little speech,
   And crowned his modest temples with applause;
They made him conscious, each one more than each,
   He still was victor, vanquished in their cause.
Sweetest of all the applause he won from thee,
O fair Almira at the Academy!

And so the dreadful massacre began
   O'er fields and orchards, and o'er woodland crests,
The ceaseless fusillade of terror ran,
   Dead fell the birds, with blood-stains on their breasts,
Or wounded crept away from sight of man,
   While the young died of famine in their nests;
A slaughter to be told in groans, not words,
The very St. Bartholomew of Birds!

The summer came, and all the birds were dead;
   The days were like hot coals; the very ground
Was burned to ashes; in the orchards fed
   Myriads of caterpillars, and around
The cultivated fields and garden beds
   Hosts of devouring insects crawled, and found
No foe to check their march, till they had made
The land a desert without leaf or shade.

Devoured by worms, like Herod, was the town,
   Because, like Herod, it had ruthlessly
Slaughtered the Innocents. From the trees spun down
   The canker-worms upon the passersby,
Upon each woman's bonnet, shawl, and gown,
   Who shook them off with just a little cry;

They were the terror of each favorite walk,
The endless theme of all the village talk.

The farmers grew impatient, but a few
    Confessed their error, and would not complain,
For after all, the best thing one can do
    When it is raining, is to let it rain.
Then they repealed the law, although they knew
    It would not call the dead to life again;
As school-boys, finding their mistake too late,
Draw a wet sponge across the accusing slate.

That year in Killingworth the Autumn came
    Without the light of his majestic look,
The wonder of the falling tongues of flame
    The illumined pages of his Doomsday book.
A few lost leaves blushed crimson with their shame,
    And drowned themselves despairing in the brook,
While the wild wind went moaning everywhere,
Lamenting the dead children of the air!

But the next Spring a stranger sight was seen,
    A sight that never yet by bard was sung,
As great a wonder as it would have been
    If some dumb animal had found a tongue!
A wagon, overarched with evergreen,
    Upon whose boughs were wicker cages hung,
All full of singing birds, came down the street,
Filling the air with music wild and sweet.

From all the country round these birds were brought,
    By order of the town, with anxious quest,
And, loosened from their wicker prisons, sought
    In woods and fields the places they loved best,
Singing loud canticles, which many thought
    Were satires to the authorities addressed,
While others, listening in green lanes, averred
Such lovely music never had been heard!

But blither still and louder carolled they
 Upon the morrow, for they seemed to know
It was the fair Almira's wedding day,
 And everywhere, around, above, below,
When the Preceptor bore his bride away,
 Their songs burst forth in joyous overflow,
And a new heaven bent over a new earth
Amid the sunny farms of Killingworth.

      —HENRY WADSWORTH LONGFELLOW

The Butterfly and the Caterpillar

A Fable Old Is Here Retold

A butterfly, one summer morn,
Sat on a spray of blossoming thorn
And, as he sipped and drank his share
Of honey from the flowered air,
Below, upon the garden wall,
A caterpillar chanced to crawl.
"Horrors!" the butterfly exclaimed,
"This must be stopped! I am ashamed
That such as I should have to be
In the same world with such as he.
Preserve me from such hideous things!
Disgusting shape! Where are his wings!
Fuzzy and gray! Eater of clay!
Won't someone take the worm away!"

The caterpillar crawled ahead,
But, as he munched a leaf, he said,
"Eight days ago, young butterfly,
You wormed about, the same as I;
Within a fortnight from today
Two wings will bear me far away,

To brighter blooms and lovelier lures,
With colors that outrival yours.
So, flutter-flit, be not so proud;
Each caterpillar is endowed
With power to make him by and by,
A blithe and brilliant butterfly.
While you, who scorn the common clay,
You, in your livery so gay,
And all the gaudy moths and millers,
Are only dressed-up caterpillars."

—JOSEPH LAUREN

The Fox and the Grapes

A Moral Tale for Those Who Fail

One summer's day a Fox was passing through
An orchard; faint he was and hungry, too.
When suddenly his keen eye chanced to fall
Upon a bunch of grapes above the wall.
"Ha! Just the thing!" he said. "Who could resist it!"
He eyed the purple cluster—jumped—and missed it.
"Ahem!" he coughed. "I'll take more careful aim,"
And sprang again. Results were much the same,
Although his leaps were desperate and high.
At length he paused to wipe a tearful eye,
And shrug a shoulder. "I am not so dry,
And lunch is bound to come within the hour . . .
Besides," he said, "I'm sure those grapes are sour."

THE MORAL is: We somehow want the peach
That always dangles just beyond our reach;
Until we learn never to be upset
With what we find too difficult to get.

—JOSEPH LAUREN

The Frogs Who Wanted a King

The frogs were living happy as could be
   In a wet marsh to which they all were suited;
From every sort of trouble they were free,
   And all night long they croaked, and honked, and hooted.
But one fine day a bull-frog said, "The thing
We never had and *must* have is a king."

So all the frogs immediately prayed;
   "Great Jove," they chorused from their swampy border,
"Send us a king and he will be obeyed,
   A king to bring a rule of Law and Order."
Jove heard and chuckled. That night in the bog
There fell a long and most impressive Log.

The swamp was silent; nothing breathed. At first
   The badly frightened frogs did never *once* stir;
But gradually some neared and even durst
   To touch, aye, even dance upon, the monster.
Whereat they croaked again, "Great Jove, oh hear!
Send us a *living* king, a king to fear."

Once more Jove smiled, and sent them down a Stork.
   "Long live—!" they croaked. But ere they framed the sentence,
The Stork bent down and, scorning knife or fork,
   Swallowed them all, with no time for repentance!

THE MORAL's this: No matter what your lot,
It might be worse. Be glad with what you've got.

                            —JOSEPH LAUREN

The Virtuous Fox and the Self-righteous Cat

The fox and the cat, as they travell'd one day,
With moral discourses cut shorter the way:

" 'Tis great," says the Fox, "to make justice our guide!"
"How god-like is mercy!" Grimalkin[1] replied.

Whilst thus they proceeded, a wolf from the wood,
Impatient of hunger, and thirsting for blood,
Rush'd forth—as he saw the dull shepherd asleep—
And seiz'd for his supper an innocent sheep.
"In vain, wretched victim, for mercy you bleat,
When mutton's at hand," says the wolf, "I must eat."

Grimalkin's astonish'd!—the fox stood aghast,
To see the fell beast at his bloody repast.
"What a wretch," says the cat, " 'tis the vilest of brutes;
Does he feed upon flesh when there's herbage and roots?"
Cries the fox, "While our oaks give us acorns so good,
What a tyrant is this to spill innocent blood!"

Well, onward they march'd, and they moraliz'd still,
Till they came where some poultry pick'd chaff by a mill.
Sly Reynard survey'd them with gluttonous eyes,
And made, spite of morals, a pullet his prize.
A mouse, too, that chanc'd from her covert to stray,
The greedy Grimalkin secured as her prey.

A spider that sat in her web on the wall,
Perceiv'd the poor victims, and pitied their fall;
She cried, "Of such murders, how guiltless am I!"
So ran to regale on a new-taken fly.

—JOHN CUNNINGHAM

The Lion and the Cub

A lion cub, of sordid mind,
Avoided all the lion kind;
Fond of applause, he sought the feasts
Of vulgar and ignoble beasts;
With asses all his time he spent,
Their club's perpetual president.

---
[1] Grimalkin: from "gray malkin," pet name for a cat.

He caught their manners, looks, and airs;
An ass in everything but ears!
If e'er his Highness meant a joke,
They grinn'd applause before he spoke;
But at each word what shouts of praise;
Goodness! how natural he brays!

Elate with flattery and conceit,
He seeks his royal sire's retreat;
Forward and fond to show his parts,
His Highness brays; the lion starts.
"Puppy! that curs'd vociferation
Betrays thy life and conversation:
Coxcombs, an ever-noisy race,
Are trumpets of their own disgrace."

"Why so severe?" the cub replies;
"Our senate always held me wise!"

"How weak is pride," returns the sire:
"All fools are vain when fools admire!
But know, what stupid asses prize,
Lions and noble beasts despise."

—JOHN GAY

The Nightingale and the Glowworm

A Nightingale that all day long
Had cheer'd the village with his song,
Nor yet at eve his note suspended,
Nor yet when eventide was ended,
Began to feel, as well he might,
The keen demands of appetite;
When looking eagerly around,
He spied far off, upon the ground,
A something shining in the dark,
And knew the Glowworm by his spark;
So, stooping down from hawthorn top,
He thought to put him in his crop.

The worm, aware of his intent,
Harangued him thus, right eloquent:
"Did you admire my lamp," quoth he,
"As much as I your minstrelsy,
You would abhor to do me wrong,
As much as I to spoil your song:
For 'twas the self-same Power Divine
Taught you to sing, and me to shine;
That you with music, I with light,
Might beautify and cheer the night."
The songster heard this short oration,
And warbling out his approbation,
Released him, as my story tells,
And found a supper somewhere else.

—WILLIAM COWPER

The Blind Men and the Elephant

A Hindoo Fable

It was six men of Indostan
    To learning much inclined,
Who went to see the Elephant
    (Though all of them were blind),
That each by observation
    Might satisfy his mind.

The *First* approached the Elephant,
    And happening to fall
Against his broad and sturdy side,
    At once began to bawl:
"God bless me! but the Elephant
    Is very like a wall!"

The *Second*, feeling of the tusk,
    Cried, "Ho! what have we here

So very round and smooth and sharp?
    To me 'tis mighty clear
This wonder of an Elephant
    Is very like a spear!"

The *Third* approached the animal,
    And happening to take
The squirming trunk within his hands,
    Thus boldly up and spake:
"I see," quoth he, "the Elephant
    Is very like a snake!"

The *Fourth* reached out an eager hand,
    And felt about the knee.
"What most this wondrous beast is like
    Is mighty plain," quoth he;
" 'Tis clear enough the Elephant
    Is very like a tree!"

The *Fifth* who chanced to touch the ear,
    Said: "E'en the blindest man
Can tell what this resembles most;
    Deny the fact who can,
This marvel of an Elephant
    Is very like a fan!"

The *Sixth* no sooner had begun
    About the beast to grope,
Than, seizing on the swinging tail
    That fell within his scope,
"I see," quoth he, "the Elephant
    Is very like a rope!"

And so these men of Indostan
    Disputed loud and long,
Each in his own opinion
    Exceeding stiff and strong,

Though each was partly in the right,
    And all were in the wrong!

        The Moral:
So oft in theologic wars,
    The disputants, I ween,
Rail on in utter ignorance
    Of what each other mean,
And prate about an Elephant
Not one of them has seen!

—JOHN GODFREY SAXE

The Pied Piper of Hamelin

Hamelin Town's in Brunswick,
By famous Hanover city;
    The river Weser, deep and wide,
    Washes its wall on the southern side;
    A pleasanter spot you never spied;
But, when begins my ditty,
    Almost five hundred years ago,
    To see the townsfolk suffer so
From vermin was a pity.

    Rats!
They fought the dogs, and kill'd the cats,
    And bit the babies in the cradles,
And ate the cheeses out of the vats,
    And lick'd the soup from the cook's own ladles,
Split open the kegs of salted sprats,
Made nests inside men's Sunday hats,
And even spoil'd the women's chats,
    By drowning their speaking
    With shrieking and squeaking
In fifty different sharps and flats.

At last the people in a body
    To the Town Hall came flocking:
" 'Tis clear," cried they, "our Mayor's a noddy;
    And as for our Corporation—shocking
To think we buy gowns lined with ermine
For dolts that can't or won't determine
What's best to rid us of our vermin!
You hope, because you're old and obese,
To find in the furry civic robe ease?
Rouse up, sirs! Give your brains a racking
To find the remedy we're lacking,
Or, sure as fate, we'll send you packing!"
At this the Mayor and Corporation
Quaked with a mighty consternation.
An hour they sate in counsel,
    At length the Mayor broke silence:
"For a gilder I'd my ermine gown sell;
    I wish I were a mile hence!
It's easy to bid one rack one's brain—
I'm sure my poor head aches again,
I've scratch'd it so, and all in vain.
Oh for a trap, a trap, a trap!"
Just as he said this, what should hap
At the chamber-door but a gentle tap?
"Bless us!" cried the Mayor, "what's that?"
(With the Corporation as he sat,
Looking little though wondrous fat;
Nor brighter was his eye, nor moister
Than a too long-open'd oyster,
Save when at noon his paunch grew mutinous
For a plate of turtle, green and glutinous)
"Only a scraping of shoes on the mat?
Anything like the sound of a rat
Makes my heart go pit-a-pat!"

"Come in!"—the Mayor cried, looking bigger:
And in did come the strangest figure!

His queer long coat from heel to head
Was half of yellow and half of red;
And he himself was tall and thin,
With sharp blue eyes, each like a pin,
And light loose hair, yet swarthy skin,
No tuft on cheek nor beard on chin,
But lips where smiles went out and in—
There was no guessing his kith and kin!
And nobody could enough admire
The tall man and his quaint attire:
Quoth one: "It's as if my great-grandsire,
Starting up at the Trump of Doom's tone,
Had walk'd this way from his painted tombstone!"

He advanced to the council-table:
And, "Please your honors," said he, "I'm able,
By means of a secret charm, to draw
All creatures living beneath the sun,
That creep, or swim, or fly, or run,
After me so as you never saw!
And I chiefly use my charm
On creatures that do people harm,
The mole, and toad, and newt, and viper;
And people call me the Pied Piper."
(And here they noticed round his neck
A scarf of red and yellow stripe,
To match with his coat of the selfsame check;
And at the scarf's end hung a pipe;
And his fingers, they noticed, were ever straying
As if impatient to be playing
Upon this pipe, as low it dangled
Over his vesture so old-fangled.)
"Yet," said he, "poor piper as I am,
In Tartary I freed the Cham,
Last June, from his huge swarm of gnats;
I eased in Asia the Nizam
Of a monstrous brood of vampyre bats;

And, as for what your brain bewilders—
If I can rid your town of rats,
Will you give me a thousand guilders?"
"One? fifty thousand!" was the exclamation
Of the astonish'd Mayor and Corporation.

Into the street the Piper stept,
  Smiling first a little smile,
As if he knew what magic slept
  In his quiet pipe the while;
Then, like a musical adept,
To blow the pipe his lips he wrinkled,
And green and blue his sharp eyes twinkled,
Like a candle-flame where salt is sprinkled;
And ere three shrill notes the pipe had utter'd,
You heard as if an army mutter'd;
And the muttering grew to a grumbling;
And the grumbling grew to a mighty rumbling;
And out of the houses the rats came tumbling.
Great rats, small rats, lean rats, brawny rats,
Brown rats, black rats, gray rats, tawny rats,
Grave old plodders, gay young friskers,
  Fathers, mothers, uncles, cousins,
Cocking tails and prickling whiskers,
  Families by tens and dozens,
Brothers, sisters, husbands, wives—
Follow'd the Piper for their lives.
From street to street he piped advancing,
And step for step they follow'd dancing,
Until they came to the river Weser,
Wherein all plunged and perish'd,
Save one who, stout as Julius Cæsar,
Swam across and lived to carry
(As the manuscript he cherish'd)
To Rat-land home his commentary,
Which was, "At the first shrill notes of the pipe,
I heard a sound as of scraping tripe,

And putting apples, wondrous ripe,
Into a cider press's gripe:
And a moving away of pickle-tub boards,
And a leaving ajar of conserve-cupboards,
And a drawing the corks of train-oil flasks,
And a breaking the hoops of butter-casks;
And it seemed as if a voice
(Sweeter far than by harp or by psaltery
Is breathed) call'd out, O rats, rejoice!
The world is grown to one vast dry-saltery!
So munch on, crunch on, take your nuncheon,
Breakfast, supper, dinner, luncheon!
And just as a bulky sugar-puncheon,
All ready staved, like a great sun shone
Glorious scarce an inch before me,
Just as methought it said, Come, bore me!
I found the Weser rolling o'er me."

You should have heard the Hamelin people
Ringing the bells till they rock'd the steeple;
"Go," cried the Mayor, "and get long poles!
Poke out the nests and block up the holes!
Consult with carpenters and builders,
And leave in our town not even a trace
Of the rats!"—when suddenly up the face
Of the Piper perk'd in the market-place,
With a, "First, if you please, my thousand guilders!"

A thousand guilders! The Mayor look'd blue;
So did the Corporation too.
For council dinners made rare havoc
With Claret, Moselle, Vin-de-Grave, Hock;
And half the money would replenish
Their cellar's biggest butt with Rhenish.
To pay this sum to a wandering fellow
With a gypsy coat of red and yellow!
"Beside," quoth the Mayor, with a knowing wink,
"Our business was done at the river's brink;

We saw with our eyes the vermin sink,
And what's dead can't come to life, I think.
So, friend, we're not the folks to shrink
From the duty of giving you something for drink,
And a matter of money to put in your poke;
But, as for the guilders, what we spoke
Of them, as you very well know, was in joke.
Beside, our losses have made us thrifty;
A thousand guilders! Come, take fifty!"

The Piper's face fell and he cried,
"No trifling! I can't wait! beside,
I've promised to visit by dinner-time
Bagdad, and accept the prime
Of the Head Cook's pottage, all he's rich in,
For having left, in the Caliph's kitchen,
Of a nest of scorpions no survivor—
With him I proved no bargain-driver.
With you, don't think I'll bate a stiver!
And folks who put me in a passion
May find me pipe to another fashion."

"How?" cried the Mayor, "d'ye think I'll brook
Being worse treated than a Cook?
Insulted by a lazy ribald
With idle pipe and vesture piebald?
You threaten us, fellow? Do your worst,
Blow your pipe there till you burst!"

Once more he stept into the street;
    And to his lips again
Laid his long pipe of smooth straight cane;
    And ere he blew three notes (such sweet
Soft notes as yet musician's cunning
    Never gave the enraptured air)
There was a rustling, that seem'd like a bustling
Of merry crowds justling at pitching and hustling,

Small feet were pattering, wooden shoes clattering,
Little hands clapping, and little tongues chattering,
And, like fowls in a farm-yard when barley is scattering,
Out came the children running.
All the little boys and girls,
With rosy cheeks and flaxen curls,
And sparkling eyes and teeth like pearls,
Tripping and skipping, ran merrily after
The wonderful music with shouting and laughter.

The Mayor was dumb, and the Council stood
As if they were changed into blocks of wood,
Unable to move a step, or cry
To the children merrily skipping by—
And could only follow with the eye
That joyous crowd at the Piper's back.
But how the Mayor was on the rack,
And the wretched Council's bosoms beat,
As the Piper turn'd from the High Street
To where the Weser roll'd its waters
Right in the way of their sons and daughters!
However, he turned from south to west,
And to Koppelberg Hill his steps address'd,
And after him the children press'd;
Great was the joy in every breast.
"He never can cross that mighty top!
He's forced to let the piping drop,
And we shall see our children stop!"
When, lo, as they reach'd the mountain's side,
A wondrous portal open'd wide,
As if a cavern was suddenly hollow'd;
And the Piper advanced and the children follow'd,
And when all were in to the very last,
The door in the mountain-side shut fast.
Did I say all? No! one was lame,
And could not dance the whole of the way,
And in after years, if you would blame
His sadness, he was used to say,

"It's dull in our town since my playmates left!
I can't forget that I'm bereft
Of all the pleasant sights they see,
Which the Piper also promised me,
For he led us, he said, to a joyous land,
Joining the town and just at hand,
Where waters gush'd and fruit trees grew,
And flowers put forth a fairer hue,
And everything was strange and new;
The sparrows were brighter than peacocks here,
And the dogs outran our fallow deer,
And honey-bees had lost their stings,
And horses were born with eagles' wings;
And just as I became assured
My lame foot would be speedily cured,
The music stopp'd, and I stood still,
And found myself outside the Hill,
Left alone against my will,
To go now limping as before,
And never hear of that country more!"

Alas, alas for Hamelin!
    There came into many a burgher's pate
    A text which says that Heaven's Gate
    Opes to the rich at as easy rate
As the needle's eye takes a camel in!
The Mayor sent east, west, north, and south
To offer the Piper by word of mouth,
    Wherever it was men's lot to find him,
Silver and gold to his heart's content,
If he'd only return the way he went,
    And bring the children behind him.
But when they saw 'twas a lost endeavor,
And Piper and dancers were gone forever,
They made a decree that lawyers never
    Should think their records dated duly
If, after the day of the month and year,
These words did not as well appear:

"And so long after what happen'd here
  On the twenty-second of July,
Thirteen hundred and Seventy-six;"
And the better in memory to fix
The place of the children's last retreat,
They call'd it the Pied Piper's Street,
Where any one playing on pipe or tabor
Was sure for the future to lose his labor.
Nor suffer'd they hostelry or tavern
  To shock with mirth a street so solemn,
But opposite the place of the cavern
  They wrote the story on a column,
And on the great church-window painted
The same, to make the world acquainted
How their children were stolen away,
And there it stands to this very day.
And I must not omit to say
That in Transylvania there's a tribe
Of alien people that ascribe
The outlandish ways and dress
On which their neighbors lay such stress,
To their fathers and mothers having risen
Out of some subterranean prison,
Into which they were trepann'd
Long time ago in a mighty band
Out of Hamelin town in Brunswick land,
But how or why, they don't understand.

So, Willy, let you and me be wipers
Of scores out with all men—especially pipers;
And, whether they pipe us free, from rats or from mice,
If we've promised them aught, let us keep our promise.
                  —ROBERT BROWNING

The Deacon's Masterpiece

Or, The Wonderful "One-Hoss Shay"

Have you heard of the wonderful one-hoss shay,
That was built in such a logical way
It ran a hundred years to a day,
And then, of a sudden, it—ah, but stay,
I'll tell you what happened without delay,
Scaring the parson into fits,
Frightening people out of their wits,—
Have you ever heard of that, I say?

Seventeen hundred and fifty-five,
Georgius Secundus was then alive,—
Snuffy old drone from the German hive;
That was the year when Lisbon-town
Saw the earth open and gulp her down,
And Braddock's army was done so brown,
Left without a scalp to its crown.
It was on the terrible Earthquake-day
That the Deacon finished the one-hoss shay.

Now in building of chaises, I tell you what,
There is always *somewhere* a weakest spot,—
In hub, tire, felloe, in spring or thill,
In panel, or crossbar, or floor, or sill,
In screw, bolt, thoroughbrace,—lurking still,
Find it somewhere you must and will,—
Above or below, within or without,—
And that's the reason, beyond a doubt,
That a chaise *breaks down,* but doesn't *wear out.*

But the Deacon swore, (as Deacons do,
With an "I dew vum," or an "I tell *yeou*,")
He would build one shay to beat the taown
'N' the keounty 'n' all the kentry raoun';
It should be so built that it couldn't break daown;

"Fur," said the Deacon, " 't's mighty plain
That the weakes' place mus' stan' the strain;
'N' the way t' fix it, uz I maintain, is only jest
T' make that place uz strong uz the rest."

So the Deacon inquired of the village folk
Where he could find the strongest oak,
That couldn't be split nor bent nor broke,—
That was for spokes and floor and sills;
He sent for lancewood to make the thills;
The crossbars were ash, from the straightest trees,
The panels of white-wood, that cuts like cheese,
But lasts like iron for things like these;
The hubs of logs from the "Settler's ellum,"—
Last of its timber,—they couldn't sell 'em,
Never an axe had seen their chips,
And the wedges flew from between their lips,
Their blunt ends frizzled like celery-tips;
Step and prop-iron, bolt and screw,
Spring, tire, axle, and linchpin too,
Steel of the finest, bright and blue;
Thoroughbrace bison-skin, thick and wide;
Boot, top, dasher, from tough old hide
Found in the pit when the tanner died.
That was the way he "put her through."—
"There!" said the Deacon, "naow she'll dew!"

Do! I tell you, I rather guess
She was a wonder, and nothing less!
Colts grew horses, beards turned gray,
Deacon and deaconess dropped away,
Children and grandchildren—where were they?
But there stood the stout old one-hoss shay
As fresh as on Lisbon-earthquake-day!

EIGHTEEN HUNDRED; it came and found
The Deacon's masterpiece strong and sound.

Eighteen hundred increased by ten;—
"Hahnsum kerridge" they called it then.
Eighteen hundred and twenty came;—
Running as usual; much the same.
Thirty and forty at last arrive,
And then came fifty, and FIFTY-FIVE.

Little of all we value here
Wakes on the morn of its hundredth year
Without both feeling and looking queer.
In fact, there's nothing that keeps its youth,
So far as I know, but a tree and truth.
(This is a moral that runs at large;
Take it.—You're welcome.—No extra charge.)

FIRST OF NOVEMBER,—The Earthquake-day
There are traces of age in the one-hoss shay,
A general flavor of mild decay,
But nothing local, as one may say.
There couldn't be,—for the Deacon's art
Had made it so like in every part
That there wasn't a chance for one to start.
For the wheels were just as strong as the thills,
And the floor was just as strong as the sills,
And the panels just as strong as the floor,
And the whipple-tree neither less nor more,
And the back-crossbar as strong as the fore,
And spring and axle and hub *encore*.
And yet, *as a whole*, it is past a doubt,
In another hour it will be *worn out!*

First of November, 'Fifty-five!
This morning the parson takes a drive.
Now, small boys, get out of the way!
Here comes the wonderful one-hoss shay,
Drawn by a rat-tailed, ewe-necked bay.
"Huddup!" said the parson.—Off went they.

The parson was working his Sunday's text,—
Had got to *fifthly*, and stopped perplexed
And what the—Moses—was coming next.
All at once the horse stood still,
Close by the meet'n'-house on the hill.
—First a shiver, and then a thrill,
Then something decidedly like a spill,—
And the parson was sitting upon a rock,
At half past nine by the meet'n'-house clock,—
Just the hour of the Earthquake shock!
—What do you think the parson found,
When he got up and stared around?
The poor old chaise in a heap or mound,
As if it had been to the mill and ground!
You see, of course, if you're not a dunce,
How it went to pieces all at once,—
All at once, and nothing first,—
Just as bubbles do when they burst.

End of the wonderful one-hoss shay.
Logic is logic. That's all I say.

—OLIVER WENDELL HOLMES

Similar Cases

There was once a little animal,
    No bigger than a fox,
And on five toes he scampered
    Over Tertiary rocks.
They called him Eohippus,
    And they called him very small,
And they thought him of no value—
    When they thought of him at all;
For the lumpish old Dinoceras
    And Coryphodon so slow
Were the heavy aristocracy
    In the days of long ago.

Said the little Eohippus,
  "I am going to be a horse!
And on my middle finger-nail:
  To run my earthly course!
I'm going to have a flowing tail!
  I'm going to have a mane!
I'm going to stand fourteen hands high
  On the psychozoic plane!"

The Coryphodon was horrified,
  The Dinoceras was shocked;
And they chased young Eohippus,
  But he skipped away and mocked.
Then they laughed enormous laughter,
  And they groaned enormous groans,
And they bade young Eohippus
  Go view his father's bones.

Said they, "You always were as small
  And mean as now we see,
And that's conclusive evidence
  That you're always going to be.
What! Be a great, tall, handsome beast,
  With hoofs to gallop on?
Why! You'd have to change your nature!"
  Said the Loxolophodon.
They considered him disposed of,
  And retired with gait serene;
That was the way they argued
  In "the early Eocene."

There was once an Anthropoidal Ape,
  Far smarter than the rest,
And everything that they could do
  He always did the best;
So they naturally disliked him,
  And they gave him shoulders cool,

And when they mentioned him at all
    They said he was a fool.

Cried this pretentious Ape one day,
    "I'm going to be a Man!
And stand upright, and hunt, and fight,
    And conquer all I can!
I'm going to cut down forest trees,
    And make my houses higher!
I'm going to kill the Mastodon!
    I'm going to make a fire!"

Loud screamed the Anthropoidal Apes
    With laughter wild and gay;
They tried to catch the boastful one,
    But he always got away.
So they yelled at him in chorus,
    Which he minded not a whit;
And they pelted him with cocoanuts,
    Which didn't seem to hit.

And then they gave him reasons
    Which they thought of much avail,
To prove how his preposterous
    Attempt was sure to fail.
Said the sages, "In the first place,
    The thing cannot be done!
And, second, if it *could* be,
    It would not be any fun!

"And third and most conclusive,
    And admitting no reply,
You would have to change your nature!
    We should like to see you try!"
They chuckled then triumphantly,
    These lean and hairy shapes,
For these things passed as arguments
    With the Anthropoidal Apes.

There was once a Neolithic Man,
   An enterprising wight,
Who made his chopping implements
   Unusually bright.
Unusually clever he,
   Unusually brave,
And he drew delightful Mammoths
   On the borders of his cave.

To his Neolithic neighbors,
   Who were startled and surprised,
Said he, "My friends, in course of time,
   We shall be civilized!
We are going to live in cities!
   We are going to fight in wars!
We are going to eat three times a day
   Without the natural cause!

"We are going to turn life upside down
   About a thing called gold!
We are going to want the earth, and take
   As much as we can hold!
We are going to wear great piles of stuff
   Outside our proper skins!
We are going to have Diseases!
   And Accomplishments!! and Sins!!!"

Then they all rose up in fury
   Against their boastful friend,
For prehistoric patience
   Cometh quickly to an end.
Said one, "This is chimerical!
   Utopian! Absurd!"
Said another, "What a stupid life!
   Too dull, upon my word!"

Cried all, "Before such things can come,
   You idiotic child,

You must alter Human Nature!"
And they all sat back and smiled.
Thought they, "An answer to that last
It will be hard to find!"
It was a clinching argument
To the Neolithic Mind.

—CHARLOTTE PERKINS STETSON GILMAN

A Turkish Legend

A certain pasha, dead five thousand years,
Once from his harem fled in sudden tears,

And had this sentence on the city's gate
Deeply engraven: "Only God is great."

So these four words above the city's noise
Hung like the accents of an angel's voice,

And evermore from the high barbican
Saluted each returning caravan.

Lost is that city's glory. Every gust
Lifts with crisp leaves the unknown pasha's dust,

And all is ruin, save one wrinkled gate
Whereon is written, "Only God is great."

—THOMAS BAILEY ALDRICH

The Forsaken Merman

Come, dear children, let us away;
Down and away below!
Now my brothers call from the bay,
Now the great winds shoreward blow,
Now the salt tides seaward flow;

Now the wild white horses play,
Champ and chafe and toss in the spray.
Children dear, let us away!
This way, this way!

Call her once before you go—
Call once yet!
In a voice that she will know:
"Margaret! Margaret!"
Children's voices should be dear
(Call once more) to a mother's ear;
Children's voices, wild with pain—
Surely she will come again!
Call her once and come away;
This way, this way!
"Mother dear, we cannot stay!
The wild white horses foam and fret."
Margaret! Margaret!

Come, dear children, come away down;
Call no more!
One last look at the white-walled town,
And the little, gray church on the windy shore,
Then come down!
She will not come though you call all day;
Come away, come away!

Children dear, was it yesterday
We heard the sweet bells over the bay?
In the caverns where we lay,
Through the surf and through the swell,
The far-off sound of a silver bell?
Sand-strewn caverns, cool and deep,
Where the winds are all asleep;
Where the spent lights quiver and gleam,
Where the salt weed sways in the stream,
Where the sea beasts, ranged all round,
Feed in the ooze of their pasture ground;

Where the sea snakes coil and twine,
Dry their mail and bask in the brine;
Where great whales come sailing by,
Sail and sail, with unshut eye,
Round the world forever and aye?
When did music come this way?
Children dear, was it yesterday?

Children dear, was it yesterday
(Call yet once) that she went away?
Once she sat with you and me,
On a red gold throne in the heart of the sea,
And the youngest sat on her knee.
She combed its bright hair, and she tended it well,
When down swung the sound of a far-off bell.
She sighed, she looked up through the clear green sea;
She said: "I must go, for my kinsfolk pray
In the little gray church on the shore today.
'Twill be Easter-time in the world—ah me!
And I lose my poor soul, Merman! here with thee."
I said: "Go up, dear heart, through the waves;
Say thy prayer, and come back to the kind sea-caves!"
She smiled, she went up through the surf in the bay.
Children dear, was it yesterday?

Children dear, were we long alone?
"The sea grows stormy, the little ones moan;
Long prayers," I said, "in the world they say;
Come!" I said; and we rose through the surf in the bay.
We went up the beach, by the sandy down
Where the sea-stocks bloom, to the white-walled town;
Through the narrow paved streets, where all was still,
To the little gray church on the windy hill.
From the church came a murmur of folk at their prayers,
But we stood without in the cold blowing airs.
We climbed on the graves, on the stones worn with rains,
And we gazed up the aisle through the small leaded panes.

She sat by the pillar; we saw her clear;
"Margaret, hist! come quick, we are here!
Dear heart," I said, "we are long alone;
The sea grows stormy, the little ones moan."
But, ah, she gave me never a look,
For her eyes were sealed to the holy book!

Loud prays the priest; shut stands the door.
Come away, children, call no more!
Come away, come down, call no more!
Down, down, down!
Down to the depths of the sea!

She sits at her wheel in the humming town,
Singing most joyfully.
Hark what she sings: "O joy, O joy,
For the humming street, and the child with its toy!
For the priest, and the bell, and the holy well;
For the wheel where I spun,
And the blessed light of the sun!"
And so she sings her fill,
Singing most joyfully,
Till the spindle drops from her hand,
And the whizzing wheel stands still.
She steals to the window, and looks at the sand,
And over the sand at the sea;
And her eyes are set in a stare;
And anon there breaks a sigh,
And anon there drops a tear,
From a sorrow-clouded eye,
And a heart sorrow-laden,
A long, long sigh;
For the cold strange eyes of a little Mermaiden
And the gleam of her golden hair.

Come away, away children;
Come children, come down!
The hoarse wind blows coldly;

Lights shine in the town.
She will start from her slumber
When gusts shake the door;
She will hear the winds howling,
Will hear the waves roar.
We shall see, while above us
The waves roar and whirl,
A ceiling of amber,
A pavement of pearl.
Singing: "Here came a mortal,
But faithless was she!
And alone dwell forever
The kings of the sea."

But, children, at midnight,
When soft the winds blow,
When clear falls the moonlight,
When spring tides are low;
When sweet airs come seaward
From heaths starred with broom,
And high rocks throw mildly
On the blanched sands a gloom;
Up the still, glistening beaches,
Up the creeks we will hie,
Over banks of bright seaweed
The ebb tide leaves dry.
We will gaze, from the sand-hills,
At the white sleeping town;
At the church on the hillside—
And then come back down,
Singing, "There dwells a loved one,
But cruel is she!
She left lonely forever
The kings of the sea."

—MATTHEW ARNOLD

The Fairies

Up the airy mountain,
  Down the rushy glen,
We daren't go a-hunting
  For fear of little men;
Wee folk, good folk,
  Trooping all together;
Green jacket, red cap,
  And white owl's feather!

Down along the rocky shore
  Some make their home,
They live on crispy pancakes
  Of yellow tide-foam;
Some in the reeds
  Of the black mountain lake,
With frogs for their watch-dogs,
  All night awake.

High on the hill-top
  The old king sits;
He is now so old and grey
  He's nigh lost his wits.
With a bridge of white mist
  Columbkill he crosses,
On his stately journeys
  From Slieveleague to Rosses;
Or going up with music
  On cold starry nights,
To sup with the queen
  Of the gay Northern Lights.

They stole little Bridget
  For seven years long;
When she came down again,
  Her friends were all gone.
They took her lightly back,

Between the night and morrow,
They thought that she was fast asleep,
    But she was dead with sorrow.
They have kept her ever since
    Deep within the lakes,
On a bed of flag leaves,
    Watching till she wakes.

By the craggy hill-side,
    Through the mosses bare
They have planted thorn-trees
    For pleasure here and there.
Is any man so daring
    As dig one up in spite,
He shall find the thornies set
    In his bed at night.

Up the airy mountain,
    Down the rushy glen,
We daren't go a-hunting
    For fear of little men;
Wee folk, good folk,
    Trooping all together;
Green jacket, red cap,
    And white owl's feather!

—WILLIAM ALLINGHAM

The Dinkey-Bird

In an ocean, 'way out yonder
    (As all sapient people know),
Is the land of Wonder-Wander,
    Whither children love to go;
It's their playing, romping, swinging,
    That give great joy to me
While the Dinkey-Bird goes singing
    In the Amfalula-tree!

There the gum-drops grow like cherries,
    And taffy's thick as peas,—
Caramels you pick like berries
    When, and where, and how you please:
Big red sugar-plums are clinging
    To the cliffs beside that sea
Where the Dinkey-Bird is singing
    In the Amfalula-tree.

So when children shout and scamper
    And make merry all the day,
When there's naught to put a damper
    To the ardor of their play;
When I hear their laughter ringing,
    Then I'm sure as sure can be
That the Dinkey-Bird is singing
    In the Amfalula-tree.

For the Dinkey-Bird's bravuras
    And staccatos are so sweet—
His roulades, appogiaturas,
    And robustos so complete,
That the youth of every nation—
    Be they near or far away—
Have especial delectation
    In that gladsome roundelay.

Their eyes grow bright and brighter,
    Their lungs begin to crow,
Their hearts get light and lighter,
    And their cheeks are all aglow;
For an echo cometh bringing
    The news to all and me.
That the Dinkey-Bird is singing
    In the Amfalula-tree.

I'm sure you'd like to go there
    To see your feathered friend—

And so many goodies grow there
  You would like to comprehend!
Speed, little dreams, your winging
  To that land across the sea
Where the Dinkey-Bird is singing
  In the Amfalula-Tree!

—EUGENE FIELD

LAUGHTER IN RHYME

The jester was welcome anywhere and everywhere. At fairs and festivals, in royal courts as well
as common courtyards, the sound of his cap and
bells brought listeners flocking eagerly. The songs
he sang and the tales he told were always punc-
tuated with laughs. The most suspenseful narratives
somehow turned into jokes, for the jester continually
mixed the plausible with the incredible; he even
had a way of combining horror and humor.

The stories in this section wear the jester's cap
and they shake their little bells of rhyme. Jokes are
scattered throughout the stanzas; there is a chuckle
on every page. The spirit is that of Milton's rollick-
ing "L'Allegro" ("The Happy Man"), full of:

> Quips and cranks and wanton wiles,
> Nods and becks and wreathèd smiles . . .
> Sport that wrinkled Care derides,
> And Laughter holding both his sides.

Some of it makes sense—definitely common sense—
while some of it is nonsense. But, according to the
proverb, "a little nonsense now and then is relished
by the best of men."

Adventures of Isabel

Isabel met an enormous bear;
Isabel, Isabel, didn't care.
The bear was hungry, the bear was ravenous,
The bear's big mouth was cruel and cavernous.
The bear said, Isabel, glad to meet you,
How do, Isabel, now I'll eat you!
Isabel, Isabel, didn't worry,
Isabel didn't scream or scurry.
She washed her hands and she straightened her hair up,
Then Isabel quietly ate the bear up.

Once on a night as black as pitch
Isabel met a wicked old witch.
The witch's face was cross and wrinkled,
The witch's gums with teeth were sprinkled.
Ho, ho, Isabel! the old witch crowed,
I'll turn you into an ugly toad!
Isabel, Isabel, didn't worry,
Isabel didn't scream or scurry.
She showed no rage and she showed no rancor,
But she turned the witch into milk and drank her.

Isabel met a hideous giant,
Isabel continued self-reliant.
The giant was hairy, the giant was horrid,
He had one eye in the middle of his forehead.
Good morning, Isabel, the giant said,
I'll grind your bones to make my bread.
Isabel, Isabel, didn't worry,
Isabel didn't scream or scurry.
She nibbled the zwieback that she always fed off,
And when it was gone, she cut the giant's head off.

Isabel met a troublesome doctor,
He punched and he poked till he really shocked her.

The doctor's talk was of coughs and chills
And the doctor's satchel bulged with pills.
The doctor said unto Isabel,
Swallow this, it will make you well.
Isabel, Isabel, didn't worry,
Isabel didn't scream or scurry.
She took those pills from the pill-concocter,
And Isabel calmly cured the doctor.

—OGDEN NASH

Ellen McJones Aberdeen

Macphairson Clonglocketty Angus McClan
Was the son of an elderly labouring man;
You've guessed him a Scotchman, shrewd reader, at sight,
And p'r'aps altogether, shrewd reader, you're right.

From the bonnie blue Forth to the beastly Deeside,
Round by Dingwall and Wrath to the mouth of the Clyde,
There wasn't a child or a woman or man
Who could pipe with Clonglocketty Angus McClan.

No other could wake such detestable groans,
With reed and with chaunter[1]—with bag and with drones:
All day and all night he delighted the chiels
With sniggering pibrochs[2] and jiggety reels.

He'd clamber a mountain and squat on the ground,
And the neighbouring maidens would gather around
To list to his pipes and to gaze in his een,
Especially Ellen McJones Aberdeen.

All loved their McClan, save a Sassenach[3] brute,
Who came to the Highlands to fish and to shoot;

[1] Chaunter: Part of the bagpiges.
[2] Pibrochs: Wild bagpipe music.
[3] Sassenach: Saxon, or Englishman.

He dressed himself up in a Highlander way;
Tho' his name it was Pattison Corby Torbay.

Torbay had incurred a good deal of expense
To make him a Scotchman in every sense;
But this is a matter, you'll readily own,
That isn't a question of tailors alone.

A Sassenach chief may be bonily built,
He may purchase a sporran,[2] a bonnet, and kilt;
Stick a skean[3] in his hose—wear an acre of stripes—
But he cannot assume an affection for pipes.

Clonglocketty's pipings all night and all day
Quite frenzied poor Pattison Corby Torbay;
The girls were amused at his singular spleen,
Especially Ellen McJones Aberdeen.

"Macphairson Clonglocketty Angus, my lad,
With pibrochs and reels you are driving me mad.
If you really must play on that cursed affair,
My goodness! play something resembling an air."

Boiled over the blood of Macphairson McClan—
The Clan of Clonglocketty rose as one man;
For all were enraged at the insult, I ween—
Especially Ellen McJones Aberdeen.

"Let's show," said McClan, "to this Sassenach loon
That the bagpipes can play him a regular tune.
Let's see," said McClan, as he thoughtfully sat,
"'In my Cottage' is easy—I'll practice at that."

He blew at his "Cottage," and blew with a will,
For a year, seven months, and a fortnight, until

---

[2] Sporran: A pouch or purse, worn hanging from the belt of Scottish Highlanders.
[3] Skean: A short sword or dagger.

(You'll hardly believe it!) McClan, I declare,
Elicited something resembling an air.

It was wild—it was fitful—as wild as the breeze—
It wandered about into several keys;
It was jerky, spasmodic, and harsh, I'm aware;
But still it distinctly suggested an air!

The Sassenach screamed, and the Sassenach danced,
He shrieked in his agony—bellowed and pranced,
And the maidens who gathered rejoiced at the scene,
Especially Ellen McJones Aberdeen.

"Hech gather, hech gather, hech gather around;
And fill a' ye lugs wi' the exquisite sound.
An air fra' the bagpipes—beat that if ye can:
Hurrah for Clonglocketty Angus McClan!"

The fame of his piping spread over the land:
Respectable widows proposed for his hand,
And maidens came flocking to sit on the green—
Especially Ellen McJones Aberdeen.

One morning the fidgetty Sassenach swore
He'd stand it no longer—he drew his claymore,
And (this was, I think, extremely bad taste)
Divided Clonglocketty close to the waist.

Oh! loud were the wailings for Angus McClan,
Oh! deep was the grief for that excellent man—
The maids stood aghast at the horrible scene,
Especially Ellen McJones Aberdeen.

It sorrowed poor Pattison Corby Torbay
To find them "take on" in this serious way;
He pitied the poor little fluttering birds,
And solaced their souls with the following words:—

"Oh, maidens," said Pattison, touching his hat,
"Don't blubber, my dears, for a fellow like that;
Observe I'm a very superior man,
A much better fellow than Angus McClan."

They smiled when he winked and addressed them as "dears,"
And they all of them vowed, as they dried up their tears,
A pleasanter gentleman never was seen—
Especially Ellen McJones Aberdeen.

—WILLIAM SCHWENCK GILBERT

The Yarn of the "Nancy Bell"

'Twas on the shores that round our coast
  From Deal to Ramsgate span,
That I found alone, on a piece of stone,
  An elderly naval man.

His hair was weedy, his beard was long,
  And weedy and long was he;
And I heard this wight on the shore recite
  In a singular minor key:

"Oh, I am a cook and a captain bold,
  And the mate of the Nancy brig,
And a bo'sun tight, and a midshipmite,
  And the crew of the captain's gig."

And he shook his fists and he tore his hair,
  Till I really felt afraid,
For I couldn't help thinking the man had been drinking,
  And so I simply said:

"O elderly man, it's little I know
  Of the duties of men of the sea,
And I'll eat my hand if I understand
  How ever you can be

"At once a cook and a captain bold,
    And the mate of the Nancy brig,
And a bo'sun tight, and a midshipmite,
    And the crew of the captain's gig!"

Then he gave a hitch to his trowsers, which
    Is a trick all seamen larn,
And having got rid of a thumping quid,
    He spun this painful yarn:

" 'Twas in the good ship Nancy Bell
    That we sail'd to the Indian sea,
And there on a reef we come to grief,
    Which has often occurr'd to me.

"And pretty nigh all o' the crew was drown'd
    (There was seventy-seven o' soul);
And only ten of the Nancy's men
    Said 'Here!' to the muster-roll.

"There was me, and the cook, and the captain bold,
    And the mate of the Nancy brig,
And the bo'sun tight and a midshipmite,
    And the crew of the captain's gig.

"For a month we'd neither wittles nor drink,
    Till a-hungry we did feel,
So we draw'd a lot, and, accordin', shot
    The captain for our meal.

"The next lot fell to the Nancy's mate,
    And a delicate dish he made;
Then our appetite with the midshipmite
    We seven survivors stay'd.

"And then we murder'd the bo'sun tight,
    And he much resembled pig;

Then we wittled free, did the cook and me,
 On the crew of the captain's gig.

"Then only the cook and me was left,
 And the delicate question, 'Which
Of us two goes to the kettle?' arose,
 And we argued it out as sich.

"For I loved that cook as a brother, I did,
 And the cook he worshipp'd me;
But we'd both be blow'd if we'd either be stow'd
 In the other chap's hold, you see.

" 'I'll be eat if you dines off me,' says Tom.
 'Yes, that,' says I, 'you'll be.
I'm boil'd if I die, my friend,' quoth I;
 And 'Exactly so,' quoth he.

"Says he: 'Dear James, to murder me
 Were a foolish thing to do,
For don't you see that you can't cook *me*,
 While I can—and will—cook *you*?'

"So he boils the water, and takes the salt
 And the pepper in portions true
(Which he never forgot), and some chopp'd shallot,
 And some sage and parsley too.

" 'Come here,' says he, with a proper pride,
 Which his smiling features tell;
' 'Twill soothing be if I let you see
 How extremely nice you'll smell.'

"And he stirr'd it round and round and round,
 And he sniff'd at the foaming froth;
When I ups with his heels, and smothers his squeals
 In the scum of the boiling broth.

"And I eat that cook in a week or less,
    And as I eating be
The last of his chops, why I almost drops,
    For a wessel in sight I see.

"And I never larf, and I never smile,
    And I never lark nor play;
But I sit and croak, and a single joke
    I have—which is to say:

"Oh, I am a cook and a captain bold,
    And the mate of the Nancy brig,
And a bo'sun tight, and a midshipmite,
    And the crew of the captain's gig!"

                    —WILLIAM SCHWENCK GILBERT

General John

The bravest names for fire and flames
    And all that mortal durst,
Were GENERAL JOHN and PRIVATE JAMES,
    Of the Sixty-seventy-first.

GENERAL JOHN was a soldier tried,
    A chief of warlike dons;
A haughty stride and a withering pride
    Were MAJOR-GENERAL JOHN's.

A sneer would play on his martial phiz,
    Superior birth to show;
"Pish!" was a favourite word of his,
    And he often said "Ho! ho!"

FULL-PRIVATE JAMES described might be,
    As a man of a mournful mind;
No characteristic trait had he
    Of any distinctive kind.

From the ranks, one day, cried PRIVATE JAMES,
　"Oh! MAJOR-GENERAL JOHN,
I've doubts of our respective names,
　My mournful mind upon.

"A glimmering thought occurs to me
　(Its source I can't unearth),
But I've a kind of a notion we
　Were cruelly changed at birth.

"I've a strange idea that each other's names
　We've each of us here got on.
Such things have been," said PRIVATE JAMES.
　"They have!" sneered GENERAL JOHN.

"My GENERAL JOHN, I swear upon
　My oath I think 'tis so——"
"Pish!" proudly sneered his GENERAL JOHN,
　And he also said "Ho! ho!"

"My GENERAL JOHN! my GENERAL JOHN!
　My GENERAL JOHN!" quoth he,
"This aristocratical sneer upon
　Your face I blush to see!

"No truly great or generous cove
　Deserving of them names,
Would sneer at a fixed idea that's drove
　In the mind of a PRIVATE JAMES!"

Said GENERAL JOHN, "Upon your claims
　No need your breath to waste;
If this is a joke, FULL-PRIVATE JAMES,
　It's a joke of doubtful taste.

"But, being a man of doubtless worth,
　If you feel certain quite

That we were probably changed at birth,
    I'll venture to say you're right."

So GENERAL JOHN as PRIVATE JAMES
    Fell in, parade upon;
And PRIVATE JAMES, by change of names,
    Was MAJOR-GENERAL JOHN.
              —WILLIAM SCHWENCK GILBERT

The Ruler of the Queen's Navee

From "Pinafore"

When I was a lad I served a term
As office boy to an attorney's firm.
I cleaned the windows and I swept the floor,
And I polished up the handle of the big front door.
    I polished up that handle so carefullee
    That now I am the Ruler of the Queen's Navee!

As office boy I made such a mark
That they gave me the post of a junior clerk.
I served the writs with a smile so bland,
And I copied all the letters in a big round hand—
    I copied all the letters in a hand so free,
    That now I am the Ruler of the Queen's Navee!

In serving writs I made such a name
That an articled clerk I soon became;
I wore clean collars and a brand-new suit
For the pass-examination at the Institute.
    And that pass-examination did so well for me,
    That now I am the Ruler of the Queen's Navee!

Of legal knowledge I acquired such a grip
That they took me into the partnership

And that junior partnership, I ween,
Was the only ship I ever had seen.
   But that kind of ship so suited me,
   That now I am the Ruler of the Queen's Navee!

I grew so rich that I was sent
By a pocket borough into Parliament.
I always voted at my party's call,
And I never thought of thinking for myself at all.
   I thought so little, they rewarded me
   By making me the Ruler of the Queen's Navee!

Now, landsmen all, whoever you may be,
If you want to rise to the top of the tree,
If your soul isn't fettered to an office stool,
Be careful to be guided by this golden rule—
   Stick close to your desk and never go to sea,
   And you *all* may be Rulers of the Queen's Navee!
               —WILLIAM SCHWENCK GILBERT

Faithless Sally Brown

Young Ben he was a nice young man,
   A carpenter by trade;
And he fell in love with Sally Brown,
   That was a lady's maid.

But as they fetched a walk one day,
   They met a press-gang crew;
And Sally she did faint away,
   Whilst Ben he was brought to.

The Boatswain swore with wicked words,
   Enough to shock a saint,
That though she did seem in a fit,
   'Twas nothing but a feint.

"Come, girl," said he, "hold up your head,
    He'll be as good as me;
For when your swain is in our boat,
    A boatswain he will be."

So when they'd made their game of her,
    And taken off her elf,
She roused, and found she only was
    A coming to herself.

"And is he gone, and is he gone?"
    She cried, and wept outright:
"Then I will to the water side,
    And see him out of sight."

A waterman came up to her,
    "Now, young woman," said he,
"If you weep on so, you will make
    Eye-water in the sea."

"Alas! they've taken my beau, Ben,
    To sail with old Benbow;"
And her woe began to run afresh,
    As if she'd said, Gee woe!

Says he, "They've only taken him
    To the Tender-ship, you see;"
"The Tender-ship," cried Sally Brown,
    "What a hard-ship that must be!

"Oh! would I were a mermaid now,
    For then I'd follow him;
But oh!—I'm not a fish-woman,
    And so I cannot swim.

"Alas! I was not born beneath
    The Virgin and the Scales,

So I must curse my cruel stars,
    And walk about in Wales."

Now Ben had sailed to many a place
    That's underneath the world;
But in two years the ship came home,
    And all her sails were furled.

But when he called on Sally Brown,
    To see how she went on,
He found she'd got another Ben,
    Whose Christian name was John.

"O Sally Brown, O Sally Brown,
    How could you serve me so,
I've met with many a breeze before,
    But never such a blow."

Then reading on his 'bacco box,
    He heaved a bitter sigh,
And then began to eye his pipe,
    And then to pipe his eye.[1]

And then he tried to sing "All's Well,"
    But could not though he tried:
His head was turned, and so he chewed
    His pigtail till he died.

His death, which happened in his berth,
    At forty-odd befell:
They went and told the sexton, and
    The sexton toll'd the bell.

                                —THOMAS HOOD

---

[1] Pipe his eye: Snivel or weep.

The Ballad of the Oysterman

It was a tall young oysterman lived by the river-side,
His shop was just upon the bank, his boat was on the tide;
The daughter of a fisherman, that was so straight and slim,
Lived over on the other bank, right opposite to him.

It was the pensive oysterman that saw a lovely maid,
Upon a moonlight evening, a-sitting in the shade;
He saw her wave her handkerchief, as much as if to say,
"I'm wide awake, young oysterman, and all the folks away."

Then up arose the oysterman, and to himself said he,
"I guess I'll leave the skiff at home, for fear that folks should
    see;
I read it in the story-book, that, for to kiss his dear,
Leander swam the Hellespont,—and I will swim this here."

And he has leaped into the waves, and crossed the shining
    stream,
And he has clambered up the bank, all in the moonlight
    gleam;
Oh there were kisses sweet as dew, and words as soft as
    rain,—
But they have heard her father's step, and in he leaps again!

Out spoke the ancient fisherman,—"Oh, what was that, my
    daughter?"
" 'T was nothing but a pebble, sir, I threw into the water."
"And what is that, pray tell me, love, that paddles off so fast?"
"It's nothing but a porpoise, sir, that's been a-swimming past."

Out spoke the ancient fisherman,—"Now bring me my
    harpoon!
I'll get into my fishing-boat, and fix the fellow soon."
Down fell that pretty innocent, as falls a snow-white lamb,
Her hair drooped round her pallid cheeks, like seaweed on a
    clam.

Alas for those two loving ones! she waked not from her
    swound,
And he was taken with the cramp, and in the waves was
    drowned;
But Fate has metamorphosed them, in pity of their woe,
And now they keep an oyster-shop for mermaids down below.

—OLIVER WENDELL HOLMES

On a Favorite Cat Drowned in a Tub of Goldfishes

'Twas on a lofty vase's side
Where China's gayest art had dyed
    The azure flowers that blow,
Demurest of the tabby kind,
The pensive Selima, reclined,
    Gazed on the lake below.

Her conscious tail her joy declared:
The fair round face, the snowy beard,
    The velvet of her paws,
Her coat that with the tortoise vies,
Her ears of jet, and emerald eyes,
    She saw, and purr'd applause.

Still had she gazed, but midst the tide
Two angel forms were seen to glide,
    The genii of the stream:
Their scaly armor's Tyrian hue,
Through richest purple, to the view
    Betray'd a golden gleam.

The hapless Nymph with wonder saw:
A whisker first, and then a claw,
    With many an ardent wish,
She stretch'd in vain to reach the prize;
What female heart can gold despise?
    What cat's averse to fish?

Presumptuous maid! with looks intent
Again she stretch'd, again she bent,
 Nor knew the gulf between—
Malignant fate sat by and smiled—
The slippery verge her feet beguiled;
 She tumbled headlong in!

Eight times emerging from the flood
She mew'd to every watery god
 Some speedy aid to send:
No dolphin came, no Nereid stirr'd,
Nor cruel Tom nor Susan heard—
 A favorite has no friend!

—THOMAS GRAY

The Well of St. Keyne

A well there is in the west country,
 And a clearer one never was seen;
There is not a wife in the west country
 But has heard of the Well of St. Keyne.

An oak and an elm tree stand beside,
 And behind doth an ash-tree grow,
And a willow from the bank above
 Droops to the water below.

A traveller came to the Well of St. Keyne;
 Joyfully he drew nigh;
For from cock-crow he had been travelling,
 And there was not a cloud in the sky.

He drank of the water so cool and clear,
 For thirsty and hot was he,
And he sat down upon the bank,
 Under the willow tree.

There came a man from the house hard by,
    At the well to fill his pail,
On the well-side he rested it,
    And bade the stranger hail.

"Now, art thou a bachelor, stranger?" quoth he,
    "For, an if thou hast a wife,
The happiest draught thou hast drank this day
    That ever thou didst in thy life.

"Or has thy good woman, if one thou hast,
    Ever here in Cornwall been?
For, an if she have, I'll venture my life
    She has drunk of the Well of St. Keyne."

"I have left a good woman who never was here,"
    The stranger he made reply;
"But that my draught should be better for that,
    I pray you answer me why."

"St. Keyne," quoth the Cornish-man, "many a time
    Drank of this crystal well;
And before the angel summoned her,
    She laid on the water a spell,—

"If the husband of this gifted well
    Shall drink before his wife,
A happy man henceforth is he,
    For he shall be master for life,—

"But if the wife should drink of it first,
    Heaven help the husband then!"—
The stranger stooped to the Well of St. Keyne,
    And drank of the water again.

"You drank of the well, I warrant, betimes?"
    He to the Cornish-man said;

But the Cornish-man smiled as the stranger spake,
  And sheepishly shook his head:—

"I hastened as soon as the wedding was done,
  And left my wife in the porch;
But i'faith, she had been wiser than me,
  For she took a bottle to church."

                                    —ROBERT SOUTHEY

Wreck of the "Julie Plante"

On wan dark night on Lac St. Pierre
De wind, she blow, blow, blow,
An' de crew of de wood-scow *Julie Plante*
Got scairt and run below.
For de wind she blow lak hurricane;
Bimeby she blow some more,
An' de scow bust up on Lac St. Pierre
Wan arpent[1] from de shore.

De captain walk on de fronte deck,
An' walk on the hin' deck too.
He call de crew from up de hole;
He call de cook also.
De cook she's name was Rosie,
She come from Montreal,
Was chambermaid on lumber barge
On de Grande Lachine Canal.

De wind she blow from nor'-eas'wes'—
De sout' wind she blow too.
Rosie cry, "Mon cher Captain;
Mon cher, what I shall do?"
Den de captain throw de big ankerre,
But still de skow, she dreef;
De crew he can't pass on de shore
Becos he lose hees skeef.

---
[1] An arpent is a Canadian measure, about 180 feet.

De night was dark lak wan black cat,
De wave run high an' fas'
When de captain tak de Rosie girl
An' tie her to de mas'.
Den he also tak de life preserve
An' jump off on de lac,
An' say, "Good-bye, my Rosie dear,
I go drown for your sak."

Next morning very early
Bout half-past two, three, four,
De captain, scow, and de poor Rosie
Was corpses on de shore.
For de wind she blow lak hurricane,
Bimeby she blow some more,
An' de scow bust up on Lac St. Pierre,
Wan arpent from de shore.

Now all good wood-scow sailorman
Tak warning from dat storm,
An' go an' marry some nice French girl
An' live on wan beeg farm.
De wind can blow lak hurricane,
An' spose she blow some more,
You can't get drown on Lac St. Pierre
So long you stay on shore.

—WILLIAM HENRY DRUMMOND

The Owl-Critic

"Who stuffed that white owl?" No one spoke in the shop,
The barber was busy, and he couldn't stop;
The customers, waiting their turns, were all reading
The "Daily," the "Herald," the "Post," little heeding
The young man who blurted out such a blunt question;
Not one raised a head, or even made a suggestion;
  And the barber kept on shaving.

"Don't you see, Mr. Brown,"
Cried the youth, with a frown,
"How wrong the whole thing is,
How preposterous each wing is,
How flattened the head is, how jammed down the neck is—
In short, the whole owl, what an ignorant wreck 't is!
I make no apology;
I've learned owl-eology.
I've passed days and nights in a hundred collections,
And cannot be blinded to any deflections
Arising from unskilful fingers that fail
To stuff a bird right, from his beak to his tail.
Mister Brown! Mister Brown!
Do take that bird down,
Or you'll soon be the laughing-stock all over town!"
    And the barber kept on shaving.
"I've *studied* owls,
And other night-fowls,
And I tell you
What I know to be true;
An owl cannot roost
With his limbs so unloosed;
No owl in this world
Ever had his claws curled,
Ever had his legs slanted,
Ever had his bill canted,
Ever had his neck screwed
Into that attitude.
He can't *do* it, because
'Tis against all bird-laws.
Anatomy teaches,
Ornithology preaches,
An owl has a toe
That *can't* turn out so!
I've made the white owl my study for years,
And to see such a job almost moves me to tears!
Mr. Brown, I'm amazed
You should be so gone crazed

As to put up a bird
In that posture absurd!
To *look* at that owl really brings on a dizziness
The man who stuffed *him* don't half know his business!"
    And the barber kept on shaving.

"Examine those eyes.
I'm filled with surprise
Taxidermists should pass
Off on you such poor glass;
So unnatural they seem
They'd make Audubon scream,
And John Burroughs laugh
To encounter such chaff.
Do take that bird down;
Have him stuffed again, Brown!"
    And the barber kept on shaving.

"With some sawdust and bark
I could stuff in the dark
An owl better than that.
I could make an old hat
Look more like an owl
Than that horrid fowl,
Stuck up there so stiff like a side of coarse leather.
In fact, about *him*, there's not one natural feather."

Just then, with a wink and a sly normal lurch,
The owl, very gravely, got down from his perch,
Walked around, and regarded his fault-finding critic
(Who thought he was stuffed) with a glance analytic,
And then fairly hooted, as if he should say:
"Your learning's at fault *this* time, anyway;
Don't waste it again on a live bird, I pray.
I'm an owl; you're another. Sir Critic, good day!"
    And the barber kept on shaving.

—JAMES THOMAS FIELDS

The Walrus and the Carpenter

The sun was shining on the sea,
    Shining with all his might:
He did his very best to make
    The billows smooth and bright—
And this was odd, because it was
    The middle of the night.

The moon was shining sulkily,
    Because she thought the sun
Had got no business to be there
    After the day was done—
"It's very rude of him," she said,
    "To come and spoil the fun!"

The sea was wet as wet could be,
    The sands were dry as dry.
You could not see a cloud, because
    No cloud was in the sky:
No birds were flying overhead—
    There were no birds to fly.

The Walrus and the Carpenter
    Were walking close at hand:
They wept like anything to see
    Such quantities of sand.
"If this were only cleared away,"
    They said, "it *would* be grand!"

"If seven maids with seven mops
    Swept it for half a year,
Do you suppose," the Walrus said,
    "That they could get it clear?"
"I doubt it," said the Carpenter,
    And shed a bitter tear.

"O Oysters, come and walk with us!"
    The Walrus did beseech.
"A pleasant talk, a pleasant walk,
    Along the briny beach:
We cannot do with more than four,
    To give a hand to each."

The eldest Oyster looked at him,
    But never a word he said:
The eldest Oyster winked his eye,
    And shook his heavy head—
Meaning to say he did not choose
    To leave the oyster-bed.

But four young Oysters hurried up,
    All eager for the treat:
Their coats were brushed, their faces washed,
    Their shoes were clean and neat—
And this was odd, because, you know,
    They hadn't any feet.

Four other Oysters followed them,
    And yet another four;
And thick and fast they came at last,
    And more, and more, and more—
All hopping through the frothy waves,
    And scrambling to the shore.

The Walrus and the Carpenter
    Walked on a mile or so,
And then they rested on a rock
    Conveniently low:
And all the little Oysters stood
    And waited in a row.

"The time has come," the Walrus said,
    "To talk of many things:

Of shoes and ships and sealing-wax,
    Of cabbages and kings;
And why the sea is boiling hot—
    And whether pigs have wings."

"But wait a bit," the Oysters cried,
    "Before we have our chat;
For some of us are out of breath,
    And all of us are fat!"
"No hurry!" said the Carpenter.
    They thanked him much for that.

"A loaf of bread," the Walrus said,
    "Is what we chiefly need:
Pepper and vinegar besides
    Are very good indeed—
Now, if you're ready, Oysters dear,
    We can begin to feed."

"But not on us!" the Oysters cried,
    Turning a little blue.
"After such kindness, that would be
    A dismal thing to do!"
"The night is fine," the Walrus said.
    "Do you admire the view?

"It was so kind of you to come!
    And you are very nice!"
The Carpenter said nothing but
    "Cut us another slice.
I wish you were not quite so deaf—
    I've had to ask you twice!"

"It seems a shame," the Walrus said,
    "To play them such a trick,
After we've brought them out so far,
    And made them trot so quick!"

The Carpenter said nothing but
　"The butter's spread too thick!"

"I weep for you," the Walrus said:
　"I deeply sympathize."
With sobs and tears he sorted out
　Those of the largest size,
Holding his pocket-handkerchief
　Before his streaming eyes.

"O Oysters," said the Carpenter,
　"You've had a pleasant run!
Shall we be trotting home again?"
　But answer came there none—
And this was scarcely odd, because
　They'd eaten every one.

　　　　　　　　　　　　—LEWIS CARROLL

The Twins

In form and feature, face and limb,
　I grew so like my brother,
That folks got taking me for him,
　And each for one another.
It puzzled all our kith and kin,
　It reached an awful pitch;
For one of us was born a twin,
　Yet not a soul knew which.

One day (to make the matter worse),
　Before our names were fixed,
As we were being washed by nurse
　We got completely mixed;
And thus, you see, by Fate's decree,
　(Or rather nurse's whim),
My brother John got christened *me*,
　And I got christened *him*.

This fatal likeness even dogged
  My footsteps when at school,
And I was always getting flogged,
  For John turned out a fool.
I put this question hopelessly
  To every one I knew—
What *would* you do, if you were me,
  To prove that you were *you?*

Our close resemblance turned the tide
  Of my domestic life;
For somehow my intended bride
  Became my brother's wife.
In short, year after year the same
  Absurd mistakes went on;
And when I died—the neighbors came
  And buried brother John!

                    —HENRY S. LEIGH

At first glance it would seem that "The Cremation of Sam McGee" should be in the same section as "The Shooting of Dan McGrew" by the same author, or side by side with some other tough-fisted and red-blooded ballad. But, although "The Cremation of Sam McGee" has the same pulse-pounding, hard-hitting manner of Robert W. Service's other poems, it is a grandiose experiment in absurdity, a gathering exaggeration that ends in a colossal joke.

The Cremation of Sam McGee

There are strange things done in the midnight sun
  By the men who moil for gold;

The Arctic trails have their secret tales
  That would make your blood run cold;
The northern lights have seen queer sights,
  But the queerest they ever did see
Was that night on the marge of Lake Lebarge
  I cremated Sam McGee.

Now Sam McGee was from Tennessee, where the cotton blooms and blows.
Why he left his home in the South to roam 'round the pole, God only knows.
He was always cold, but the land of gold seemed to hold him like a spell,
Though he'd often say in his homely way that "he'd sooner live in hell."

On Christmas Day we were mushing our way over the Dawson Trail.
Talk of your cold! Through the parka's fold it stabbed like a driven nail.
If our eyes we'd close, then the lashes froze till sometimes we couldn't see;
It wasn't much fun, but the only one to whimper was Sam McGee.

And that very night, as we lay packed tight in our robes beneath the snow,
And the dogs were fed, and the stars o'erhead were dancing heel and toe,
He turned to me, and "Cap," says he, "I'll cash in this trip, I guess;
And if I do, I'm asking that you won't refuse my last request."

Well, he seemed so low that I couldn't say no; then he says with a sort of moan:
"It's the cursèd cold, and it's got right hold till I'm chilled clean through to the bone.

Yet 'taint being dead—it's my awful dread of the icy grave
that pains;
So I want you to swear that, foul or fair, you'll cremate my
last remains."

A pal's last need is a thing to heed, so I swore I would not
fail;
And we started on at the streak of dawn; but God! he looked
ghastly pale.
He crouched on the sleigh, and he raved all day of his home
in Tennessee;
And before nightfall a corpse was all that was left of Sam
McGee.

There wasn't a breath in that land of death, and I hurried,
horror-driven,
With a corpse half hid that I couldn't get rid, because of a
promise I'd given;
It was lashed to the sleigh, and it seemed to say: "You may
tax your brawn and brains,
But you promised true, and it's up to you to cremate those
last remains."

Now a promise made is a debt unpaid, and the trail has its
own stern code;
In the days to come, though my lips were dumb, in my heart
how I cursed that load.
In the long, long night, by the lone firelight, while the
huskies, 'round in a ring,
Howled out their woes to the homeless snows—O God! how
I loathed the thing.

And every day that quiet clay seemed to heavy and heavier
grow;
And on I went, though the dogs were spent and the grub was
getting low;

The trail was bad, and I felt half mad, but I swore I would
    not give in;
And I'd often sing to the hateful thing, and it harkened with
    a grin.

Till I came to the marge of Lake Lebarge, and a derelict
    there lay;
It was jammed in the ice, but I saw in a trice it was called
    the *Alice May*.
And I looked at it, and I thought a bit, and I looked at my
    frozen chum;
Then "Here," said I, with a sudden cry, "is my cre-ma-tor-
    i-um."

Some planks I tore from the cabin floor, and I lit the boiler
    fire;
Some coal I found that was lying around, and I heaped the
    fuel higher;
The flames just soared, and the furnace roared—such a blaze
    you seldom see;
And I burrowed a hole in the glowing coal, and I stuffed
    in Sam McGee.

Then I made a hike, for I didn't like to hear him sizzle so;
And the heavens scowled, and the huskies howled, and the
    wind began to blow.
It was icy cold, but the hot sweat rolled down my cheeks,
    and I don't know why;
And the greasy smoke in an inky cloak went streaking down
    the sky.

I do not know how long in the snow I wrestled with grisly
    fear;
But the stars came out and they danced about ere again I
    ventured near;

I was sick with dread, but I bravely said: "I'll just take a
    peep inside.
I guess he's cooked, and it's time I looked"; . . . then the
    door I opened wide.

And there sat Sam, looking cold and calm, in the heart of
    the furnace roar;
And he wore a smile you could see a mile, and he said:
    "Please close that door!
It's fine in here, but I greatly fear you'll let in the cold and
    storm—
Since I left Plumtree, down in Tennessee, it's the first time
    I've been warm."

> *There are strange things done in the midnight sun*
>   *By the men who moil for gold;*
> *The Arctic trails have their secret tales*
>   *That would make your blood run cold;*
> *The northern lights have seen queer sights,*
>   *But the queerest they ever did see*
> *Was that night on the marge of Lake Lebarge*
>   *I cremated Sam McGee.*

—ROBERT W. SERVICE

The Jackdaw of Rheims

The Jackdaw sat on the Cardinal's chair!
Bishop and abbot and prior were there;
    Many a monk, and many a friar,
    Many a knight, and many a squire,
With a great many more of lesser degree,—
In sooth, a goodly company;
And they served the Lord Primate on bended knee.
    Never, I ween,
    Was a prouder seen,
Read of in books, or dreamt of in dreams,
Than the Cardinal Lord Archbishop of Rheims!

In and out,
Through the motley rout,
That little Jackdaw kept hopping about:
Here and there,
Like a dog in a fair,
Over comfits and cates,
And dishes and plates,
Cowl and cope, and rochet and pall,
Mitre and crosier, he hopped upon all.
With a saucy air,
He perched on the chair
Where, in state, the great Lord Cardinal sat,
In the great Lord Cardinal's great red hat;
And he peered in the face
Of his Lordship's Grace,
With a satisfied look, as if he would say,
"We two are the greatest folks here to-day!"
And the priests, with awe,
As such freaks they saw,
Said, "The Devil must be in that little Jackdaw!"

The feast was over, the board was cleared,
The flawns and the custards had all disappeared,
And six little Singing-boys,—dear little souls
In nice clean faces, and nice white stoles,—
Came, in order due,
Two by two,
Marching that grand refectory through!
A nice little boy held a golden ewer,
Embossed and filled with water, as pure
As any that flows between Rheims and Namur.
Which a nice little boy stood ready to catch
In a fine golden hand-basin made to match.
Two nice little boys, rather more grown,
Carried lavender-water and eau-de-Cologne;
And a nice little boy had a nice cake of soap,
Worthy of washing the hands of the Pope!

One little boy more
A napkin bore,
Of the best white diaper, fringed with pink,
And a cardinal's hat marked in "permanent ink."

The great Lord Cardinal turns at the sight
Of these nice little boys dressed all in white;
From his finger he draws
His costly turquoise:
And, not thinking at all about little Jackdaws
Deposits it straight
By the side of his plate,
While the nice little boys on his Eminence wait
Till, when nobody's dreaming of any such thing,
That little Jackdaw hops off with the ring!

There's a cry and a shout,
And a deuce of a rout,
And nobody seems to know what they're about,
But the monks have their pockets all turned inside out;
The friars are kneeling,
And hunting and feeling
The carpet, the floor, and the walls, and the ceiling.
The Cardinal drew
Off each plum-colored shoe,
And left his red stockings exposed to the view;
He peeps, and he feels
In the toes and the heels.
They turn up the dishes,—they turn up the plates,—
They take up the poker and poke out the grates,
—They turn up the rugs,
They examine the mugs;
But, no!—no such thing,—
They can't find the Ring!
And the Abbot declared that "when nobody twigged it,
Some rascal or other had popped in and prigged it!"

The Cardinal rose with a dignified look,
He called for his candle, his bell, and his book!
   In holy anger and pious grief
   He solemnly cursed that rascally thief!
He cursed him at board, he cursed him in bed;
From the sole of his foot to the crown of his head;
He cursed him in sleeping, that every night
He should dream of the Devil, and wake in a fright.
He cursed him in eating, he cursed him in drinking,
He cursed him in coughing, in sneezing, in winking;
He cursed him in sitting, in standing, in lying;
He cursed him in walking, in riding, in flying;
He cursed him living, he cursed him dying!—
Never was heard such a terrible curse!
    But what gave rise
    To no little surprise,
Nobody seemed one penny the worse!

    The day was gone,
    The night came on,
The monks and the friars they searched till dawn;
    When the sacristan saw,
    On crumpled claw,
Come limping a poor little lame Jackdaw!
    No longer gay,
    As on yesterday;
His feathers all seemed to be turned the wrong way;—
His pinions drooped,—he could hardly stand,—
His head was as bald as the palm of your hand;
    His eye so dim,
    So wasted each limb,
That, heedless of grammar, they all cried, "That's Him!—
That's the scamp that has done this scandalous thing,
That's the thief that has got my Lord Cardinal's Ring!"
    The poor little Jackdaw,
    When the monks he saw,
Feebly gave vent to the ghost of a caw;

And turned his bald head as much as to say,
"Pray be so good as to walk this way!"
    Slower and slower
    He limped on before,
Till they came to the back of the belfry-door,
    Where the first thing they saw,
    Midst the sticks and the straw,
Was the Ring, in the nest of that little Jackdaw!

Then the great Lord Cardinal called for his book,
And off that terrible curse he took:
    The mute expression
    Served in lieu of confession,
And, being thus coupled with full restitution,
The Jackdaw got plenary absolution!
    —When those words were heard,
    That poor little bird
Was so changed in a moment, 't was really absurd:
    He grew sleek and fat;
    In addition to that,
A fresh crop of feathers, came thick as a mat!
    His tail wagged more
    Even than before;
But no longer it wagged with an impudent air,
No longer he perched on the Cardinal's chair:
    He hopped now about
    With a gait devout;
At Matins, at Vespers, he never was out;
And, so far from any more pilfering deeds,
He always seemed telling the Confessor's beads.
If any one lied, or if any one swore,
Or slumbered in prayer-time and happened to snore
    That good Jackdaw
    Would give a great "Caw!"
As much as to say, "Don't do so any more!"
While many remarked, as his manners they saw,
That they "never had known such a pious Jackdaw!"

He long lived the pride
Of that country side,
And at last in the odor of sanctity died;
When, as words were too faint
His merits to paint,
The Conclave determined to make him a Saint.
And on newly made Saints and Popes, as you know,
It's the custom of Rome new names to bestow,
So they canonized him by the name of Jim Crow!

—RICHARD HARRIS BARHAM

Won't You Marry Me?

"Soldier, soldier, won't you marry me?
It's O, for a fife and a drum."
"How can I marry such a pretty girl as you
When I've got no hat to put on?"

Off to the tailor she did go
As hard as she could run,
Brought him back the finest was there.
"Now, soldier, put it on."

"Soldier, soldier, won't you marry me?
It's O, for a fife and a drum."
"How can I marry such a pretty girl as you
When I've got no coat to put on?"

Off to the tailor she did go
As hard as she could run,
Brought him back the finest was there.
"Now, soldier, put it on."

"Soldier, soldier, won't you marry me?
It's O, for a fife and a drum."

"How can I marry such a pretty girl as you
When I've got no shoes to put on?"

Off to the shoe shop she did go
    As hard as she could run,
Brought him back the finest was there.
    "Now, soldier, put them on."

"Soldier, soldier, won't you marry me?
    It's O, for a fife and a drum."
"How can I marry such a pretty girl as you—
    And a wife and baby at home?"

AUTHOR UNKNOWN

Abdul Abulbul Amir

The sons of the Prophet are valiant and bold,
    And quite unaccustomed to fear;
And the bravest of all was a man, so I'm told,
    Called Abdul Abulbul Amir.

When they wanted a man to encourage the van,
    Or harass the foe from the rear,
Storm fort or redoubt, they were sure to call out
    For Abdul Abulbul Amir.

There are heroes in plenty, and well known to fame,
    In the legions that fight for the Czar;
But none of such fame as the man by the name
    Of Ivan Petrofsky Skovar.

He could imitate Irving, tell fortunes by cards,
    And play on the Spanish guitar;
In fact, quite the cream of the Muscovite guards
    Was Ivan Petrofsky Skovar.

One day this bold Muscovite shouldered his gun,
    Put on his most cynical sneer,
And was walking downtown when he happened to run
    Into Abdul Abulbul Amir.

"Young man," said Abulbul, "is existence so dull
    That you're anxious to end your career?
Then, infidel, know you have trod on the toe
    Of Abdul Abulbul Amir.

"So take your last look at the sea, sky and brook,
    Make your latest report on the war;
For I mean to imply you are going to die,
    O, Ivan Petrofsky Skovar."

So this fierce man he took his trusty chibouk,[1]
    And murmuring, "Allah Akbar!"
With murder intent he most savagely went
    For Ivan Petrofsky Skovar.

The Sultan rose up, the disturbance to quell,
    Likewise, give the victor a cheer.
He arrived just in time to bid hasty farewell
    To Abdul Abulbul Amir.

A loud-sounding splash from the Danube was heard
    Resounding o'er meadows afar;
It came from the sack fitting close to the back
    Of Ivan Petrofsky Skovar.

There lieth a stone where the Danube doth roll,
    And on it in characters queer
Are: "Stranger, when passing by, pray for the soul
    Of Abdul Abulbul Amir."

---

[1] Chibouk: a heavy Turkish tobacco pipe, often four or five feet long.

A Muscovite maiden her vigil doth keep
    By the light of the pale northern star,
And the name she repeats every night in her sleep
    Is Ivan Petrofsky Skovar.

AUTHOR UNKNOWN

    A plowman and the son of a plowman, Robert Burns wrote poetry that was close to the soil. For a short period in his life he was courted by leaders of society, but he was most at home with "the sons and daughters of labor and poverty," and his straightforward verse speaks to them as well as for them. When he wrote "Tam O' Shanter" he remembered the tales he heard in his childhood, legends of ghosts and goblins, brownies and bogeys, and brought them to life again in a headlong gallop of high-spirited rhyme.

Tam O' Shanter

When chapman billies[1] leave the street,
And drouthy neibors neibors meet;
As market days are wearing late,
And folk begin to tak the gate,
While we sit bousing at the nappy,[2]
An' getting fou and unco happy,
We think na on the lang Scots miles,
The mosses, waters, slaps[3] and stiles,
That lie between us and our hame,
Where sits our sulky, sullen dame,
Gathering her brows like gathering storm,
Nursing her wrath to keep it warm.

---

[1] Peddlers. [2] Drinking ale. [3] Hedge gaps.

This truth fand honest Tam o' Shanter,
As he frae Ayr ae night did canter
(Auld Ayr, wham ne'er a town surpasses,
For honest men and bonie lasses).

O Tam! had'st thou but been sae wise,
As taen thy ain wife Kate's advice!
She tauld thee weel thou was a skellum,[4]
A blethering, blustering, drunken blellum;[5]
That frae November till October,
Ae market-day thou was no sober;
That ilka melder[6] wi' the Miller,
Thou sat as lang as thou had siller;[7]
That ev'ry nag was ca'd a shoe on[8]
The Smith and thee gat roarin fou on;
That at the Lord's house, ev'n on Sunday,
Thou drank wi' Kirkton Jean till Monday;
She prophesied that late or soon,
Thou wad be found, deep drowned in Doon,
Or catched wi' warlocks in the mirk,
By Alloway's auld, haunted kirk.

Ah, gentle dames! it gars me greet,[9]
To think how mony counsels sweet,
How mony lengthened, sage advices,
The husband frae the wife despises!

But to our tale:—Ae market night,
Tam had got planted unco right,
Fast by an ingle, bleezing finely,
Wi' reaming swats [10] that drank divinely;
And at his elbow, Souter [11] Johnie,
His ancient, trusty, drouthy crony:
Tam lo'ed him like a very brither;
They had been fou for weeks thegither.

---

[4] Rascal.   [5] Babbler.   [6] Every corn-grinding.   [7] Silver, i.e. money.   [8] Called for another drink.   [9] Makes me weep.   [10] Tankards of foaming ale.   [11] Cobbler.

The night drave on wi' sangs an' clatter;
And aye the ale was growing better:
The Landlady and Tam grew gracious,
Wi' favors secret, sweet and precious:
The Souter tauld his queerest stories;
The Landlord's laugh was ready chorus:
The storm without might rair and rustle,
Tam did na mind the storm a whistle.

Care, mad to see a man sae happy,
E'en drowned himsel amang the nappy.
As bees flee hame wi' lades [12] o' treasure,
The minutes winged their way wi' pleasure:
Kings may be blest, but Tam was glorious,
O'er a' the ills o' life victorious!
But pleasures are like poppies spread,
You seize the flow'r, its bloom is shed;
Or like the snow falls in the river,
A moment white—then melts for ever;
Or like the borealis race,
That flit ere you can point their place;
Or like the rainbow's lovely form
Evanishing amid the storm.
Nae man can tether time or tide;—
The hour approaches Tam maun ride;
That hour, o' night's black arch the key-stane,
That dreary hour he mounts his beast in;
And sic a night he taks the road in,
As ne'er poor sinner was abroad in.

The wind blew as 'twad blawn its last;
The rattling showers rose on the blast;
The speedy gleams the darkness swallowed;
Loud, deep, and lang, the thunder bellowed:
That night, a child might understand,
The Deil had business on his hand.

---

[12] Loads.

Weel mounted on his gray mare, Meg,
A better never lifted leg,
Tam skelpit [13] on through dub [14] and mire,
Despising wind, and rain, and fire;
Whiles holding fast his guid blue bonnet;
Whiles crooning o'er some auld Scots sonnet;
Whiles glowering round wi' prudent cares,
Lest bogles [15] catch him unawares;
Kirk Alloway was drawing nigh,
Whare ghaists and houlets [16] nightly cry.

By this time he was cross the ford,
Whare in the snaw the chapman smoored, [17]
And past the birks and meikle stane, [18]
Whare drunken Charlie brak's neckbane;
And through the whins, [19] and by the cairn, [20]
Whare hunters fand the murdered bairn;
And near the thorn, aboon the well,
Whare Mungo's mither hanged hersel.
Before him Doon pours all his floods;
The doubling storm roars through the woods;
The lightnings flash from pole to pole;
Near and more near the thunders roll:
When, glimmering through the groaning trees,
Kirk Alloway seemed in a bleeze;
Through ilka bore [21] the beams were glancing;
And loud resounded mirth and dancing.

Inspiring bold John Barleycorn!
What dangers thou canst make us scorn!
Wi' tippenny, [22] we fear nae evil;
Wi' usquebae, [23] we'll face the Devil!
The swats sae reamed in Tammie's noddle,
Fair play, he cared na deils a boddle. [24]

---

[13] Splashed.   [14] Puddle.   [15] Goblins.   [16] Owls.   [17] Smothered.   [18] Huge
stone.   [19] Bushes.   [20] Stone pile.   [21] Chink.   [22] Twopenny ale.   [23] Whisky.
[24] Didn't care a farthing.

But Maggie stood right sair astonished,
Till, by the heel and hand admonished,
She ventured forward on the light;
And, wow! Tam saw an unco sight!

Warlocks and witches in a dance;
Nae cotillion brent-new frae France,
But hornpipes, jigs, strathspeys, and reels,
Put life and mettle in their heels.
At winnock-bunker [25] in the east,
There sat auld Nick, in shape o' beast;
A towzie tyke,[26] black, grim, and large,
To gie them music was his charge:
He screwed the pipes and gart them skirl,[27]
Till roof and rafters a' did dirl.—[28]
Coffins stood round, like open presses,
That shawed the dead in their last dresses;
And by some devilish cantrip sleight,[29]
Each in its cauld hand held a light—
By which heroic Tam was able
To note upon the holy table
A murderer's banes in gibbet-airns;[30]
Two span-lang, wee, unchristened bairns;
A thief, new-cutted frae a rape,
Wi' his last gasp his gab did gape;
Five tomahawks wi' blude red-rusted;
Five scimitars wi' murder crusted;
A garter which a babe had strangled;
A knife a father's throat had mangled,
Whom his ain son of life bereft,
The gray hairs sticking to the heft;
Wi' mair of horrible and awfu',
Which even to name wad be unlawfu'.

As Tammie glowered, amazed and curious,
The mirth and fun grew fast and furious;

[25] Window seat. [26] Shaggy cur. [27] Made them squeal. [28] Rattle. [29] Magic
trick. [30] Gallow's irons.

The Piper loud and louder blew,
The dancers quick and quicker flew,
They reeled, they set, they crossed, they cleekit,[31]
Till ilka carlin swat and reekit,[32]
And coost her duddies to the wark,[33]
And linkit at it in her sark! [34]

· · · · · · ·

But Tam kent what was what fu' brawlie:
There was ae winsome wench and waulie [35]
That night enlisted in the core
(Lang after kenned on Carrick shore
For mony a beast to dead she shot,
And perished mony a bonie boat,
And shook baith meikle corn and bear,[36]
And kept the country-side in fear);
Her cutty-sark,[37] o' Paisley harn,
That while a lassie she had worn,
In longitude though sorely scanty,
It was her best, and she was vauntie.[38]
Ah! little kenned thy reverend grannie,
That sark she coft [39] for her wee Nannie,
Wi' twa pund Scots ('twas a' her riches),
Wad ever graced a dance of witches!

But here my Muse her wing maun cower,
Sic flights are far beyond her power;
To sing how Nannie lap and flang
(A souple jade she was and strang),
And how Tam stood, like ane bewitched,
And thought his very een enriched:
Even Satan glowered, and fidged fu' fain,
And hotched [40] and blew wi' might and main:
Till first ae caper, syne anither,
Tam tint [41] his reason a' thegither,

---

[31] Joined hands. [32] Every hag sweat and smoked.
[33] Cast off her clothes for the work. [34] Danced in her shirt. [35] Jolly.
[36] Barley. [37] Short shirt. [38] Proud. [39] Bought. [40] Squirmed. [41] Lost.

And roars out, "Weel done, Cutty-sark!"
And in an instant all was dark:
And scarcely had he Maggie rallied,
When out the hellish legion sallied.

As bees bizz out wi' angry fyke,[42]
When plundering herds assail their byke;[43]
As open pussie's[44] mortal foes,
When, pop! she starts before their nose;
As eager runs the market-crowd,
When "Catch the thief!" resounds aloud;
So Maggie runs, the witches follow,
Wi' mony an eldritch[45] skreich and hollo.

Ah, Tam! Ah, Tam! thou'll get thy fairin![46]
In hell they'll roast thee like a herrin!
In vain thy Kate awaits thy comin!
Kate soon will be a woefu' woman!
Now, do thy speedy utmost, Meg,
And win the key-stane o' the brig;[47]
There, at them thou thy tail may toss,
A running stream they dare na cross;
But ere the key-stane she could make,
The fiend a tail she had to shake!
For Nannie, far before the rest,
Hard upon noble Maggie prest,
And flew at Tam wi' furious ettle;[48]
But little wist she Maggie's mettle!
Ae spring brought off her master hale,
But left behind her ain gray tail:
The carlin claught her by the rump,
And left poor Maggie scarce a stump.

Now wha this tale o' truth shall read,
Ilk' man and mother's son, take heed:

---

[42] Fuss.   [43] Hive.   [44] The hare's.   [45] Unearthly.   [46] Reward.   [47] Bridge.
[48] Intent.

Whene'er to drink you are inclined,
Or cutty-sarks run in your mind,
Think, ye may buy the joys o'er dear,
Remember Tam o' Shanter's mare!

—ROBERT BURNS

OF MYSTERY AND TERROR

Here are stories which emanate from the unfet-
tered imagination, out of dreams and darkness,
visions that are full of beauty and consternation.
Red-handed murder is here, fearful as in Hood's
"The Dream of Eugene Aram," in Tennyson's
"Rizpah" and his "The Sisters." These gory crimes are
contrasted with situations as fearful but as humorous-
ly impossible as Benét's "Metropolitan Nightmare"
and as poignantly compassionate as Gibson's "The
Stone." Natural life gives way to the supernatural in
Robert Frost's "The Witch of Coös," Roy Helton's
"Old Christmas," Goethe's "The Erl-King," and
Heine's "A Meeting"—the latter two appearing here
in new translations.

Although the category may be limited, there are
continual differences. It might be interesting to com-
pare Byron's treatment of the biblical story of Bel-
shazzar with Heine's, and Keats's fantastic "La Belle
Dame Sans Merci" with the anonymous "True
Thomas" in "Ballads of Long Ago." The wide range
is further indicated by the otherworldly wonder of
Poe's "Israfel," Moody's frighteningly casual "The
Menagerie," Hardy's brief but bitterly ironic "Ah,
Are You Digging on My Grave?" and John David-
son's melodramatic tale of betrayal and triumph, "A
Ballad of Hell."

A Ballad of Hell

"A letter from my love to-day!
    Oh, unexpected, dear appeal!"
She struck a happy tear away
    And broke the crimson seal.

"My love, there is no help on earth,
    No help in heaven; the dead man's bell
Must toll our wedding; our first hearth
    Must be the well-paved floor of hell."

The colour died from out her face,
    Her eyes like ghostly candles shone;
She cast dread looks about the place,
    Then clenched her teeth, and read right on.

"I may not pass the prison door;
    Here must I rot from day to day,
Unless I wed whom I abhor,
    My cousin, Blanche of Valencay.

"At midnight with my dagger keen
    I'll take my life; it must be so.
Meet me in hell to-night, my queen,
    For weal and woe."

She laughed although her face was wan,
    She girded on her golden belt,
She took her jewelled ivory fan,
    And at her glowing missal knelt.

Then rose, "And am I mad?" she said,
    She broke her fan, her belt untied;
With leather girt herself instead,
    And stuck a dagger at her side.

She waited, shuddering in her room
  Till sleep had fallen on all the house.
She never flinched; she faced her doom:
  They two must sin to keep their vows.

Then out into the night she went;
  And stooping, crept by hedge and tree;
Her rose-bush flung a snare of scent,
  And caught a happy memory.

She fell, and lay a minute's space;
  She tore the sward in her distress;
The dewy grass refreshed her face;
  She rose and ran with lifted dress.

She started like a morn-caught ghost
  Once when the moon came out and stood
To watch; the naked road she crossed,
  And dived into the murmuring wood.

The branches snatched her streaming cloak;
  A live thing shrieked; she made no stay!
She hurried to the trysting-oak—
  Right well she knew the way.

Without a pause she bared her breast
  And drove her dagger home and fell,
And lay like one that takes her rest,
  And died and wakened up in hell.

She bathed her spirit in the flame,
  And near the centre took her post;
From all sides to her ears there came
  The dreary anguish of the lost.

The devil started at her side
  Comely, and tall, and black as jet.

"I am young Malespina's bride;
    Has he come hither yet?"

"My poppet, welcome to your bed."
    "Is Malespina here?"
"Not he! To-morrow he must wed
    His cousin Blanche, my dear!"

"You lie; he died with me to-night."
    "Not he! It was a plot." "You lie."
"My dear, I never lie outright."
    "We died at midnight, he and I."

The devil went. Without a groan
    She, gathered up in one fierce prayer,
Took root in hell's midst all alone,
    And waited for him there.

She dared to make herself at home,
    Amidst the wail, the uneasy stir.
The blood-stained flame that filled the dome,
    Scentless and silent, shrouded her.

How long she stayed I cannot tell;
    But when she felt his perfidy,
She marched across the floor of hell;
    And all the damned stood up to see.

The devil stopped her at the brink;
    She shook him off; she cried, "Away!"
"My dear, you have gone mad, I think."
    "I was betrayed: I will not stay."

Across the weltering deep she ran—
    A stranger thing was never seen:
The damned stood silent to a man;
    They saw the great gulf set between.

To her it seemed a meadow fair;
   And flowers sprang up about her feet;
She entered heaven; she climbed the stair;
   And knelt down at the mercy-seat.

Seraphs and saints with one great voice
   Welcomed that soul that knew not fear;
Amazed to find it could rejoice,
   Hell raised a hoarse half-human cheer.

                     —JOHN DAVIDSON

The Stone

"And will you cut a stone for him,
   To set above his head?
And will you cut a stone for him—
   A stone for him?" she said.

Three days before, a splintered rock
   Had struck her lover dead—
   Had struck him in the quarry dead,
Where, careless of the warning call,
   He loitered, while the shot was fired—
A lively stripling, brave and tall,
   And sure of all his heart desired . . .
A flash, a shock,
   A rumbling fall . . .
And, broken 'neath the broken rock,
   A lifeless heap, with face of clay;
And still as any stone he lay,
   With eyes that saw the end of all.

I went to break the news to her;
   And I could hear my own heart beat
With dread of what my lips might say
But, some poor fool had sped before;
   And flinging wide her father's door,

Had blurted out the news to her,
Had struck her lover dead for her,
Had struck the girl's heart dead in her,
Had struck life lifeless at a word,
And dropped it at her feet:
Then hurried on his witless way,
Scarce knowing she had heard.

And when I came, she stood alone,
A woman turned to stone:
And, though no word at all she said,
I knew that all was known.
Because her heart was dead,
She did not sigh nor moan,
His mother wept:
She could not weep.
Her lover slept:
She could not sleep.
Three days, three nights,
She did not stir:
Three days, three nights,
Were one to her,
Who never closed her eyes
From sunset to sunrise,
From dawn to evenfall:
Her tearless, staring eyes,
That seeing naught, saw all.

The fourth night when I came from work,
I found her at my door.
"And will you cut a stone for him?"
She said: and spoke no more:
But followed me, as I went in,
And sank upon a chair;
And fixed her gray eyes on my face,
With still, unseeing stare.
And, as she waited patiently,
I could not bear to feel

Those still, gray eyes that followed me,
Those eyes that plucked the heart from me,
Those eyes that sucked the breath from me
And curdled the warm blood in me,
Those eyes that cut me to the bone,
And pierced my marrow like cold steel.

And so I rose, and sought a stone;
And cut it, smooth and square:
And, as I worked, she sat and watched,
Beside me, in her chair.
Night after night, by candlelight,
I cut her lover's name:
Night after night, so still and white,
And like a ghost she came;
And sat beside me in her chair;
And watched with eyes aflame.
She eyed each stroke;
And hardly stirred:
She never spoke
A single word:
And not a sound or murmur broke
The quiet, save the mallet-stroke.
With still eyes ever on my hands,
With eyes that seemed to burn my hands,
My wincing, overwearied hands,
She watched, with bloodless lips apart,
And silent, indrawn breath:
And every stroke my chisel cut,
Death cut still deeper in her heart:
The two of us were chiseling,
Together, I and death.

And when at length the job was done,
And I had laid the mallet by,
As if, at last, her peace were won,
She breathed his name; and, with a sigh,

Passed slowly through the open door:
And never crossed my threshold more.

Next night I labored late, alone,
To cut her name upon the stone.

—W. W. GIBSON

Old Christmas

"Where are you coming from, Lomey Carter,
    So airly over the snow?
And what's them pretties you got in your hand,
    And where you aiming to go?

"Step in, Honey: Old Christmas morning
    I ain't got nothing much;
Maybe a bite of sweetness and corn bread,
    A little ham meat and such.

"But come in, Honey! Sally Anne Barton's
    Hungering after your face.
Wait till I light my candle up:
    Set down! There's your old place.

"Now where you been so airly this morning?"
    "*Graveyard, Sally Anne.*
Up by the trace in the salt lick meadows
    Where Taulbe kilt my man."

"Taulbe ain't to home this morning . . .
    I can't scratch up a light:
Dampness gets on the heads of the matches;
    But I'll blow up the embers bright."

"*Needn't trouble. I won't be stopping:*
    Going a long ways still."

"You didn't see nothing, Lomey Carter,
　　Up on the graveyard hill?"

"*What should I see there, Sally Anne Barton?*"
　　"Well, sperits do walk last night."
"*There were an elder bush a-blooming
　　While the moon still give some light.*"

"Yes, elder bushes, they bloom, Old Christmas,
　　And critters kneel down in their straw.
Anything else up in the graveyard?"
　　"*One thing more I saw:*

"*I saw my man with his head all bleeding
　　Where Taulbe's shot went through.*"
"What did he say?"　"*He stooped and kissed me.*"
　　"What did he say to you?"

"Said, Lord Jesus forguv your Taulbe;
　　But he told me another word;
He said it soft when he stooped and kissed me.
　　That were the last I heard."

"Taulbe ain't to home this morning."
　　"*I know that, Sally Anne,
For I kilt him, coming down through the meadow
　　Where Taulbe kilt my man.*

"*I met him upon the meadow trace
　　When the moon were fainting fast,
And I had my dead man's rifle gun
　　And kilt him as he come past.*"

"But I heard two shots."　"'*Twas his was second:
　　He shot me 'fore he died:
You'll find us at daybreak, Sally Anne Barton:
　　I'm laying there dead at his side.*"

　　　　　　　　　　　　　　—ROY HELTON

The Listeners

"Is there anybody there?" said the Traveler,
  Knocking on the moonlit door;
And his horse in the silence champed the grasses
  Of the forest's ferny floor.
And a bird flew up out of the turret,
  Above the Traveler's head:
And he smote upon the door again a second time;
  "Is there anybody there?" he said.
But no one descended to the Traveler;
  No head from the leaf-fringed sill
Leaned over and looked into his gray eyes,
  Where he stood perplexed and still.
But only a host of phantom listeners
  That dwelt in the lone house then
Stood listening in the quiet of the moonlight
  To that voice from the world of men:
Stood thronging the faint moonbeams on the dark stair
  That goes down to the empty hall,
Hearkening in an air stirred and shaken
  By the lonely Traveler's call.
And he felt in his heart their strangeness,
  Their stillness answering his cry,
While his horse moved, cropping the dark turf,
  'Neath the starred and leafy sky;
For he suddenly smote on the door, even
  Louder, and lifted his head:—
"Tell them I came, and no one answered,
  That I kept my word," he said.
Never the least stir made the listeners,
  Though every word he spake
Fell echoing through the shadowiness of the still house
  From the one man left awake:
Aye, they heard his foot upon the stirrup,
  And the sound of iron on stone,

And how the silence surged softly backward,
　　When the plunging hoofs were gone.

　　　　　　　　　　　　　　　　　—WALTER DE LA MARE

Metropolitan Nightmare

It rained quite a lot that spring. You woke in the morning
And saw the sky still clouded, the streets still wet,
But nobody noticed so much, except the taxis
And the people who parade. You don't, in a city.
The parks got very green. All the trees were green
Far into July and August, heavy with leaf,
Heavy with leaf and the long roots boring and spreading,
But nobody noticed that but the city gardeners
And they don't talk.

　　　　　　　　Oh, on Sundays, perhaps you'd notice:
Walking through certain blocks, by the shut, proud houses
With the windows boarded, the people gone away,
You'd suddenly see the queerest small shoots of green
Poking through cracks and crevices in the stone
And a bird-sown flower, red on a balcony,
But then you made jokes about grass growing in the streets
And politics and grass-roots—and there were songs
And gags and a musical show called "Hot and Wet."
It all made a good box for the papers. When the flamingo
Flew into a meeting of the Board of Estimate,
The new mayor acted at once and called the photographers.
When the first green creeper crawled upon Brooklyn Bridge,
They thought it was ornamental. They let it stay.

That was the year the termites came to New York
And they don't do well in cold climates—but listen, Joe,
They're only ants, and ants are nothing but insects.
It was funny and yet rather wistful, in a way
(As Heywood Broun pointed out in the *World-Telegram*)
To think of them looking for wood in a steel city.
It made you feel about life. It was too divine.
There were funny pictures by all the smart, funny artists

And Macy's ran a terribly clever ad:
"The Widow's Termite" or something.
                                    There was no
Disturbance. Even the Communists didn't protest
And say they were Morgan hirelings. It was too hot,
Too hot to protest, too hot to get excited,
An even African heat, lush, fertile and steamy,
That soaked into bone and mind and never once broke.
The warm rain fell in fierce showers and ceased and fell.
Pretty soon you got used to its always being that way.

You got used to the changed rhythm, the altered beat,
To people walking slower, to the whole bright
Fierce pulse of the city slowing, to men in shorts,
To the new sun-helmets from Best's and the cops' white
    uniforms,
And the long noon-rest in the offices, everywhere.
It wasn't a plan or anything. It just happened.
The fingers tapped slower, the office-boys
Dozed on their benches, the bookkeeper yawned at his desk.
The A.T.&T. was the first to change the shifts
And establish an official siesta-room;
But they were always efficient. Mostly it just
Happened like sleep itself, like a tropic sleep,
Till even the Thirties were deserted at noon
Except for a few tourists and one damp cop.
They ran boats to see the big lilies on the North River
But it was only the tourists who really noticed
The flocks of rose-and-green parrots and parrakeets
Nesting in the stone crannies of the Cathedral.
The rest of us had forgotten when they first came.

There wasn't any real change, it was just a heat spell,
A rain spell, a funny summer, a weather-man's joke,
In spite of the geraniums three feet high
In the tin-can gardens of Hester and Desbrosses.
New York was New York. It couldn't turn inside out.

When they got the news from Woods Hole about the Gulf
    Stream,
The *Times* ran an adequate story.
But nobody reads those stories but science-cranks.

Until, one day, a somnolent city-editor
Gave a new cub the termite yarn to break his teeth on.
The cub was just down from Vermont, so he took his time.
He was serious about it. He went around.
He read all about termites in the Public Library
And it made him sore when they fired him.
                                        So, one evening,
Talking with an old watchman, beside the first
Raw girders of the new Planetopolis Building
(Ten thousand brine-cooled offices, each with shower)
He saw a dark line creeping across the rubble
And turned a flashlight on it.
                        "Say, buddy," he said,
"You better look out for those ants. They eat wood, you know,
They'll have your shack down in no time."
                                The watchman spat.
"Oh, they've quit eating wood," he said, in a casual voice,
"I thought everybody knew that."
                                —And, reaching down,
He pried from the insect jaws the bright crumb of steel.
                                —STEPHEN VINCENT BENÉT

The Witch of Coös

I staid the night for shelter at a farm
Behind the mountain, with a mother and son,
Two old-believers. They did all the talking.

MOTHER. Folks think a witch who has familiar spirits
She could call up to pass a winter evening,
But won't, should be burned at the stake or something.

Summoning spirits isn't "Button, button,
Who's got the button," I would have them know.

SON. Mother can make a common table rear
And kick with two legs like an army mule.

MOTHER. And when I've done it, what good have I done?
Rather than tip a table for you, let me
Tell you what Ralle the Sioux Control once told me.
He said the dead had souls, but when I asked him
How could that be—I thought the dead were souls,
He broke my trance. Don't that make you suspicious
That there's something the dead are keeping back?
Yes, there's something the dead are keeping back.

SON. You wouldn't want to tell him what we have
Up attic, mother?

MOTHER. Bones—a skeleton.

SON. But the headboard of mother's bed is pushed
Against the attic door: the door is nailed.
It's harmless. Mother hears it in the night
Halting perplexed behind the barrier
Of door and headboard. Where it wants to get
Is back into the cellar where it came from.

MOTHER. We'll never let them, will we, son! We'll never!

SON. It left the cellar forty years ago
And carried itself like a pile of dishes
Up one flight from the cellar to the kitchen,
Another from the kitchen to the bedroom,
Another from the bedroom to the attic,
Right past both father and mother, and neither stopped it.
Father had gone upstairs; mother was downstairs.
I was a baby: I don't know where I was.

MOTHER. The only fault my husband found with me—
I went to sleep before I went to bed,
Especially in winter when the bed
Might just as well be ice and the clothes snow.
The night the bones came up the cellar-stairs
Toffile had gone to bed alone and left me,
But left an open door to cool the room off
So as to sort of turn me out of it.
I was just coming to myself enough
To wonder where the cold was coming from,
When I heard Toffile upstairs in the bedroom
And thought I heard him downstairs in the cellar.
The board we had laid down to walk dry-shod on
When there was water in the cellar in spring
Struck the hard cellar bottom. And then someone
Began the stairs, two footsteps for each step,
The way a man with one leg and a crutch,
Or a little child, comes up. It wasn't Toffile:
It wasn't anyone who could be there.
The bulkhead double-doors were double-locked
And swollen tight and buried under snow.
The cellar windows were banked up with sawdust
And swollen tight and buried under snow.
It was the bones. I knew them—and good reason.
My first impulse was to get to the knob
And hold the door. But the bones didn't try
The door; they halted helpless on the landing,
Waiting for things to happen in their favor.
The faintest restless rustling ran all through them.
I never could have done the thing I did
If the wish hadn't been too strong in me
To see how they were mounted for this walk.
I had a vision of them put together
Not like a man, but like a chandelier.
So suddenly I flung the door wide on him.
A moment he stood balancing with emotion,
And all but lost himself. (A tongue of fire
Flashed out and licked along his upper teeth.

Smoke rolled inside the sockets of his eyes.)
Then he came at me with one hand outstretched,
The way he did in life once; but this time
I struck the hand off brittle on the floor,
And fell back from him on the floor myself.
The finger-pieces slid in all directions.
(Where did I see one of those pieces lately?
Hand me my button-box—it must be there.)
I sat up on the floor and shouted, "Toffile,
It's coming up to you." It had its choice
Of the door to the cellar or the hall.
It took the hall door for the novelty,
And set off briskly for so slow a thing,
Still going every which way in the joints, though,
So that it looked like lightning or a scribble,
From the slap I had just now given its hand.
I listened till it almost climbed the stairs
From the hall to the only finished bedroom,
Before I got up to do anything;
Then ran and shouted, "Shut the bedroom door,
Toffile, for my sake!" "Company?" he said,
"Don't make me get up; I'm too warm in bed."
So lying forward weakly on the handrail
I pushed myself upstairs, and in the light
(The kitchen had been dark) I had to own
I could see nothing. "Toffile, I don't see it.
It's with us in the room though. It's the bones."
"What bones?" "The cellar bones—out of the grave."
That made him throw his bare legs out of bed
And sit up by me and take hold of me.
I wanted to put out the light and see
If I could see it, or else mow the room,
With our arms at the level of our knees,
And bring the chalk-pile down. "I'll tell you what—
It's looking for another door to try.
The uncommonly deep snow has made him think
Of his old song, *The Wild Colonial Boy*,
He always used to sing along the tote-road.

He's after an open door to get out-doors.
Let's trap him with an open door up attic."
Toffile agreed to that, and sure enough,
Almost the moment he was given an opening,
The steps began to climb the attic stairs.
I heard them. Toffile didn't seem to hear them.
"Quick!" I slammed to the door and held the knob.
"Toffile, get nails." I made him nail the door shut
And push the headboard of the bed against it.
Then we asked was there anything
Up attic that we'd ever want again.
The attic was less to us than the cellar.
If the bones liked the attic, let them have it.
Let them stay in the attic. When they sometimes
Come down the stairs at night and stand perplexed
Behind the door and headboard of the bed,
Brushing their chalky skull with chalky fingers,
With sounds like the dry rattling of a shutter,
That's what I sit up in the dark to say—
To no one any more since Toffile died.
Let them stay in the attic since they went there.
I promised Toffile to be cruel to them
For helping them be cruel once to him.

SON. We think they had a grave down in the cellar.

MOTHER. We know they had a grave down in the cellar.

SON. We never could find out whose bones they were.

MOTHER. Yes, we could too, son. Tell the truth for once.
They were a man's his father killed for me.
I mean a man he killed instead of me.
The least I could do was to help dig their grave.
We were about it one night in the cellar.
Son knows the story: but 'twas not for him
To tell the truth, suppose the time had come.
Son looks surprised to see me end a lie

We'd kept all these years between ourselves
So as to have it ready for outsiders.
But tonight I don't care enough to lie—
I don't remember why I ever cared.
Toffile, if he were here, I don't believe
Could tell you why he ever cared himself . . .

She hadn't found the finger-bone she wanted
Among the buttons poured out in her lap.
I verified the name next morning: Toffile.
The rural letter-box said Toffile Lajway.

—ROBERT FROST

In "La Belle Dame Sans Merci" Keats harks back
to the spirit of the ancient ballads, and particularly to
the ballad of "True Thomas" (see page 47), com-
posed three centuries before Keats's poem. Keats is
concerned with a knight rather than a prophecying
poet and, instead of the ensnaring Queen of Elfland, the enchantress is a lady, "a faëry's child."
Both poems are about a mortal bewitched by an
immortal who casts a spell of magic over her not too
unwilling victim. The same wonder and doom—the
doom of love—establish a kinship between the great
lyric poet of the nineteenth century and the unknown
balladist of the sixteenth.

La Belle Dame Sans Merci

"Oh, what can ail thee, knight-at-arms,
    Alone and palely loitering?
The sedge has withered from the lake,
    And no birds sing.

"Oh, what can ail thee, knight-at-arms,
   So haggard and so woebegone?
The squirrel's granary is full,
   And the harvest's done.

"I see a lily on thy brow,
   With anguish moist and fever dew;
And on thy cheeks a fading rose
   Fast withereth, too."

I met a lady in the meads,
   Full beautiful—a faëry's child;
Her hair was long, her foot was light,
   And her eyes were wild.

I made a garland for her head,
   And bracelets too, and fragrant zone;
She looked at me as she did love,
   And made sweet moan.

I set her on my pacing steed,
   And nothing else saw, all day long.
For sidelong would she bend, and sing
   A faëry's song.

She found me roots of relish sweet,
   And honey wild, and manna dew;
And sure in language strange she said,
   "I love thee true."

She took me to her elfin grot,
   And there she wept, and sighed full sore;
And there I shut her wild, wild eyes
   With kisses four.

And there she lullèd me asleep,
   And there I dreamed, ah, woe betide!

The latest dream I ever dreamt
   On the cold hill's side.

I saw pale kings, and princes, too,
   Pale warriors, death-pale were they all;
They cried, "La Belle Dame Sans Merci
   Hath thee in thrall!"

I saw their starved lips in the gloam
   With horrid warning gapèd wide—
And I awoke, and found me here,
   On the cold hill's side.

And this is why I sojourn here,
   Alone and palely loitering,
Though the sedge is withered from the lake
   And no birds sing.

—JOHN KEATS

A Meeting

Under the linden the music is gay,
   The couples are gossiping loudly;
And two are dancing whom nobody knows,
   They carry themselves so proudly.

Now here, now there, they glide and sway
   In wave-like measures beguiling.
They bow to each other, and as they nod,
   She whispers, gently smiling:

"A water-pink is hanging from
   Your cap, my fair young dancer;
It only grows in the depths of the sea—
   You are no mortal man, sir.

"You are a merman, and to lure
   These village maids your wish is.
I knew you at once by your watery eyes
   And your teeth as sharp as the fishes'."

Now here, now there, they glide and sway
   In wave-like measures beguiling.
They bow to each other, and as they nod,
   He answers, gently smiling:

"My lovely lady, tell me why
   Your hand's so cold and shiny?
And why is the border of your gown
   So damp and draggled and briny?

"I knew you at once by your watery eyes,
   And your bow so mocking and tricksy—
You're never a daughter of earth, my dear;
   You are my cousin, the nixie."

The fiddles are silent, the dancing is done;
   They part with a ripple of laughter.
They know each other too well, and will try
   To avoid such a meeting hereafter.
              —HEINRICH HEINE
            Translated by Louis Untermeyer

The Erl-King

Who rides so late in a night so wild?
A father is riding with his child.
He clasps the boy close in his arm;
He holds him tightly, he keeps him warm.

"My son, you are trembling. What do you fear?"
"Look, father, the Erl-King! He's coming near!

With his crown and his shroud! Yes, that is he!"
"My son, it's only the mist you see."

"O lovely child, oh, come with me,
Such games we'll play! So glad we'll be!
Such flowers to pick! Such sights to behold!
My mother will make you clothes of gold!"

"O father, my father, did you not hear
The Erl-King whispering in my ear?"
"Lie still, my child, lie quietly.
It's only the wind in the leaves of the tree."

"Dear boy, if you will come away,
My daughters will wait on you every day;
They'll give you the prettiest presents to keep;
They'll dance when you wake and they'll sing you asleep."

"My father! My father! Do you not see
The Erl-King's pale daughters waiting for me?"
"My son, my son, I see what you say—
The willow is waving its branches of gray."

"I love you—so come without fear or remorse.
And if you're not willing, I'll take you by force!"
"My father! My father! Tighten your hold!
The Erl-King has caught me—his fingers are cold!"

The father shudders. He spurs on his steed.
He carries the child with desperate speed.
He reaches the courtyard, and looks down with dread.
There in his arms the boy lies dead.

—JOHANN WOLFGANG VON GOETHE
Translated by Louis Untermeyer

The Wreck of the Hesperus

It was the schooner Hesperus,
    That sailed the wintry sea;
And the skipper had taken his little daughter,
    To bear him company.

Blue were her eyes as the fairy-flax,
    Her cheeks like the dawn of day,
And her bosom white as the hawthorn buds
    That ope in the month of May.

The skipper he stood beside the helm,
    His pipe was in his mouth,
And he watched how the veering flaw did blow
    The smoke now West, now South.

Then up and spake an old sailòr,
    Had sailed the Spanish Main,
"I pray thee, put into yonder port,
    For I fear a hurricane.

"Last night, the moon had a golden ring,
    And to-night no moon we see!"
The skipper, he blew a whiff from his pipe,
    And a scornful laugh laughed he.

Colder and louder blew the wind,
    A gale from the Northeast,
The snow fell hissing in the brine,
    And the billows frothed like yeast.

Down came the storm, and smote amain
    The vessel in its strength;
She shuddered and paused, like a frighted steed,
    Then leaped her cable's length.

"Come hither! come hither! my little daughtèr,
   And do not tremble so;
For I can weather the roughest gale
   That ever wind did blow."

He wrapped her warm in his seaman's coat
   Against the stinging blast;
He cut a rope from a broken spar,
   And bound her to the mast.

"O father! I hear the church-bells ring,
   Oh say, what may it be?"
" 'Tis a fog-bell on a rock-bound coast!"—
   And he steered for the open sea.

"O father! I hear the sound of guns,
   Oh say, what may it be?"
"Some ship in distress, that cannot live
   In such an angry sea!"

"O father! I see a gleaming light,
   Oh say, what may it be?"
But the father answered never a word,
   A frozen corpse was he.

Lashed to the helm, all stiff and stark,
   With his face turned to the skies,
The lantern gleamed through the gleaming snow
   On his fixed and glassy eyes.

Then the maiden clasped her hands and prayed
   That savèd she might be;
And she thought of Christ, who stilled the wave,
   On the Lake of Galilee.

And fast through the midnight dark and drear,
   Through the whistling sleet and snow,

Like a sheeted ghost, the vessel swept
    Towards the reef of Norman's Woe.

And ever the fitful gusts between
    A sound came from the land;
It was the sound of the trampling surf,
    On the rocks and the hard sea-sand.

The breakers were right beneath her bows,
    She drifted a dreary wreck,
And a whooping billow swept the crew
    Like icicles from her deck.

She struck where the white and fleecy waves
    Looked soft as carded wool,
But the cruel rocks, they gored her side
    Like the horns of an angry bull.

Her rattling shrouds, all sheathed in ice,
    With the masts went by the board;
Like a vessel of glass, she stove and sank,
    Ho! ho! the breakers roared!

At daybreak, on the bleak sea-beach,
    A fisherman stood aghast,
To see the form of a maiden fair,
    Lashed close to a drifting mast.

The salt sea was frozen on her breast,
    The salt tears in her eyes;
And he saw her hair, like the brown sea-weed,
    On the billows fall and rise.

Such was the wreck of the Hesperus,
    In the midnight and the snow!
Christ save us all from a death like this
    On the reef of Norman's Woe!

            —HENRY WADSWORTH LONGFELLOW

The Menagerie

Thank God my brain is not inclined to cut
Such capers every day! I'm just about
Mellow, but then—There goes the tent-flap shut.
Rain's in the wind. I thought so: every snout
Was twitching when the keeper turned me out.

That screaming parrot makes my blood run cold.
Gabriel's trump! the big bull elephant
Squeals "Rain!" to the parched herd. The monkeys scold.
And jabber that it's rain water they want.
(It makes me sick to see a monkey pant.)

I'll foot it home, to try and make believe
I'm sober. After this I stick to beer,
And drop the circus when the sane folks leave.
A man's a fool to look at things too near:
They look back, and begin to cut up queer.

Beasts do, at any rate; especially
Wild devils caged. They have the coolest way
Of being something else than what you see:
You pass a sleek young zebra nosing hay,
A nylghau looking bored and distingué—

And think you've seen a donkey and a bird.
Not on your life! Just glance back, if you dare.
The zebra chews, the nylghau hasn't stirred;
But something's happened, Heaven knows what or where,
To freeze your scalp and pompadour your hair.

I'm not precisely an aeolian lute
Hung in the wandering winds of sentiment,
But drown me if the ugliest, meanest brute
Grunting and fretting in that sultry tent
Didn't just floor me with embarrassment!

'Twas like a thunder-clap from out the clear—
One minute they were circus beasts, some grand,
Some ugly, some amusing, and some queer:
Rival attractions to the hobo band,
The flying jenny, and the peanut stand.

Next minute they were old hearth-mates of mine!
Lost people, eyeing me with such a stare!
Patient, satiric, devilish, divine;
A gaze of hopeless envy, squalid care,
Hatred, and thwarted love, and dim despair.

Within my blood my ancient kindred spoke—
Grotesque and monstrous voices, heard afar
Down ocean caves when behemoth awoke,
Or through fern forests roared the plesiosaur
Locked with the giant-bat in ghastly war.

And suddenly, as in a flash of light,
I saw great Nature working out her plan;
Through all her shapes from mastodon to mite
Forever groping, testing, passing on
To find at last the shape and soul of Man.

Till in the fullness of accomplished time,
Comes brother Forepaugh, upon business bent,
Tracks her through frozen and through torrid clime,
And shows us, neatly labeled in a tent,
The stages of her huge experiment;

Blabbing aloud her shy and reticent hours;
Dragging to light her blinking, slothful moods;
Publishing fretful seasons when her powers
Worked wild and sullen in her solitudes,
Or when her mordant laughter shook the woods.

Here, round about me, were her vagrant births;
Sick dreams she had, fierce projects she essayed;

Her qualms, her fiery prides, her crazy mirths;
The troublings of her spirit as she strayed,
Cringed, gloated, mocked, was lordly, was afraid.

On that long road she went to seek mankind;
Here were the darkling coverts that she beat
To find the Hider she was sent to find;
Here the distracted footprints of her feet
Whereby her soul's Desire she came to greet.

But why should they, her botch-work, turn about
And stare disdain at me, her finished job?
Why was the place one vast suspended shout
Of laughter? Why did all the daylight throb
With soundless guffaw and dumb-stricken sob?

Helpless I stood among those awful cages;
The beasts were walking loose, and I was bagged!
I, I, last product of the toiling ages,
Goal of heroic feet that never lagged—
A little man in trousers, slightly jagged.

Deliver me from such another jury!
The Judgment-day will be a picnic to't.
Their satire was more dreadful than their fury,
And worst of all was just a kind of brute
Disgust, and giving up, and sinking mute.

Survival of the fittest, adaptation,
And all their other evolution terms,
Seem to omit one small consideration,
To wit, that tumblebugs and angleworms
Have souls: there's soul in everything that squirms.

And souls are restless, plagued, impatient things,
All dream and unaccountable desire;

Crawling, but pestered with the thought of wings;
Spreading through every inch of earth's old mire
Mystical hanker after something higher.

Wishes *are* horses, as I understand.
I guess a wistful polyp that has strokes
Of feeling fain to gallivant on land
Will come to be a scandal to his folks;
Legs he will sprout, in spite of threats and jokes.

And at the core of every life that crawls
Or runs or flies or swims or vegetates—
Churning the mammoth's heart-blood, in the galls
Of shark and tiger planting gorgeous hates,
Lighting the love of eagles for their mates;

Yes, in the dim brain of the jellied fish
That is and is not living—moved and stirred
From the beginning a mysterious wish,
A vision, a command, a fatal Word:
The name of Man was uttered, and they heard.

Upward along the aeons of old war
They sought him: wing and shank-bone, claw and bill
Were fashioned and rejected; wide and far
They roamed the twilight jungles of their will;
But still they sought him, and desired him still.

Man they desired, but mind you, Perfect Man,
The radiant and the loving, yet to be!
I hardly wonder, when they came to scan
The upshot of their strenuosity,
They gazed with mixed emotions upon *me*.

Well, my advice to you is, Face the creatures,
Or spot them sideways with your weather eye,

Just to keep tab on their expansive features;
It isn't pleasant when you're stepping high
To catch a giraffe smiling on the sly.

If nature made you graceful, don't get gay
Back-to before the hippopotamus;
If meek and godly, find some place to play
Besides right where three mad hyenas fuss;
You may hear language that we won't discuss.

If you're a sweet thing in a flower-bed hat,
Or her best fellow with your tie tucked in,
Don't squander love's bright springtime girding at
An old chimpanzee with an Irish chin:
There may be hidden meaning in his grin.

—WILLIAM VAUGHN MOODY

The Legend of Rabbi Ben Levi

Rabbi Ben Levi, on the Sabbath, read
A volume of the Law, in which it said,
"No man shall look upon my face and live."
And as he read, he prayed that God would give
His faithful servant grace with mortal eye
To look upon His face and yet not die.

Then fell a sudden shadow on the page,
And, lifting up his eyes, grown dim with age,
He saw the Angel of Death before him stand,
Holding a naked sword in his right hand.

Rabbi Ben Levi was a righteous man,
Yet through his veins a chill of terror ran.
With trembling voice he said, "What wilt thou here?"
The Angel answered, "Lo! the time draws near

When thou must die; yet first, by God's decree,
Whate'er thou askest shall be granted thee."
Replied the Rabbi, "Let these living eyes
First look upon my place in Paradise."

Then said the Angel, "Come with me and look."
Rabbi Ben Levi closed the sacred book,
And rising, and uplifting his gray head,
"Give me thy sword," he to the Angel said,
"Lest thou shouldst fall upon me by the way."
The Angel smiled and hastened to obey,
Then led him forth to the Celestial Town,
And set him on the wall, whence, gazing down,
Rabbi Ben Levi, with his living eyes,
Might look upon his place in Paradise.

Then straight into the city of the Lord
The Rabbi leaped with the Death-Angel's sword,
And through the streets there swept a sudden breath
Of something there unknown, which men call death.
Meanwhile the Angel stayed without, and cried,
"Come back!" To which the Rabbi's voice replied,
"No! in the name of God, whom I adore,
I swear that hence I will depart no more!"

Then all the Angels cried, "O Holy One,
See what the son of Levi here hath done!
The kingdom of Heaven he takes by violence,
And in Thy name refuses to go hence!"
The Lord replied, "My Angels, be not wroth;
Did e'er the son of Levi break his oath?
Let him remain; for he with mortal eye
Shall look upon my face and yet not die."

Beyond the outer wall the Angel of Death
Heard the great voice, and said, with panting breath,
"Give back the sword, and let me go my way."
Whereat the Rabbi paused, and answered, "Nay!

Anguish enough already hath it caused
Among the sons of men." And while he paused
He heard the awful mandate of the Lord
Resounding through the air, "Give back the sword!"

The Rabbi bowed his head in silent prayer;
Then said he to the dreadful Angel, "Swear,
No human eye shall look on it again;
But when thou takest away the souls of men,
Thyself unseen, and with an unseen sword,
Thou wilt perform the bidding of the Lord."

The Angel took the sword again, and swore,
And walks on earth unseen for evermore.

—HENRY WADSWORTH LONGFELLOW

Israfel

And the angel Israfel, whose heart-strings are a lute, and who has the sweetest voice of all God's creatures. —*Koran*

In Heaven a spirit doth dwell
    "Whose heart-strings are a lute";
None sing so wildly well
As the angel Israfel,
And the giddy stars (so legends tell),
Ceasing their hymns, attend the spell
    Of his voice, all mute.

Tottering above
    In her highest noon,
    The enamoured moon
Blushes with love,
    While, to listen, the red levin
    (With the rapid Pleiads, even,
    Which were seven,)
    Pauses in Heaven.

And they say (the starry choir
   And the other listening things)
That Israfeli's fire
Is owing to that lyre
   By which he sits and sings—
The trembling living wire
   Of those unusual strings.

But the skies that angel trod,
   Where deep thoughts are a duty—
Where Love's a grown-up God—
   Where the Houri glances are
Imbued with all the beauty
   Which we worship in a star.

Therefore thou art not wrong,
   Israfeli, who despisest
An unimpassioned song;
To thee the laurels belong,
   Best bard, because the wisest!
Merrily live, and long!

The ecstasies above
   With thy burning measures suit—
Thy grief, thy joy, thy hate, thy love,
   With the fervour of thy lute—
   Well may the stars be mute!

Yes, Heaven is thine; but this
   Is a world of sweets and sours;
   Our flowers are merely—flowers,
And the shadow of thy perfect bliss
   Is the sunshine of ours.

If I could dwell
Where Israfel
   Hath dwelt, and he where I,
He might not sing so wildly well

A mortal melody,
While a bolder note than this might swell
From my lyre within the sky.

—EDGAR ALLAN POE

Belshazzar

The noon of night was drawing on;
Dark silence lay on Babylon.

Yet in the castle of the King
Were flaring lights and reveling;

There, in the royal banquet hall,
Belshazzar held high festival.

He saw his brilliant court recline
And empty bowl on bowl of wine.

He heard cups ring and vassals sing;
And all the brawling pleased the King.

The wine awoke and made him bold;
He flushed; his words grew uncontrolled.

Wine was his passion, wine his prod;
With obscene oaths he mocked at God.

He blasphemed Heaven and all its laws,
While the court echoed with applause.

The King commanded, his brow was black;
The servants vanished, but hurried back,

Carrying treasures, rich and rare;
The holy Temple's spoil was there.

The King laid hands on a sacred cup;
With a lewd laugh he filled it up.

He drained the goblet in one quick draught,
And then, with slobbering lips, he laughed:

"Jehovah! I drink to your greatness gone;
I am the King of Babylon!"

The blasphemous words had scarce been said
When something struck the King with dread.

The ribald laugh died in the hall;
Silence fell like a deathly pall,

While on the white wall there appeared
A human hand, abrupt and weird;

And then, in letters of red flame,
It wrote, and vanished the way it came.

The King's pale features seemed to freeze;
He could not quiet his knocking knees.

Stone-cold about him his courtiers were.
They gave no sound; they made no stir.

Magicians came, yet none of all
Could read that writing upon the wall.

And in the night death came to one
Belshazzar, King of Babylon.

—HEINRICH HEINE
Translated by Louis Untermeyer

The Vision of Belshazzar

The King was on his throne,
   The Satraps thronged the hall;
A thousand bright lamps shone
   O'er that high festival.
A thousand cups of gold,
   In Judah deemed divine,—
Jehovah's vessels hold
   The godless Heathen's wine!

In that same hour and hall,
   The fingers of a hand
Came forth against the wall,
   And wrote as if on sand:
The fingers of a man;—
   A solitary hand
Along the letters ran,
   And traced them like a wand.

The monarch saw, and shook,
   And bade no more rejoice;
All bloodless waxed his look,
   And tremulous his voice.
"Let the men of lore appear,
   The wisest of the earth,
And expound the words of fear,
   Which mar our royal mirth."

Chaldea's seers are good,
   But here they have no skill;
And the unknown letters stood,
   Untold and awful still.
And Babel's men of age
   Are wise and deep in lore;
But now they were not sage,
   They saw,—but knew no more.

A captive in the land,
  A stranger and a youth,
He heard the King's command,
  He saw that writing's truth.
The lamps around were bright,
  The prophecy in view:
He read it on that night,—
  The morrow proved it true.

"Belshazzar's grave is made,
  His kingdom passed away,
He, in the balance weighed,
  Is light and worthless clay;
The shroud, his robe of state,
  His canopy, the stone:
The Mede is at his gate!
  The Persian on his throne!"

—GEORGE GORDON, LORD BYRON

The Conqueror Worm

Lo! 'tis a gala night
  Within the lonesome latter years!
An angel throng, bewinged, bedight
  In veils, and drowned in tears,
Sit in a theatre, to see
  A play of hopes and fears,
While the orchestra breathes fitfully
  The music of the spheres.

Mimes, in the form of God on high,
  Mutter and mumble low,
And hither and thither fly—
  Mere puppets they, who come and go
At bidding of vast formless things
  That shift the scenery to and fro,

Flapping from out their Condor wings
    Invisible Woe!

That motley drama—oh, be sure
    It shall not be forgot!
With its Phantom chased for evermore,
    By a crowd that seize it not,
Through a circle that ever returneth in
    To the self-same spot,
And much of Madness, and more of Sin,
    And Horror the soul of the plot.

But see, amid the mimic rout
    A crawling shape intrude!
A blood-red thing that writhes from out
    The scenic solitude!
It writhes!—it writhes!—with mortal pangs
    The mimes become its food,
And seraphs sob at vermin fangs
    In human gore imbued.

Out—out are the lights—out all!
    And, over each quivering form,
The curtain, a funeral pall,
    Comes down with the rush of a storm,
While the angels, all pallid and wan,
    Uprising, unveiling, affirm
That the play is the tragedy, "Man,"
    And its hero the Conqueror Worm.

—EDGAR ALLAN POE

The Laboratory

Ancien Régime

Now that I, tying thy glass-mask tightly,
May gaze thro' these faint smokes curling whitely,

As thou pliest thy trade in this devil's smithy—
Which is the poison to poison her, prithee?

He is with her; and they know that I know
Where they are, what they do; they believe my tears flow
While they laugh, laugh at me, at me fled to the drear
Empty church, to pray God in, for them!—I am here.

Grind away, moisten and mash up thy paste,
Pound at thy powder,—I am not in haste!
Better sit thus, and observe thy strange things,
Than go where men wait me and dance at the King's.

That in the mortar—you call it a gum?
Ah, the brave tree whence such gold oozings come!
And yonder soft phial, the exquisite blue,
Sure to taste sweetly,—is that poison too?

Had I but all of them, thee and thy treasures,
What a wild crowd of invisible pleasures!
To carry pure death in an earring, a casket,
A signet, a fan-mount, a filigree-basket!

Soon, at the King's, a mere lozenge to give
And Pauline should have just thirty minutes to live!
But to light a pastille, and Elise, with her head,
And her breast, and her arms, and her hands, should drop
   dead!

Quick—is it finished? The color's too grim!
Why not soft like the phial's, enticing and dim?
Let it brighten her drink, let her turn it and stir,
And try it and taste, ere she fix and prefer!

What a drop! She's not little, no minion like me—
That's why she ensnared him. This never will free
The soul from those strong, great eyes, say "no!"
To that pulse's magnificent come-and-go.

For only last night, as they whispered, I brought
My own eyes to bear on her so, that I thought
Could I keep them one half minute fixed, she would fall,
Shrivelled; she fell not; yet this does it all!

Not that I bid you spare her the pain!
Let death be felt and the proof remain;
Brand, burn up, bite into its grace—
He is sure to remember her dying face!

It is done? Take my mask off! Nay, be not morose,
It kills her, and this prevents seeing it close:
The delicate droplet, my whole fortune's fee—
If it hurts her, beside, can it ever hurt me?

Now, take all my jewels, gorge gold to your fill,
You may kiss me, old man, on my mouth if you will!
But brush this dust off me, lest horror it brings
Ere I know it—next moment I dance at the King's.

—ROBERT BROWNING

"Ah, Are You Digging on My Grave?"

"Ah, are you digging on my grave
   My loved one?—planting rue?"
—"No: yesterday he went to wed
One of the brightest wealth has bred.
'It cannot hurt her now,' he said,
   'That I should not be true.'"

"Then who is digging on my grave?
   My nearest dearest kin?"
—"Ah, no; they sit and think, 'What use!
What good will planting flowers produce?
No tendance of her mound can loose
   Her spirit from Death's gin.'"

"But some one digs upon my grave?
   My enemy?—prodding sly?"
—"Nay: when she heard you had passed the Gate
That shuts on all flesh soon or late,
She thought you no more worth her hate,
   And cares not where you lie."

"Then, who is digging on my grave?
   Say—since I have not guessed!"
—"Oh, it is I, my mistress dear,
Your little dog, who still lives near,
And much I hope my movements here
   Have not disturbed your rest?"

"Ah, yes! *You* dig upon my grave ...
   Why flashed it not on me
That one true heart was left behind!
What feeling do we ever find
To equal among human kind
   A dog's fidelity!"

"Mistress, I dug upon your grave
   To bury a bone, in case
I should be hungry near this spot
When passing on my daily trot.
I am sorry, but I quite forgot
   It was your resting-place."

—THOMAS HARDY

The Dream of Eugene Aram

'Twas in the prime of summer time,
   An evening calm and cool,
And four-and-twenty happy boys
   Came bounding out of school;
There were some that ran, and some that leapt
   Like troutlets in a pool.

Away they sped with gamesome minds
   And souls untouched by sin;
To a level mead they came, and there
   They drove the wickets in:
Pleasantly shone the setting sun
   Over the town of Lynn.

Like sportive deer they coursed about,
   And shouted as they ran,
Turning to mirth all things of earth
   As only boyhood can;
But the usher sat remote from all,
   A melancholy man!

His hat was off, his vest apart,
   To catch heaven's blessèd breeze;
For a burning thought was in his brow,
   And his bosom ill at ease,
So he leaned his head on his hands, and read
   The book between his knees.

Leaf after leaf he turned it o'er,
   Nor ever glanced aside—
For the peace of his soul he read that book
   In the golden eventide;
Much study had made him very lean,
   And pale, and leaden-eyed.

At last he shut the ponderous tome;
   With a fast and fervent grasp
He strained the dusky covers close,
   And fixed the brazen hasp:
"O God! could I so close my mind,
   And clasp it with a clasp!"

Then leaping on his feet upright,
   Some moody turns he took—

Now up the mead, then down the mead,
 And past a shady nook;
And, lo! he saw a little boy
 That pored upon a book.

"My gentle lad, what is 't you read—
 Romance or fairy fable?
Or is it some historic page,
 Of kings and crowns unstable?"
The young boy gave an upward glance—
 "It is 'The Death of Abel.'"

The usher took six hasty strides,
 As smit with sudden pain—
Six hasty strides beyond the place,
 Then slowly back again;
And down he sat beside the lad,
 And talked with him of Cain;

And, long since then, of bloody men,
 Whose deeds tradition saves;
And lonely folk cut off unseen,
 And hid in sudden graves;
And horrid stabs, in groves forlorn,
 And murders done in caves;

And how the sprites of injured men
 Shriek upward from the sod;
Ay, how the ghostly hand will point
 To show the burial-clod;
And unknown facts of guilty acts
 Are seen in dreams from God.

He told how murderers walked the earth
 Beneath the curse of Cain—
With crimson clouds before their eyes,
 And flames about their brain;

For blood has left upon their souls
   Its everlasting stain!

"And well," quoth he, "I know, for truth,
   Their pangs must be extreme—
Woe, woe, unutterable woe!—
   Who spill life's sacred stream!
For why? Methought, last night I wrought
   A murder, in a dream!

"One that had never done me wrong—
   A feeble man and old;
I led him to a lonely field—
   The moon shone clear and cold;
Now here, said I, this man shall die;
   And I will have his gold!

"Two sudden blows with a ragged stick,
   And one with a heavy stone,
One hurried gash with a hasty knife—
   And then the deed was done:
There was nothing lying at my feet
   But lifeless flesh and bone!

"Nothing but lifeless flesh and bone,
   That could not do me ill;
And yet I feared him all the more
   For lying there so still:
There was a manhood in his look
   That murder could not kill!

"And lo! the universal air
   Seemed lit with ghastly flame—
Ten thousand thousand dreadful eyes
   Were looking down in blame;
I took the dead man by his hand,
   And called upon his name.

"O God! it made me quake to see
    Such sense within the slain;
But when I touched the lifeless clay,
    The blood gushed out amain!
For every clot a burning spot
    Was scorching in my brain!

"My head was like an ardent coal,
    My heart as solid ice;
My wretched, wretched soul, I knew,
    Was at the Devil's price:
A dozen times I groaned—the dead
    Had never groaned but twice.

"And now, from forth the frowning sky,
    From the heaven's topmost height,
I heard a voice—the awful voice
    Of the blood-avenging sprite:
'Thou guilty man! take up thy dead,
    And hide it from my sight!'

"I took the dreary body up,
    And cast it in a stream—
The sluggish water black as ink,
    The depth was so extreme:
My gentle boy, remember, this
    Is nothing but a dream!

"Down went the corse with a hollow plunge,
    And vanished in the pool;
Anon I cleansed my bloody hands,
    And washed my forehead cool,
And sat among the urchins young,
    That evening, in the school.

"O Heaven! to think of their white souls,
    And mine so black and grim!

I could not share a childish prayer,
  Nor join in evening hymn;
Like a devil of the pit I seemed,
  'Mid holy cherubim!

"And peace went with them, one and all,
  And each calm pillow spread;
But Guilt was my grim chamberlain,
  That lighted me to bed,
And drew my midnight curtains round
  With fingers bloody red!

"All night I lay in agony,
  In anguish dark and deep;
My fevered eyes I dared not close,
  But stared aghast at Sleep:
For sin had rendered unto her
  The keys of hell to keep!

"All night I lay in agony,
  From weary chime to chime;
With one besetting horrid hint
  That racked me all the time—
A mighty yearning, like the first
  Fierce impulse unto crime—

"One stern tyrannic thought, that made
  All other thoughts its slave!
Stronger and stronger every pulse
  Did that temptation crave—
Still urging me to go and see
  The dead man in his grave!

"Heavily I rose up, as soon
  As light was in the sky,
And sought the black accursèd pool
  With a wild, misgiving eye:

And I saw the dead in the river-bed,
    For the faithless stream was dry.

"Merrily rose the lark, and shook
    The dew-drop from its wing;
But I never marked its morning flight,
    I never heard it sing:
For I was stooping once again
    Under the horrid thing.

"With breathless speed, like a soul in chase,
    I took him up and ran;
There was no time to dig a grave
    Before the day began—
In a lonesome wood, with heaps of leaves,
    I hid the murdered man!

"And all that day I read in school,
    But my thought was otherwhere;
As soon as the midday task was done,
    In secret I was there—
And a mighty wind had swept the leaves,
    And still the corse was bare!

"Then down I cast me on my face,
    And first began to weep,
For I knew my secret then was one
    That earth refused to keep—
Or land or sea, though he should be
    Ten thousand fathoms deep.

"So wills the fierce avenging sprite,
    Till blood for blood atones!
Ay, though he's buried in a cave,
    And trodden down with stones,
And years have rotted off his flesh—
    The world shall see his bones!

"O God! that horrid, horrid dream
　　Besets me now awake!
Again—again, with dizzy brain,
　　The human life I take;
And my red right hand grows raging hot,
　　Like Cranmer's at the stake.

"And still no peace for the restless clay
　　Will wave or mold allow;
The horrid thing pursues my soul—
　　It stands before me now!"
The fearful boy looked up, and saw
　　Huge drops upon his brow.

That very night, while gentle sleep
　　The urchin eyelids kissed,
Two stern-faced men set out from Lynn,
　　Through the cold and heavy mist;
And Eugene Aram walked between,
　　With gyves upon his wrist.

　　　　　　　　　　　—THOMAS HOOD

The Haystack in the Floods

Had she come all the way for this,
To part at last without a kiss?
Yea, had she borne the dirt and rain
That her own eyes might see him slain
Beside the haystack in the floods?

Along the dripping leafless woods,
The stirrup touching either shoe,
She rode astride as troopers do;
With kirtle kilted to her knee,
To which the mud splashed wretchedly;
And the wet dripped from every tree

Upon her head and heavy hair,
And on her eyelids broad and fair;
The tears and rain ran down her face.
By fits and starts they rode apace,
And very often was his place
Far off from her; he had to ride
Ahead, to see what might betide
When the roads crossed; and sometimes, when
There rose a murmuring from his men,
Had to turn back with promises.
Ah me! she had but little ease;
And often for pure doubt and dread
She sobbed, made giddy in the head
By the swift riding; while, for cold,
Her slender fingers scarce could hold
The wet reins; yea, and scarcely, too,
She felt the foot within her shoe
Against the stirrup: all for this,
To part at last without a kiss
Beside the haystack in the floods.

For when they neared that old soaked hay,
They saw across the only way
That Judas, Godmar, and the three
Red running lions dismally
Grinned from his pennon, under which
In one straight line along the ditch,
They counted thirty heads.
                    So then
While Robert turned round to his men,
She saw at once the wretched end,
And, stooping down, tried hard to rend
Her coif the wrong way from her head,
And hid her eyes; while Robert said:
"Nay, love, 'tis scarcely two to one;
At Poictiers where we made them run
So fast—why, sweet my love, good cheer,

The Gascon frontier is so near,
Nought after us."
                    But: "O!" she said
"My God! my God! I have to tread
The long way back without you; then
The court at Paris; those six men;
The gratings of the Chatelet;
The swift Seine on some rainy day
Like this, and people standing by,
And laughing, while my weak hands try
To recollect how strong men swim.
All this, or else a life with him,
For which I should be damned at last,
Would God that this next hour were past!"

He answered not, but cried his cry,
"St. George for Marny!" cheerily;
And laid his hand upon her rein.
Alas! no man of all his train
Gave back that cheery cry again;
And, while for rage his thumb beat fast
Upon his sword-hilt, some one cast
About his neck a kerchief long,
And bound him.
                    Then they went along
To Godmar, who said: "Now, Jehane,
Your lover's life is on the wane
So fast, that, if this very hour
You yield not as my paramour,
He will not see the rain leave off:
Nay, keep your tongue from gibe and scoff,
Sir Robert, or I slay you now."
She laid her hand upon her brow,
Then gazed upon the palm, as though
She thought her forehead bled, and: "No!"
She said, and turned her head away,
As there was nothing else to say,

And everything was settled: red
Grew Godmar's face from chin to head:
"Jehane, on yonder hill there stands
My castle, guarding well my lands;
What hinders me from taking you,
And doing that I list to do
To your fair wilful body, while
Your knight lies dead?"
                 A wicked smile
Wrinkled her face, her lips grew thin,
A long way out she thrust her chin:
"You know that I should strangle you
While you were sleeping; or bite through
Your throat, by God's help: ah!" she said,
"Lord Jesus, pity your poor maid!
For in such wise they hem me in,
I cannot choose but sin and sin,
Whatever happens: yet I think
They could not make me eat or drink,
And so should I just reach my rest."
"Nay, if you do not my behest,
O Jehane! though I love you well,"
Said Godmar, "would I fail to tell
All that I know?" "Foul lies," she said.
"Eh? lies, my Jehane? by God's head,
At Paris folk would deem them true!

Do you know, Jehane, they cry for you:
'Jehane the brown! Jehane the brown!
Give us Jehane to burn or drown!'
Eh!—gag me, Robert!—sweet my friend,
This were indeed a piteous end
For those long fingers, and long feet,
And long neck, and smooth shoulders sweet;
An end that few men would forget
That saw it. So, an hour yet:
Consider, Jehane, which to take
Of life or death!"

So, scarce awake,
Dismounting, did she leave that place,
And totter some yards: with her face
Turned upward to the sky she lay,
Her head on a wet heap of hay,
And fell asleep: and while she slept,
And did not dream, the minutes crept
Around to twelve again; but she,
Being waked at last, sighed quietly,
And strangely childlike came, and said:
"I will not." Straightway Godmar's head,
As though it hung on strong wires, turned
Most sharply round, and his face burned.

For Robert, both his eyes were dry,
He could not weep, but gloomily
He seemed to watch the rain; yea, too,
His lips were firm; he tried once more
To touch her lips; she reached out, sore
And vain desire so tortured them,
The poor gray lips, and now the hem
Of his sleeve brushed them.
                              With a start
Up Godmar rose, thrust them apart;
From Robert's throat he loosed the bands
Of silk and mail. With empty hands
Held out, she stood and gazed, and saw,
The long bright blade without a flaw
Glide out from Godmar's sheath, his hand
In Robert's hair; she saw him bend
Back Robert's head; she saw him send
The thin steel down; the blow told well,
Right backward the knight Robert fell,
And moaned as dogs do, being half dead,
Unwitting, as I deem: so then
Godmar turned grinning to his men,
Who ran, some five or six, and beat
His head to pieces at their feet.

Then Godmar turned again and said:
"So, Jehane, the first fitte is read!
Take note, my lady, that your way
Lies backward to the Chatelet!"
She shook her head and gazed awhile
At her cold hands with a rueful smile,
As though this thing had made her mad.

This was the parting that they had
Beside the haystack in the floods.

—WILLIAM MORRIS

The Inchcape Rock

No stir in the air, no stir in the sea—
The ship was as still as she could be;
Her sails from heaven received no motion;
Her keel was steady in the ocean.

Without either sign or sound of their shock,
The waves flowed over the Inchcape rock;
So little they rose, so little they fell,
They did not move the Inchcape bell.

The holy Abbot of Aberbrothok
Had placed that bell on the Inchcape rock;
On a buoy in the storm it floated and swung,
And over the waves its warning rung.

When the rock was hid by the surges' swell,
The mariners heard the warning bell;
And then they knew the perilous rock,
And blessed the Abbot of Aberbrothok.

The sun in heaven was shining gay—
All things were joyful on that day;

The sea-birds screamed as they wheeled around,
And there was joyance in their sound.

The buoy of the Inchcape bell was seen,
A darker speck on the ocean green;
Sir Ralph, the rover, walked his deck,
And he fixed his eye on the darker speck.

He felt the cheering power of spring—
It made him whistle, it made him sing;
His heart was mirthful to excess;
But the rover's mirth was wickedness.

His eye was on the bell and float:
Quoth he, "My men, put out the boat;
And row me to the Inchcape rock,
And I'll plague the priest of Aberbrothok."

The boat is lowered, the boatmen row,
And to the Inchcape rock they go;
Sir Ralph bent over from the boat,
And cut the warning bell from the float.

Down sank the bell with a gurgling sound;
The bubbles rose, and burst around.
Quoth Sir Ralph, "The next who comes to the rock
Will not bless the Abbot of Aberbrothok."

Sir Ralph, the rover, sailed away—
He scoured the seas for many a day;
And now, grown rich with plundered store,
He steers his course to Scotland's shore.

So thick a haze o'erspreads the sky
They cannot see the sun on high;
The wind hath blown a gale all day;
At evening it hath died away.

On the deck the rover takes his stand;
So dark it is they see no land.
Quoth Sir Ralph, "It will be lighter soon,
For there is the dawn of the rising moon."

"Canst hear," said one, "the breakers roar?
For yonder, methinks, should be the shore.
Now where we are I cannot tell,
But I wish we could hear the Inchcape bell."

They hear no sound; the swell is strong;
Though the wind hath fallen, they drift along;
Till the vessel strikes with a shivering shock—
O Christ! it is the Inchcape rock!

Sir Ralph, the rover, tore his hair;
He cursed himself in his despair.
The waves rush in on every side;
The ship is sinking beneath the tide.

But ever in his dying fear
One dreadful sound he seemed to hear—
A sound as if with the Inchcape bell
The Devil below was ringing his knell.

—ROBERT SOUTHEY

Fitz-James O'Brien, born in Ireland and brought up in England, became an American journalist, short story writer, and author of occasional poetry, most of which is forgotten. A few of his tales have been compared to Poe, and his macabre poem, "The Demon of the Gibbet," has something of the ghastly urgency and sense of doom which is in Goethe's "The Erl-King" on page 361.

The Demon of the Gibbet

There was no west, there was no east,
    No star abroad for eyes to see;
And Norman spurred his jaded beast
    Hard by the terrible gallows-tree.

"O, Norman, haste across this waste,—
    For something seems to follow me!"
"Cheer up, dear Maud, for, thanked be God,
    We nigh have passed the gallows-tree!"

He kissed her lip: then—spur and whip!
    And fast they fled across the lea.
But vain the heel, and rowel steel,—
    For something leaped from the gallows-tree!

"Give me your cloak, your knightly cloak,
    That wrapped you oft beyond the sea!
The wind is bold, my bones are old,
    And I am cold on the gallows-tree."

"O holy God! O dearest Maud,
    Quick, quick, some prayers—the best that be!
A bony hand my neck has spanned,
    And tears my knightly cloak from me!"

"Give me your wine,—the red, red wine,
    That in the flask hangs by your knee!
Ten summers burst on me accurst,
    And I'm athirst on the gallows-tree!"

"O Maud, my life, my loving wife!
    Have you no prayer to set us free?
My belt unclasps,—a demon grasps,
    And drags my wine-flask from my knee!"

"Give me your bride, your bonnie bride,
  That left her nest with you to flee!
O she hath flown to be my own,
  For I'm alone on the gallows-tree!"

"Cling closer, Maud, and trust in God!
  Cling close!—Ah, heaven, she slips from me!"
A prayer, a groan, and he alone
  Rode on that night from the gallows-tree.

                    —FITZ-JAMES O'BRIEN

The Sisters

We were two daughters of one race:
She was the fairest in the face:
  The wind is blowing in turret and tree.
They were together, and she fell;
Therefore revenge became me well.
  O the Earl was fair to see!

She died: she went to burning flame:
She mix'd her ancient blood with shame.
  The wind is howling in turret and tree.
Whole weeks and months, and early and late,
To win his love I lay in wait:
  O the Earl was fair to see!

I made a feast; I bad him come;
I won his love, I brought him home.
  The wind is roaring in turret and tree.
And after supper, on a bed,
Upon my lap he laid his head:
  O the Earl was fair to see!

I kiss'd his eyelids into rest:
His ruddy cheek upon my breast.
  The wind is raging in turret and tree.

I hated him with the hate of hell,
But I loved his beauty passing well.
    O the Earl was fair to see!

I rose up in the silent night:
I made my dagger sharp and bright.
    The wind is raving in turret and tree.
As half-asleep his breath he drew,
Three times I stabb'd him thro' and thro'.
    O the Earl was fair to see!

I curl'd and comb'd his comely head,
He look'd so grand when he was dead.
    The wind is blowing in turret and tree.
I wrapt his body in the sheet,
And laid him at his mother's feet.
    O the Earl was fair to see!

—ALFRED, LORD TENNYSON

Rizpah

Wailing, wailing, wailing, the wind over land and sea—
And Willy's voice in the wind, "O mother, come out to me!"
Why should he call me tonight, when he knows that I cannot
    go?
For the downs are as bright as day, and the full moon stares
    at the snow.

We should be seen, my dear; they would spy us out of the
    town.
The loud black nights for us, and the storm rushing over the
    down,
When I cannot see my own hand, but am led by the creak
    of the chain,
And grovel and grope for my son till I find myself drenched
    with the rain.

Anything fallen again? Nay—what was there left to fall?
I have taken them home, I have numbered the bones, I have
    hidden them all.
What am I saying—and what are *you*? Do you come as a spy?
Falls? What falls! Who knows? As the tree falls so must it lie.

Who let her in? How long has she been? You—what have you
    heard?
Why did you sit so quiet? You never have spoken a word.
Oh—to pray with me—yes—a lady—none of their spies—
But the night has crept into my heart, and begun to darken
    my eyes.

Ah—you that have lived so soft, what should *you* know of the
    night,
The blast and the burning shame and the bitter frost and the
    fright?
I have done it, while you were asleep—you were only made
    for the day.
I have gathered my baby together—and now you may go
    your way.

Nay—for it's kind of you, madam, to sit by an old dying wife.
But say nothing hard of my boy, I have only an hour of life.
I kissed my boy in the prison, before he went out to die.
"They dared me to do it," he said, and he never has told me
    a lie.
I whipped him for robbing an orchard once when he was
    but a child—
"The farmer dared me to do it," he said; he was always so
    wild—
And idle—and couldn't be idle—my Willy—he never could rest.
The king should have made him a soldier, he would have
    been one of his best.

But he lived with a lot of wild mates, and they never would
    let him be good;
They swore that he dare not rob the mail, and he swore that
    he would;
And he took no life, but he took one purse, and when all was
    done
He flung it among his fellows—"I'll none of it," said my son.

I came into court to the judge and the lawyers. I told them
    my tale,
God's own truth—but they killed him, they killed him for
    robbing the mail.
They hanged him in chains for a show—we had always borne
    a good name—
To be hanged for a thief—and then put away—isn't that
    enough shame?
Dust to dust—low down—let us hide! But they set him so high
That all the ships of the world could stare at him, passing by.
God'll pardon the hell-black raven and horrible fowls of the
    air,
But not the black heart of the lawyer who killed him and
    hanged him there.

And the jailer forced me away. I had bid him my last good-by;
They had fastened the door of his cell. "O mother!" I heard
    him cry.
I couldn't get back though I tried, he had something further
    to say,
And now I never shall know it. The jailer forced me away.

Then since I couldn't but hear that cry of my boy that was
    dead,
They seized me and shut me up: they fastened me down on
    my bed.
"Mother, O mother!"—he called in the dark to me year after
    year—
They beat me for that, they beat me—you know that I couldn't
    but hear;

And then at the last they found I had grown so stupid and
  still
They let me abroad again—but the creatures had worked their
  will.

Flesh of my flesh was gone, but bone of my bone was left—
I stole them all from the lawyers—and you, will you call it a
  theft?—
My baby, the bones that had sucked me, the bones that had
  laughed and had cried—
Theirs? Oh no! They are mine—not theirs—they had moved
  in my side.
Do you think I was scared by the bones? I kissed 'em, I
  buried 'em all—
I can't dig deep, I am old—in the night by the churchyard
  wall.
My Willy 'll rise up whole when the trumpet of judgment 'll
  sound,
But I charge you never to say that I laid him in holy ground.

They would scratch him up—they would hang him again on
  the cursèd tree.
Sin? Oh, yes, we are sinners, I know—let all that be,
And read me a Bible verse of the Lord's goodwill toward
  men—
"Full of compassion and mercy, the Lord"—let me hear it
  again;
"Full of compassion and mercy—long-suffering." Yes, oh, yes!
For the lawyer is born but to murder—the Saviour lives but
  to bless.

He'll never put on the black cap except for the worst of the
  worst,
And the first may be last—I have heard it in church—and the
  last may be first.
Suffering—O long-suffering—yes, as the Lord must know,
Year after year in the mist and the wind and the shower and
  the snow.

Heard, have you? what? They have told you he never re-
pented his sin.

How do they know it? Are *they* his mother? Are *you* of his
kin?

Heard! Have you ever heard, when the storm on the downs
began,

The wind that'll wail like a child and the sea that'll moan
like a man?

Election, Election, and Reprobation—it's all very well.

But I go tonight to my boy, and I shall not find him in hell.

For I cared so much for my boy that the Lord has looked
into my care,

And He means me I'm sure to be happy with Willy, I know
not where.

And if *he* be lost—but to save *my* soul, that is all your desire—

Do you think that I care for *my* soul if my boy be gone to the
fire?

I have been with God in the dark—go, go, you may leave me
alone—

You never have borne a child—you are just as hard as a stone.

Madam, I beg your pardon! I think that you mean to be kind.

But I cannot hear what you say for my Willy's voice in the
wind—

The snow and the sky so bright—he used but to call in the
dark,

And he calls to me now from the church and not from the
gibbet—for hark!

Nay—you can hear it yourself—it is coming—shaking the walls—

Willy—the moon's in a cloud—Good-night. I am going. He
calls.

—ALFRED, LORD TENNYSON

HEROES AND LEGENDS OF
THE NEW WORLD

It is logical that this volume should conclude with a section devoted to the New World. The poems which follow deal with fabulous figures as well as historic personalities who have their roots in native soil. Many of the story-poems, such as "The Landing of the Pilgrim Fathers," "Pocahontas," "Paul Revere's Ride," and "The High Tide at Gettysburg," among others, reflect momentous events in our history. Others, such as "The Ballad of William Sycamore" and "Jim Bludso," are composite personalities, a synthesis of the American spirit. The indigenous folk-songs, with which the book ends, recall the tone of the ballads with which this volume begins.

Altogether these poems trace the course of a developing country; they are memorials and mile-stones in the progress of a nation. Whether they are written by great poets or anonymous ballad-makers, they are a vital part of our common heritage.

The Landing of the Pilgrim Fathers

The breaking waves dashed high
   On a stern and rock-bound coast,
And the woods against a stormy sky
   Their giant branches tossed;

And the heavy night hung dark
   The hills and waters o'er,
When a band of exiles moored their bark
   On the wild New England shore.

Not as the conqueror comes,
   They, the true-hearted, came;
Not with the roll of the stirring drums,
   And the trumpet that sings of fame:

Not as the flying come,
   In silence and in fear;
They shook the depths of the desert gloom
   With their hymns of lofty cheer.

Amidst the storm they sang,
   And the stars heard, and the sea;
And the sounding aisles of the dim woods rang
   To the anthem of the free.

The ocean eagle soared
   From his nest by the white wave's foam,
And the rocking pines of the forest roared,—
   This was their welcome home.

There were men with hoary hair
   Amidst that pilgrim-band:
Why had they come to wither there,
   Away from their childhood's land?

There was woman's fearless eye,
 Lit by her deep love's truth;
There was manhood's brow serenely high,
 And the fiery heart of youth.

What sought they thus afar?
 Bright jewels of the mine?
The wealth of seas, the spoils of war?—
 They sought a faith's pure shrine!

Ay, call it holy ground,
 The soil where first they trod;
They have left unstained what there they found,—
 Freedom to worship God.

—FELICIA D. HEMANS

Pocahontas

Wearied arm and broken sword
 Wage in vain the desperate fight;
Round him press a countless horde,
 He is but a single knight.
Hark! a cry of triumph shrill
 Through the wilderness resounds,
 As, with twenty bleeding wounds,
Sinks the warrior, fighting still.

Now they heap the funeral pyre,
 And the torch of death they light;
Ah! 't is hard to die by fire!
 Who will shield the captive knight?
Round the stake with fiendish cry
 Wheel and dance the savage crowd,
 Cold the victim's mien and proud,
And his breast is bared to die.

Who will shield the fearless heart?
  Who avert the murderous blade?
From the throng with sudden start
  See, there springs an Indian maid.
Quick she stands before the knight:
  "Loose the chain, unbind the ring!
  I am daughter of the king,
And I claim the Indian right!"

Dauntlessly aside she flings
  Lifted axe and thirsty knife,
Fondly to his heart she clings,
  And her bosom guards his life!
In the woods of Powhatan,
  Still 't is told by Indian fires
  How a daughter of their sires
Saved a captive Englishman.

—WILLIAM MAKEPEACE THACKERAY

The Ballad of William Sycamore

(1790–1871)

My father, he was a mountaineer,
His fist was a knotty hammer;
He was quick on his feet as a running deer,
And he spoke with a Yankee stammer.

My mother, she was merry and brave,
And so she came to her labor,
With a tall green fir for her doctor grave
And a stream for her comforting neighbor.

And some are wrapped in the linen fine,
And some like a godling's scion;

But I was cradled on twigs of pine
In the skin of a mountain lion.

And some remember a white, starched lap
And a ewer with silver handles;
But I remember a coonskin cap
And the smell of bayberry candles.

The cabin logs, with the bark still rough,
And my mother who laughed at trifles,
And the tall, lank visitors, brown as snuff,
With their long, straight squirrel-rifles.

I can hear them dance, like a foggy song,
Through the deepest one of my slumbers,
The fiddle squeaking the boots along
And my father calling the numbers.

The quick feet shaking the puncheon-floor,
The fiddle squeaking and squealing,
Till the dried herbs rattled above the door
And the dust went up to the ceiling.

There are children lucky from dawn till dusk,
But never a child so lucky!
For I cut my teeth on "Money Musk"
In the Bloody Ground of Kentucky!

When I grew tall as the Indian corn,
My father had little to lend me,
But he gave me his great, old powder-horn
And his woodsman's skill to befriend me.

With a leather shirt to cover my back,
And a redskin nose to unravel
Each forest sign, I carried my pack
As far as a scout could travel.

Till I lost my boyhood and found my wife,
A girl like a Salem clipper!
A woman straight as a hunting-knife
With eyes as bright as the Dipper!

We cleared our camp where the buffalo feed,
Unheard-of streams were our flagons;
And I sowed my sons like apple-seed
On the trail of the Western wagons.

They were right, tight boys, never sulky or slow,
A fruitful, a goodly muster.
The eldest died at the Alamo.
The youngest fell with Custer.

The letter that told it burned my hand.
Yet we smiled and said, "So be it!"
But I could not live when they fenced the land,
For it broke my heart to see it.

I saddled a red, unbroken colt
And rode him into the day there;
And he threw me down like a thunderbolt
And rolled on me as I lay there.

The hunter's whistle hummed in my ear
As the city-men tried to move me,
And I died in my boots like a pioneer
With the whole wide sky above me.

Now I lie in the heart of the fat, black soil,
Like the seed of a prairie-thistle;
It has washed my bones with honey and oil
And picked them clean as a whistle.

And my youth returns, like the rains of Spring,
And my sons, like the wild-geese flying;

And I lie and hear the meadow-lark sing
And have much content in my dying.

Go play with the towns you have built of blocks
The towns where you would have bound me!
I sleep in my earth like a tired fox,
And my buffalo have found me.
                              —STEPHEN VINCENT BENÉT

Paul Revere's Ride

Listen, my children, and you shall hear
Of the midnight ride of Paul Revere,
On the eighteenth of April, in Seventy-five;
Hardly a man is now alive
Who remembers that famous day and year.

He said to his friend, "If the British march
By land or sea from the town to-night,
Hang a lantern aloft in the belfry arch
Of the North Church tower as a signal light,—
One, if by land, and two, if by sea;
And I on the opposite shore will be,
Ready to ride and spread the alarm
Through every Middlesex village and farm,
For the country folk to be up and to arm."
Then he said "Good-night," and with muffled oar
Silently row'd to the Charlestown shore,
Just as the moon rose over the bay,
Where swinging wide at her moorings lay
The Somerset, British man-of-war;
A phantom ship, with each mast and spar
Across the moon like a prison bar,
And a huge black hulk, that was magnified
By its own reflection in the tide.

Meanwhile his friend, through alley and street,
Wanders and watches with eager ears,
Till in the silence around him he hears
The master of men at the barrack-door,
The sound of arms, and the tramp of feet,
And the measured tread of the grenadiers
Marching down to their boats on the shore.
Then he climb'd the tower of the Old North Church,
By the wooden stairs, with stealthy tread,
To the belfry-chamber overhead,
And started the pigeons from their perch
On the sombre rafters, that round him made
Masses of moving shapes of shade,—
By the trembling ladder, steep and tall,
To the highest window in the wall,
Where he paused to listen and look down
A moment on the roofs of the town,
And the moonlight flowing over all.

Beneath, in the churchyard, lay the dead,
In their night-encampment on the hill,
Wrapp'd in silence so deep and still
That he could hear, like a sentinel's tread,
The watchful night-wind, as it went
Creeping along from tent to tent,
And seeming to whisper, "All is well!"
A moment only he feels the spell
Of the place and the hour, and the secret dread
Of the lonely belfry and the dead;
For suddenly all his thoughts are bent
On a shadowy something far away,
Where the river widens to meet the bay,
A line of black that bends and floats
On the rising tide like a bridge of boats.

Meanwhile, impatient to mount and ride,
Booted and spurr'd, with a heavy stride
On the opposite shore walk'd Paul Revere.

Now he patted his horse's side,
Now he gazed at the landscape far and near,
Then, impetuous, stamp'd the earth,
And turn'd and tighten'd his saddle-girth;
But mostly he watch'd with eager search
The belfry-tower of the Old North Church,
As it rose above the graves on the hill,
Lonely and spectral and sombre and still.
And lo! as he looks, on the belfry's height
A glimmer, and then a gleam of light!
He springs to the saddle, the bridle he turns,
But lingers and gazes, till full on his sight
A second lamp in the belfry burns.

A hurry of hoofs in a village street,
A shape in the moonlight, a bulk in the dark,
And beneath, from the pebbles, in passing, a spark
Struck out by a steed flying fearless and fleet:
That was all; and yet, through the gloom and the light,
The fate of a nation was riding that night;
And the spark struck out by that steed in his flight
Kindled the land into flame with its heat.

He had left the village and mounted the steep,
And beneath him, tranquil and broad and deep,
Is the Mystic, meeting the ocean tides,
And under the alders that skirts its edge,
Now soft on the sand, now loud on the ledge,
Is heard the tramp of his steed as he rides.

It was twelve by the village clock
When he crossed the bridge into Medford town.
He heard the crowing of the cock,
And the barking of the farmer's dog,
And felt the damp of the river fog,
That rises after the sun goes down.

It was one by the village clock
When he galloped into Lexington.
He saw the gilded weathercock
Swim in the moonlight as he pass'd,
And the meeting-house windows, blank and bare,
Gaze at him with a spectral glare,
As if they already stood aghast
At the bloody work they would look upon.

It was two by the village clock
When he came to the bridge in Concord town.
He heard the bleating of the flock,
And the twitter of birds among the trees,
And felt the breath of the morning breeze
Blowing over the meadows brown.
And one was safe and asleep in his bed
Who at the bridge would be first to fall,
Who that day would be lying dead,
Pierced by a British musket-ball.

You know the rest; in the books you have read,
How the British regulars fired and fled,—
How the farmers gave them ball for ball,
From behind each fence and farmyard wall,
Chasing the red-coats down the lane,
Then crossing the fields to emerge again
Under the trees at the turn of the road,
And only pausing to fire and load.

So through the night rode Paul Revere,
And so through the night went his cry of alarm
To every Middlesex village and farm,—
A cry of defiance, and not of fear,
A voice in the darkness, a knock at the door,
And a word that shall echo for evermore!
For, borne on the night-wind of the Past,
Through all our history, to the last,

In the hour of darkness, and peril, and need,
The people will waken and listen to hear
The hurrying hoof-beats of that steed,
And the midnight message of Paul Revere.
                    —HENRY WADSWORTH LONGFELLOW

Abraham Davenport

In the old days (a custom laid aside
With breeches and cocked hats) the people sent
Their wisest men to make the public laws.
And so, from a brown homestead, where the Sound
Drinks the small tribute of the Mianas,
Waved over by the woods of Rippowams,
And hallowed by pure lives and tranquil deaths,
Stamford sent up to the councils of the State
Wisdom and grace in Abraham Davenport.

'T was on a May-day of the far old year
Seventeen hundred eighty, that there fell
Over the bloom and sweet life of the Spring,
Over the fresh earth and the heaven of noon,
A horror of great darkness, like the night
In day of which the Norland sagas tell,—
The Twilight of the Gods. The low-hung sky
Was black with ominous clouds, save where its rim
Was fringed with a dull glow, like that which climbs
The crater's sides from the red hell below.
Birds ceased to sing, and all the barn-yard fowls
Roosted; the cattle at the pasture bars
Lowed, and looked homeward; bats on leathern wings
Flitted abroad; the sounds of labor died;
Men prayed, and women wept; all ears grew sharp
To hear the doom-blast of the trumpet shatter
The black sky, that the dreadful face of Christ
Might look from the rent clouds, not as He looked
A loving guest at Bethany, but stern
As Justice and inexorable Law.

Meanwhile in the old State House, dim as ghosts,
Sat the lawgivers of Connecticut,
Trembling beneath their legislative robes.
"It is the Lord's Great Day! Let us adjourn,"
Some said; and then, as if with one accord,
All eyes were turned to Abraham Davenport.
He rose, slow cleaving with his steady voice
The intolerable hush. "This well may be
The Day of Judgment which the world awaits;
But be it so or not, I only know
My present duty, and my Lord's command
To occupy till He come. So at the post
Where He hath set me in His providence,
I choose, for one, to meet Him face to face,—
No faithless servant frightened from my task,
But ready when the Lord of the harvest calls;
And therefore, with all reverence, I would say,
Let God do His work, we will see to ours.
Bring in the candles." And they brought them in.

Then by the flaring lights the Speaker read,
Albeit with husky voice and shaking hands,
An act to amend an act to regulate
The shad and alewive fisheries. Whereupon
Wisely and well spake Abraham Davenport,
Straight to the question, with no figures of speech
Save the ten Arab signs, yet not without
The shrewd dry humor natural to the man:
His awe-struck colleagues listening all the while,
Between the pauses of his argument,
To hear the thunder of the wrath of God
Break from the hollow trumpet of the cloud.

And there he stands in memory to this day,
Erect, self-poised, a rugged face, half seen
Against the background of unnatural dark,
A witness to the ages as they pass,
That simple duty hath no place for fear.

—JOHN GREENLEAF WHITTIER

Grandmother's Story of Bunker Hill Battle

(*As she saw it from the belfry*)

'Tis like stirring living embers when, at eighty, one remembers
All the aching and the quakings of "the times that tried men's
 souls";
When I talk of "Whig" and "Tory," when I tell the "Rebel"
 story,
To you the words are ashes, but to me they're burning
 coals.

I had heard the muskets' rattle of the April running battle;
Lord Percy's hunted soldiers, I can see their red coats still;
But a deadly chill comes o'er me, as the day looms up
 before me,
When a thousand men lay bleeding on the slopes of Bunker's
 Hill.

'Twas a peaceful summer's morning, when the first thing
 gave us warning
Was the booming of the cannon from the river and the shore:
"Child," says grandma, "what's the matter, what is all this
 noise and clatter?
Have those scalping Indian devils come to murder us once
 more?"

Poor old soul! my sides were shaking in the midst of all my
 quaking,
To hear her talk of Indians when the guns began to roar;
She had seen the burning village, and the slaughter and the
 pillage,
When the Mohawks killed her father with their bullets
 through his door.

Then I said, "Now, dear old granny, don't you fret and
    worry any,
For I'll soon come back and tell you whether this is work
    or play;
There can't be mischief in it, so I won't be gone a minute"—
For a minute then I started. I was gone the livelong day!

No time for bodice-lacing or for looking-glass grimacing;
Down my hair went as I hurried, tumbling half-way to my
    heels;
God forbid your ever knowing, when there's blood around
    her flowing,
How the lonely, helpless daughter of a quiet household feels!

In the street I heard a thumping; and I knew it was the
    stumping
Of the Corporal, our old neighbor, on that wooden leg he
    wore,
With a knot of women round him,—it was lucky I had found
    him,
So I followed with the others, and the Corporal marched
    before.

They were making for the steeple,—the old soldier and his
    people;
The pigeons circled round us as we climbed the creaking
    stair.
Just across the narrow river—oh, so close it made me shiver!—
Stood a fortress on the hill-top that but yesterday was bare.

Not slow our eyes to find it; well we knew who stood
    behind it,
Though the earthwork hid them from us, and the stubborn
    walls were dumb:
Here were sister, wife, and mother, looking wild upon each
    other,
And their lips were white with terror as they said, THE HOUR
    HAS COME!

The morning slowly wasted, not a morsel had we tasted,
And our heads were almost splitting with the cannons' deafen-
    ing thrill,
When a figure tall and stately round the rampart strode
    sedately;
It was PRESCOTT, one since told me; he commanded on the
    hill.

Every woman's heart grew bigger when we saw his manly
    figure,
With the banyan buckled round it, standing up so straight
    and tall;
Like a gentleman of leisure who is strolling out for pleasure,
Through the storm of shells and cannon-shot he walked
    around the wall.

At eleven the streets were swarming, for the redcoats' ranks
    were forming;
At noon in marching order they were moving to the piers;
How the bayonets gleamed and glistened, as we looked far
    down, and listened
To the trampling and the drum-beat of the belted grenadiers!

At length the men have started, with a cheer (it seemed
    faint-hearted),
In their scarlet regimentals, with their knapsacks on their
    backs,
And the reddening, rippling water, as after a sea-fight's
    slaughter,
Round the barges gliding onward blushed like blood along
    their tracks.

So they crossed to the other border, and again they formed
    in order;
And the boats came back for soldiers, came for soldiers,
    soldiers still:
The time seemed everlasting to us women faint and fasting,—
At last they're moving, marching, marching proudly up the
    hill.

We can see the bright steel glancing all along the lines
    advancing,—

Now the front rank fires a volley,—they have thrown away
    their shot;

For behind their earthwork lying, all the balls above them
    flying,

Our people need not hurry; so they wait and answer not.

Then the Corporal, our old cripple (he would swear some-
    times and tipple),—

He had heard the bullets whistle (in the old French war)
    before,—

Calls out in words of jeering, just as if they all were hearing,—

And his wooden leg thumps fiercely on the dusty belfry
    floor:—

"Oh! fire away, ye villains, and earn King George's shillin's,

But ye'll waste a ton of powder afore a 'rebel' falls;

You may bang the dirt and welcome, they're as safe as Dan'l
    Malcolm

Ten foot beneath the gravestone that you've splintered with
    your balls!"

In the hush of expectation, in the awe and trepidation

Of the dread approaching moment, we are well-nigh breath-
    less all;

Though the rotten bars are failing on the rickety belfry
    railing,

We are crowding up against them like the waves against
    a wall.

Just a glimpse (the air is clearer), they are nearer,—nearer,
    —nearer,

When a flash,—a curling smoke-wreath,—then a crash,—the
    steeple shakes,—

The deadly truce is ended; the tempest's shroud is rended;

Like a morning mist it gathered, like a thunder-cloud it
    breaks!

O the sight our eyes discover as the blue-black smoke blows
over!

The red-coats stretched in windrows as a mower rakes his
hay;

Here a scarlet heap is lying, there a headlong crowd is
flying

Like a billow that has broken and is shivered into spray.

Then we cried, "The troops are routed! they are beat,—it
can't be doubted!

God be thanked, the fight is over!"—Ah! the grim old soldier's
smile!

"Tell us, tell us why you look so?" (we could hardly speak,
we shook so),—

"Are they beaten? *Are* they beaten? ARE they beaten?"—
"Wait a while."

O the trembling and the terror! For too late we saw our
error:

They are baffled, not defeated; we have driven them back
in vain.

And the columns that were scattered, round the colors that
were tattered,

Toward the sullen silent fortress turn their belted breasts
again.

All at once, as we are gazing, lo the roofs of Charlestown
blazing!

They have fired the harmless village; in an hour it will be
down!

The Lord in heaven confound them, rain his fire and brim-
stone round them,—

The robbing, murdering red-coats, that would burn a peaceful
town!

They are marching, stern and solemn; we can see each
massive column

As they near the naked earth-mound with the slanting walls
so steep.

Have our soldiers got faint-hearted, and in noiseless haste
    departed?
Are they panic-struck and helpless? Are they palsied or
    asleep?

Now! the walls they're almost under! scarce a rod the foes
    asunder!
Not a firelock flashed against them! up the earthwork they
    will swarm!
But the words have scarce been spoken, when the ominous
    calm is broken,
And a bellowing crash has emptied all the vengeance of the
    storm!

So again, with murderous slaughter, pelted backwards to the
    water,
Fly Pigot's running heroes and the frightened braves of
    Howe;
And we shout, "At last they're done for, it's their barges they
    have run for:
They are beaten, beaten, beaten; and the battle's over now!"

And we looked, poor timid creatures, on the rough old soldier's
    features,
Our lips afraid to question, but he knew what we would ask:
"Not sure," he said; "keep quiet,—once more, I guess, they'll
    try it,—
Here's damnation to the cut-throats!"——then he handed me
    his flask,

Saying, "Gal, you're looking shaky; have a drop of old
    Jamaiky;
I'm afeard there'll be more trouble afore the job is done";
So I took one scorching swallow; dreadful faint I felt and
    hollow,
Standing there from early morning when the firing was
    begun.

All through those hours of trial I had watched a calm clock
  dial,
As the hands kept creeping, creeping,—they were creeping
  round to four,
When the old man said, "They're forming with their bayonets
  fixed for storming;
It's the death-grip that's a-coming—they will try the works
  once more."

With brazen trumpets blaring, the flames behind them
  glaring,
The deadly wall before them in close array they come;
Still onward, upward toiling, like a dragon's fold uncoiling,
Like the rattlesnake's shrill warning the reverberating drum!

Over heaps all torn and gory—Shall I tell the fearful story,
How they surged above the breastwork, as a sea breaks over
  a deck;
How driven, yet scarce defeated, our wornout men retreated,
With their powder-horns all emptied, like the swimmers from
  a wreck.

It has all been told and painted; as for me, they say I fainted,
And the wooden-legged old Corporal stumped with me down
  the stair:
When I woke from dreams affrighted the evening lamps were
  lighted,—
On the floor a youth was lying; his bleeding breast was bare.

And I heard through all the flurry, "Send for WARREN! hurry!
  hurry!
Tell him here's a soldier bleeding, and he'll come and dress
  his wound."
Ah, we knew not till the morrow told its tale of death and
  sorrow,
How the starlight found him stiffened on the dark and bloody
  ground.

Who the youth was, what his name was, where the place
    from which he came was,
Who had brought him from the battle, and had left him at
    our door,
He could not speak to tell us; but 'twas one of our brave
    fellows,
As the homespun plainly showed us which the dying soldier
    wore.

For they all thought he was dying, as they gathered round
    him crying,—
And they said, "Oh, how they'll miss him!" and, "What *will*
    his mother do?"
Then, his eyelids just unclosing like a child's that has been
    dozing,
He faintly murmured, "Mother!"—and—I saw his eyes were
    blue.

"Why, grandma, how you're winking!" Ah, my child, it sets
    me thinking
Of a story not like this one. Well, he somehow lived along;
So we came to know each other, and I nursed him like a—
    mother,
Till at last he stood before me, tall, and rosy-cheeked, and
    strong.

And we sometimes walked together in the pleasant summer
    weather,—
"Please to tell us what his name was?" Just your own, my
    little dear.
There's his picture Copley painted. We became so well
    acquainted,
That—in short, that's why I'm grandma, and you children
    all are here!

—OLIVER WENDELL HOLMES

Skipper Ireson's Ride

Of all the rides since the birth of time,
Told in story or sung in rhyme,—
On Apuleius's Golden Ass,
Or one-eyed Calender's horse of brass,
Witch astride of a human back,
Islam's prophet on Al-Borák,—
The strangest ride that ever was sped
Was Ireson's, out of Marblehead!
    Old Floyd Ireson, for his hard heart,
        Tarred and feathered and carried in a cart
            By the women of Marblehead!

Body of turkey, head of owl,
Wings a-droop like a rained-on fowl,
Feathered and ruffled in every part,
Skipper Ireson stood in the cart.
Scores of women, old and young,
Strong of muscle, and glib of tongue,
Pushed and pulled up the rocky lane,
Shouting and singing the shrill refrain:
    "Here's Flud Oirson, fur his horrd horrt,
        Torr'd an' futherr'd an' corr'd in a corrt
            By the women o' Morble'eadl"

Wrinkled scolds with hands on hips,
Girls in bloom of cheek and lips,
Wild-eyed, free-limbed, such as chase
Bacchus round some antique vase,
Brief of skirt, with ankles bare,
Loose of kerchief and loose of hair,
With conch-shells blowing and fish-horns' twang,
Over and over the Maenads sang:
    "Here's Flud Oirson, fur his horrd horrt,
        Torr'd an' futherr'd an' corr'd in a corrt
            By the women o' Morble'eadl"

Small pity for him!—He sailed away
From a leaking ship in Chaleur Bay,—
Sailed away from a sinking wreck,
With his own town's-people on her deck!
"Lay by! lay by!" they called to him.
Back he answered, "Sink or swim!
Brag of your catch of fish again!"
And off he sailed through the fog and rain!
   Old Floyd Ireson, for his hard heart,
    Tarred and feathered and carried in a cart
      By the women of Marblehead!

Fathoms deep in dark Chaleur
That wreck shall lie forevermore.
Mother and sister, wife and maid,
Looked from the rocks of Marblehead
Over the moaning and rainy sea,—
Looked for the coming that might not be!
What did the winds and the sea-birds say
Of the cruel captain who sailed away?—
   Old Floyd Ireson, for his hard heart,
    Tarred and feathered and carried in a cart
      By the women of Marblehead!

Through the street, on either side,
Up flew windows, doors swung wide;
Sharp-tongued spinsters, old wives gray,
Treble lent the fish-horn's bray.
Sea-worn grandsires, cripple-bound,
Hulks of old sailors run aground,
Shook head, and fist, and hat, and cane,
And cracked with curses the hoarse refrain:
   "Here's Flud Oirson, fur his horrd horrt,
    Torr'd an' futherr'd an' corr'd in a corrt
      By the women o' Morble'ead!"

Sweetly along the Salem road
Bloom of orchard and lilac showed.
Little the wicked skipper knew
Of the fields so green and the sky so blue.
Riding there in his sorry trim,
Like an Indian idol glum and grim,
Scarcely he seemed the sound to hear
Of voices shouting, far and near:
   "Here's Flud Oirson, fur his horrd horrt,
   Torr'd an' futherr'd an' corr'd in a corrt
     By the women o' Morble'ead!"

"Hear me, neighbors!" at last he cried,—
"What to me is this noisy ride?
What is the shame that clothes the skin
To the nameless horror that lives within?
Waking or sleeping, I see a wreck,
And hear a cry from a reeling deck!
Hate me and curse me,—I only dread
The hand of God and the face of the dead!"
   Said old Floyd Ireson, for his hard heart,
   Tarred and feathered and carried in a cart
     By the women of Marblehead!

Then the wife of the skipper lost at sea
Said, "God has touched him! why should we!"
Said an old wife mourning her only son,
"Cut the rogue's tether and let him run!"
So with soft relentings and rude excuse,
Half scorn, half pity, they cut him loose,
And gave him a cloak to hide him in,
And left him alone with his shame and sin.
   Poor Floyd Ireson, for his hard heart,
   Tarred and feathered and carried in a cart
     By the women of Marblehead!
               —JOHN GREENLEAF WHITTIER

The War Between the States has had many recorders; even the smallest incident has been celebrated in song. Perhaps the most widely quoted poem of this period is "Barbara Frietchie." In September, 1862, General Lee's army marched through Maryland. Stonewall Jackson led the troops, and it was in Frederick, Maryland, that an incident occurred which was immortalized by the New England poet, John Greenleaf Whittier. The authenticity of the story has been disputed—some say that nothing of the sort actually occurred—but "Barbara Frietchie" remains in American literature not only as a fearless heroine but as a symbol of indomitable womanhood.

Barbara Frietchie

Up from the meadows rich with corn,
Clear in the cool September morn,

The clustered spires of Frederick stand
Green-walled by the hills of Maryland.

Round about them orchards sweep,
Apple and peach tree fruited deep,

Fair as the garden of the Lord
To the eyes of the famished rebel horde,

On that pleasant morn of the early fall
When Lee marched over the mountain wall;

Over the mountains winding down,
Horse and foot, into Frederick town.

Forty flags with their silver stars,
Forty flags with their crimson bars,

Flapped in the morning wind: the sun
Of noon looked down, and saw not one.

Up rose old Barbara Frietchie then,
Bowed with her fourscore years and ten;

Bravest of all in Frederick town,
She took up the flag the men hauled down;

In her attic window the staff she set,
To show that one heart was loyal yet.

Up the street came the rebel tread.
Stonewall Jackson riding ahead.

Under his slouched hat left and right
He glanced; the old flag met his sight.

"Halt!"—the dust-brown ranks stood fast,
"Fire"—out blazed the rifle-blast.

It shivered the window, pane and sash;
It rent the banner with seam and gash.

Quick as it fell, from the broken staff
Dame Barbara snatched the silken scarf.

She leaned far out on the window-sill,
And shook it forth with a royal will.

"Shoot, if you must, this old gray head,
But spare your country's flag," she said.

A shade of sadness, a blush of shame,
Over the face of the leader came;

The nobler nature within him stirred
To life at that woman's deed and word;

"Who touches a hair of yon gray head
Dies like a dog! March on!" he said.

All day long through Frederick street
Sounded the tread of marching feet:

All day long that free flag tossed
Over the heads of the rebel host.

Ever its torn folds rose and fell
On the loyal winds that loved it well;

And through the hill-gaps sunset light
Shone over it with a warm good-night.

Barbara Frietchie's work is o'er,
And the Rebel rides on his raids no more.

Honor to her! and let a tear
Fall, for her sake, on Stonewall's bier.

Over Barbara Frietchie's grave,
Flag of Freedom and Union, wave!

Peace and order and beauty draw
Round thy symbol of light and law;

And ever the stars above look down
On thy stars below in Frederick town!

—JOHN GREENLEAF WHITTIER

The High Tide at Gettysburg

A cloud possessed the hollow field,
The gathering battle's smoky shield:
    Athwart the gloom the lightning flashed,
    And through the cloud some horsemen dashed,
And from the heights the thunder pealed.

Then, at the brief command of Lee,
Moved out that matchless infantry,
   With Pickett leading grandly down,
   To rush against the roaring crown
Of those dread heights of destiny.

Far heard above the angry guns,
A cry across the tumult runs:
   The voice that rang through Shiloh's woods,
   And Chickamauga's solitudes:
The fierce South cheering on her sons!

Ah, how the withering tempest blew
Against the front of Pettigrew!
   A Khamsin wind that scorched and singed,
   Like that infernal flame that fringed
The British squares at Waterloo!

A thousand fell where Kemper led;
A thousand died where Garnett bled;
   In blinding flame and strangling smoke,
   The remnant through the batteries broke,
And crossed the works with Armistead.

"Once more in Glory's van with me!"
Virginia cried to Tennessee:
   "We two together, come what may,
   Shall stand upon those works today!"
The reddest day in history.

Brave Tennessee! In reckless way
Virginia heard her comrade say:
   "Close round this rent and riddled rag!"
   What time she set her battle flag
Amid the guns of Doubleday.

But who shall break the guards that wait
Before the awful face of Fate?

The tattered standards of the South
Were shriveled at the cannon's mouth,
And all her hopes were desolate.

In vain the Tennesseean set
His breast against the bayonet;
    In vain Virginia charged and raged,
    A tigress in her wrath uncaged,
Till all the hill was red and wet!

Above the bayonets, mixed and crossed,
Men saw a gray, gigantic ghost
    Receding through the battle cloud,
    And heard across the tempest loud
The death cry of a nation lost!

The brave went down! Without disgrace
They leaped to Ruin's red embrace;
    They only heard Fame's thunders wake,
    And saw the dazzling sunburst break
In smiles on Glory's bloody face!

They fell, who lifted up a hand
And bade the sun in heaven to stand;
    They smote and fell, who set the bars
    Against the progress of the stars,
And stayed the march of Motherland!

They stood, who saw the future come
On through the fight's delirium;
    They smote and stood, who held the hope
    Of nations on that slippery slope,
Amid the cheers of Christendom!

God lives! He forged the iron will
That clutched and held that trembling hill!
    God lives and reigns! He built and lent
    The heights for Freedom's battlement,
Where floats her flag in triumph still!

Fold up the banners! Smelt the guns!
Love rules. Her gentler purpose runs.
  A mighty mother turns in tears
  The pages of her battle years,
Lamenting all her fallen sons!

—WILL HENRY THOMPSON

Ever since songs were made, singers delighted to glorify exceptional people. Men and women have always liked to hear about other men and women who lived dangerously and dared death in a dozen different ways. It made little difference whether the subjects celebrated were noble warriors, shining heroes, or out-and-out villains. Just as hundreds of years ago ballad-singers wove legends around Robin Hood, who (according to tradition) "robbed the rich to help the poor," so in our own time cowboys and other anonymous poets sang about the deeds done by fictional characters like "Jim Bludso" and "Dan McGrew" or by such genuine outlaws as Jesse James, Billy the Kid, and Sam Bass.

The roar of modern industry has not silenced the ballad-maker. He finds heroes in the men who swing hammers, dig tunnels, and run the railroads, such as John Henry. Even the baseball field furnishes material for poetry in the near-tragic tale of "Casey at the Bat."

Jim Bludso

Wall, no! I can't tell whar he lives,
  Bekase he don't live, you see;
Leastways, he's got out of the habit
  Of livin' like you an' me.

Whar have you been for the last three year
    That you haven't heard folks tell
How Jimmy Bludso passed in his checks
    The night of the Prairie Belle?

He weren't no saint—them engineers
    Is pretty much all alike—
One wife in Natchez-under-the-Hill
    And another one here in Pike;
A keerless man in his talk was Jim,
    And an awkward hand in a row,
But he never flunked, an' he never lied—
    I reckon he never knowed how.

And this was all the religion he had—
    To treat his engine well;
Never be passed on the river;
    To mind the pilot's bell;
And if ever the Prairie Belle took fire,
    A thousand times he swore
He'd hold her nozzle agin the bank
    Till the last soul got ashore.

All the boats has their day on the Mississip',
    And her day come at last,—
The Movastar was a better boat,
    But the Belle she *wouldn't* be passed.
And so she come tearin' along that night—
    The oldest craft on the line—
With a nigger squat on her safety-valve,
    And her furnace crammed, rosin an' pine.

The fire bust out as she cl'ared the bar
    And burnt a hole in the night,
And quick as a flash she turned, an' made
    For that willer-bank on the right.
There was runnin' an' cursin', but Jim yelled out
    Over all the infernal roar,

"I'll hold her nozzle agin the bank
   Till the last galoot's ashore!"

Through the hot black breath of the burnin' boat
   Jim Bludso's voice was heard,
An' they all had trust in his cussedness,
   And knowed he would keep his word.
And, sure's you're born, they all got off
   Afore the smokestack fell,—
And Bludso's ghost went up alone
   In the smoke of the Prairie Belle.

He weren't no saint—but at Jedgement
   I'd run my chance with Jim,
'Longside of some pious gentlemen
   That wouldn't shook hands with him.
He seen his duty, a dead-sure thing,—
   And went for it, thar an' then:
And Christ ain't a-goin' to be too hard
   On a man that died for men.

                       —JOHN HAY

Little Breeches

I don't go much on religion,
   I never ain't had no show;
But I've got a middlin' tight grip, sir,
   On the handful o' things I know.
I don't pan out on the prophets
   An' free-will, an' that sort of thing—
But I b'lieve in God an' the angels,
   Ever sence one night last spring.

I come to town with some turnips,
   An' my little Gabe come along—
No four-year-old in the county
   Could beat him for pretty an' strong,

Peart an' chipper an' sassy.
  Always ready to swear and fight,—
And I'd l'arnt him to chaw terbacker,
  Jest to keep his milk-teeth white.

The snow come down like a blanket
  As I passed by Taggart's store;
I went in for a jug of molasses
  An' left the team at the door.
They scared at something an' started—
  I heard one little squall,
An' hell-to-split over the prairie
  Went team, Little Breeches an' all.

Hell-to-split over the prairie!
  I was almost froze with skeer;
But we rousted up some torches,
  An' s'arched for 'em far an' near.
At last we struck horse an' wagon,
  Snowed under a soft white mound,
Upsot, dead beat—but of little Gabe
  No hide nor hair was found.

And here all hope soured on me,
  Of my feller-critter's aid—
I jest flopped down on my marrow-bones
  Crotch-deep in the snow, an' prayed. . . .
By this, the torches wuz played out,
  An' me an' Isrul Parr
Went off for some wood to a sheepfold
  That he said wuz somewhar thar.

We found it at last, an' a little shed
  Where they shut up the lamb at night.
We looked in an' seen them huddled thar,
  So warm an' sleepy an' white;
An' thar sot Little Breeches an' chirped,
  As peart as ever you see,

"I wants a chaw of terbacky,
　　An' that's what's the matter of me."

How did he git thar? Angels.
　　He could never have walked in that storm.
They jest scooped down an' toted him
　　To whar it was safe an' warm.
An' I think that savin' a little child,
　　An' bringin' him to his own,
Is a derned sight better business
　　Than loafin' around The Throne.

　　　　　　　　　　　　　　　　　—JOHN HAY

The Shooting of Dan McGrew

A bunch of the boys were whooping it up in the Malamute
　　saloon;
The kid that handles the music-box was hitting a jag-time
　　tune;
Back of the bar, in a solo game, sat Dangerous Dan McGrew,
And watching his luck was his light-o'-love, the lady that's
　　known as Lou.

When out of the night, which was fifty below, and into the
　　din and the glare,
There stumbled a miner fresh from the creeks, dog-dirty, and
　　loaded for bear.
He looked like a man with a foot in the grave and scarcely
　　the strength of a louse,
Yet he tilted a poke of dust on the bar, and he called for
　　drinks for the house.
There was none could place the stranger's face, though we
　　searched ourselves for a clue;
But we drank his health, and the last to drink was Dangerous
　　Dan McGrew.

There's men that somehow just grip your eyes, and hold
 them hard like a spell;
And such was he, and he looked to me like a man who had
 lived in hell;
With a face most hair, and the dreary stare of a dog whose
 day is done,
As he watered the green stuff in his glass, and the drops fell
 one by one.
Then I got to figgering who he was, and wondering what
 he'd do,
And I turned my head—and there watching him was the lady
 that's known as Lou.

His eyes went rubbering round the room, and he seemed in
 a kind of daze,
Till at last that old piano fell in the way of his wandering
 gaze.
The rag-time kid was having a drink; there was no one else
 on the stool,
So the stranger stumbles across the room, and flops down
 there like a fool.
In a buckskin shirt that was glazed with dirt he sat, and I
 saw him sway;
Then he clutched the keys with his talon hands—my God! but
 that man could play.

Were you ever out in the Great Alone, when the moon was
 awful clear,
And the icy mountains hemmed you in with a silence you
 most could *hear;*
With only the howl of a timber wolf, and you camped there
 in the cold,
A half-dead thing in a stark, dead world, clean mad for the
 muck called gold;
While high overhead, green, yellow and red, the North Lights
 swept in bars?—
Then you've a hunch what the music meant . . . hunger and
 night and the stars.

And hunger not of the belly kind, that's banished with bacon
    and beans,
But the gnawing hunger of lonely men for a home and all that
    it means;
For a fireside far from the cares that are, four walls and a roof
    above;
But oh! so cramful of cosy joy, and crowned with a woman's
    love—
A woman dearer than all the world, and true as Heaven is
    true—
(God! how ghastly she looks through her rouge,—the lady
    that's known as Lou.)

Then on a sudden the music changed, so soft that you scarce
    could hear;
But you felt that your life had been looted clean of all that it
    once held dear;
That someone had stolen the woman you loved; that her love
    was a devil's lie;
That your guts were gone, and the best for you was to crawl
    away and die.
'Twas the crowning cry of a heart's despair, and it thrilled you
    through and through—
"I guess I'll make it a spread misere," said Dangerous Dan
    McGrew.

The music almost died away . . . then it burst like a pent-up
    flood;
And it seemed to say, "Repay! repay!" and my eyes were blind
    with blood.
The thought came back of an ancient wrong, and it stung
    like a frozen lash,
And the lust awoke to kill, to kill . . . then the music stopped
    with a crash,
And the stranger turned, and his eyes they burned in a most
    peculiar way;
In a buckskin shirt that was glazed with dirt he sat, and I
    saw him sway;

Then his lips went in in a kind of grin, and he spoke, and his
    voice was calm,
And "Boys," says he, "you don't know me, and none of you
    care a damn;
But I want to state, and my words are straight, and I'll bet
    my poke they're true,
That one of you is a hound of hell . . . and that one is Dan
    McGrew."

Then I ducked my head, and the lights went out, and two
    guns blazed in the dark,
And a woman screamed, and the lights went up, and two men
    lay stiff and stark.
Pitched on his head, and pumped full of lead, was Dangerous
    Dan McGrew,
While the man from the creeks lay clutched to the breast of
    the lady that's known as Lou.

These are the simple facts of the case, and I guess I ought to
    know.
They say that the stranger was crazed with "hooch," and I'm
    not denying it's so.
I'm not so wise as the lawyer guys, but strictly between us
    two—
The woman that kissed him—and pinched his poke—was the
    lady that's known as Lou.

—ROBERT W. SERVICE

Jesse James

It was on a Wednesday night, the moon was shining bright,
    They robbed the Glendale train.
And the people they did say, for many miles away,
    'Twas the outlaws Frank and Jesse James.

Jesse had a wife to mourn for his life,
    Three children, they were brave;

But the dirty little coward who shot Mister Howard
  Has laid Jesse James in his grave.

It was Robert Ford, the dirty little coward,
  I wonder how he does feel,
For he ate of Jesse's bread and he slept in Jesse's bed,
  Then he laid Jesse James in his grave.

Jesse was a man, a friend to the poor,
  He'd never see a man suffer pain,
And with his brother Frank he robbed the Gallatin bank,
  And stopped the Glendale train.

They went to the crossing not very far from there,
  And there they did the same;
And the agent on his knees he delivered up the keys
  To the outlaws Frank and Jesse James.

It was on a Saturday night, Jesse was at home
  Talking to his family brave,
When the thief and the coward, little Robert Ford,
  Laid Jesse James in his grave.

The people held their breath when they heard of Jesse's
    death,
  And wondered how he ever came to die.
'Twas one of the gang, dirty Robert Ford,
  That shot Jesse James on the sly.

Jesse went to his rest with his hand on his breast.
  The devil will be upon his knee.
He was born one day in the county of Clay,
  And he came from a solitary race.

                                        AUTHOR UNKNOWN

Billy the Kid

I'll sing you a true song of Billy the Kid,
I'll sing of the desperate deeds that he did
Way out in New Mexico long, long ago,
When a man's only chance was his own forty four.

When Billy the Kid was a very young lad,
In old Silver City he went to the bad;
Way out in the West with a gun in his hand
At the age of twelve years he killed his first man.

Fair Mexican maidens play guitars and sing
A song about Billy, their boy bandit king,
How ere his young manhood had reached its sad end
He'd a notch on his pistol for twenty-one men.

'Twas on the same night when poor Billy died
He said to his friends: "I am not satisfied;
There are twenty-one men I have put bullets through
And Sheriff Pat Garrett must make twenty-two."

Now, this is how Billy the Kid met his fate:
The bright moon was shining, the hour was late.
Shot down by Pat Garrett, who once was his friend,
The young outlaw's life had now come to its end.

There's many a man with a face fine and fair
Who starts out in life with a chance to be square,
But just like poor Billy he wanders astray
And loses his life in the very same way.

AUTHOR UNKNOWN

Sam Bass

Sam Bass was born in Indiana—it was his native home.
Before he reached young manhood, the boy began to roam.

Sam first came out to Texas a cowboy for to be,
A kinder hearted fellow you seldom ever see.

Sam used to deal in race stock. One called the Denton mare,
He matched in all the races, and took her to the fair.
He fairly coined the money and spent it frank and free,
He always drank good whiskey, wherever he might be.

Sam left the Collins' ranch one pretty summer day,
With a herd of Texas cattle the Black Hills for to stray;
Sold out in Custer City and then went on a spree—
His chums a lot of cowboys as tough as they could be.

On their way to Texas they robbed the U P train,
For safety split in couples and started out again.
Joe Collins and his partner were overtaken soon.
With all their hard-earned money they had to meet their
    doom.

Sam made it back to Texas all right-side-up with care,
Rode in the town of Denton with all his friends to share.
But there he was so reckless, three robberies did he do,
He robbed the passenger, the express, and U.S. mail cars, too.

Sam had four companions—four bold and daring lads—
They were Richardson and Jackson, Joe Collins, and Old
    Dad;
Such bold and daring cowboys the rangers never knew;
They whipped the Texas rangers and ran the boys in blue.

Sam had another companion called Arkansaw for short,
Was shot by a Texas ranger by the name of Thomas Floyd;
Tom is a big six footer and thinks he's mighty fly,
But let me tell you this sir, he's a dead beat on the sly.

Jim Murphy was arrested and then released on bail;
He jumped his bond at Tyler, then jumped the northbound
    mail;

But Mayor Jones stood in with Jim so it was all a stall.
A put-up job to capture Sam before the coming fall.

Sam met his fate at Round Rock, July the twenty-first,
They dropped poor Sam with rifle balls and emptied out his
    purse.
Poor Sam he is a corpse now and six feet under clay.
And Jackson's in the bushes trying hard to get away.

Jim had borrowed Sam's good gold and didn't want to pay;
The only idea that he had was to give poor Sam away.
He sold out Sam and Barnes and left their friends to mourn—
Oh, what a scorching Jim will get when Gabriel blows his
    horn!

AUTHOR UNKNOWN

    Roy Bean liked to call himself "the Law west of the
Pecos," and his followers claimed he had a right to
the title. He was a fabled character in Texas, where
many things are fabulous—the story goes that he was
a cook, a cobbler, a barber, a bartender, a teacher
and a lawyer before he became a judge. Many songs
were made up about him; the following is one of the
favorite versions.

Roy Bean

Cowboys, come and hear a story of Roy Bean in all his glory,
"All the Law west of the Pecos," was his line:
You must let our ponies take us, to a town on Lower Pecos
Where the High Bridge spans the cañon thin and fine.

He was born one day near Toyah where he learned to be a
    lawyer,
And a teacher and a barber for his fare;

He was cook and old shoe-mender, sometimes preacher and
    bartender:
It cost two bits to have him cut your hair.

He was certain sure a hustler and considerably a rustler,
And at mixing up an egg nog he was grand.
He was lively, he was merry, he could drink a Tom and
    Jerry;
On occasion at a round-up took a hand.

You may find the story funny, but once he had no money
Which for him was not so very strange and rare,
And he went to help Pap Wyndid but he got so absent
    minded,
That he put his RB brand on old Pap's steer.

Now Pap was right smart angry, so Roy Bean went down to
    Langtry
Where he opened up an office and a store.
There he'd sell you drinks or buttons or another rancher's
    muttons,
Though the latter made the other feller sore.

Once there came from Austin city a young dude reputed
    witty,
Out of Bean he thought he'd quickly take a rise:
And he got frisky as he up and called for whiskey
And he said to Bean, "Now hurry, damn your eyes."

On the counter threw ten dollars and it very quickly follers
That the bar-keep took full nine and gave back one,
Then the stranger give a holler as he viewed his single dollar,
And at that commenced the merriment and fun.

For the dude he slammed the table just as hard as he was able,
That the price of whiskey was too high he swore.
Said Roy Bean, "Cause of your fussin' and your most out-
    rageous cussin'
You are fined the other dollar by the law.

"On this place I own a lease, sir, I'm the justice of the peace,
    sir,
And the Law west of the Pecos all is here,
For you've acted very badly." Then the stranger went off
    sadly,
While down his cheek there rolled a bitter tear.

AUTHOR UNKNOWN

Little Mohee

As I was a-walking down by the seashore,
The waves were a-playing, the wind it did roar.

There I sat a-musing by myself on the grass,
And who did I spy but a young Indian lass.

She came and sat by me, took hold of my hand
And said, "You're a stranger and in a strange land.

"But if you will follow you're welcome to come
And dwell in the cottage that I call my home."

The sun was a-sinking far over the sea,
As I went along with my little Mohee.

Together we wandered, together we roamed,
Till I came to the cottage that she called her home.

She asked me to marry and offered her hand,
Saying, "My father's the chieftain that rules o'er this land.

"My father's a chieftain; you a ruler can be;
I'm his only daughter, my name is Mohee."

"O no, my dear maiden, that never can be,
I have a dear sweetheart in my own countree.

"It was early one morning, one morning in May,
I broke her poor heart by going away.

"I'm going to leave you, so fare well, my dear,
My ship's sails are spreading, and home I must steer."

The last time I saw her she knelt on the sand,
And as my boat passed her she waved me her hand.

Saying, "When you get over with the girl that you love,
O remember Mohee, in the cocoanut grove."

And when I had landed with my girl on the shore,
Both friends and relations gathered round me once more.

I gazed all about me, not one did I see
That could ever compare with my little Mohee.

And the girl I had trusted had proved untrue to me,
So I said, "I'll turn courses back over the sea.

"I'll turn my courses and backward I'll flee,
And spend all my days with the little Mohee."

AUTHOR UNKNOWN

One of the most famous of American folk-songs, "Frankie and Johnny" originated about 1850. Since that time, like a true ballad, it has undergone many changes; it has been expanded into a motion picture, a folk-opera, several ballets, and at least two plays. It has been sung as a solo, as a kind of modern cantata, and as a musical comedy number in various versions. The version which follows is one of the most popular.

Frankie and Johnny

Frankie and Johnny were lovers, O lordy how they could love.
Swore to be true to each other, true as the stars above;
   He was her man, but he done her wrong.

Frankie she was his woman, everybody knows.
She spent one hundred dollars for a suit of Johnny's clothes.
   He was her man, but he done her wrong.

Frankie and Johnny went walking, Johnny in his brand new
   suit,
"O good Lord," says Frankie, "but don't my Johnny look
   cute?"
   He was her man, but he done her wrong.

Frankie went down to Memphis, she went on the evening train;
She paid one hundred dollars for Johnny a watch and chain.
   He was her man, but he done her wrong.

Frankie went down to the corner to buy a glass of beer;
She says to the fat bartender, "Has my loving man been here?
   He was my man, but he done me wrong."

"Ain't goin' to tell you no story; ain't goin' to tell you no lie.
I seen your man 'bout an hour ago with a girl named Nellie
   Bly.
   If he's your man, he's doin' you wrong."

Frankie went down to the pawnshop; she didn't go there for
   fun.
She hocked all her jewelry, bought a pearl-handled forty-four
   gun
   For to get her man who was doing her wrong.

Frankie went down to the hotel, looked in the window so high;
There she saw her lovin' Johnny makin' love to Nellie Bly.
   He was her man, but he was doin' her wrong.

Frankie threw back her kimono, took out that old forty-four.
Root-a-toot-toot three times she shot, right through the hotel
   door.
   She was after her man who was doin' her wrong.

Johnny grabbed off his Stetson, cried, "O Lord, Frankie, don't
   shoot!"
But Frankie put her finger on the trigger, and the gun went
   root-a-toot-toot.
   He was her man, but she shot him down.

"Roll me over easy, roll me over slow,
Roll me over easy, boys, 'cause my wounds are hurting me so,
   I was her man, but I done her wrong."

"Oh, my baby, kiss me once before I go.
Turn me over on my right side, baby, where de bullet hurts
   me so.
   I was your man, but I done you wrong."

Frankie went to his coffin, she looked down on his face.
She said, "O Lord, have mercy on me, I wish I could take his
   place,
   He was my man, and I done him wrong."

Oh, bring on your rubber-tired hearses, bring on your rubber-
   tired hacks,
They're takin' Johnny to the cemetery, but they'll never bring
   him back.
   He was her man, but he done her wrong.

The judge said to the jury, "It's as plain as plain can be;
This woman shot her lover, so it's murder in the second
   degree.
   He was her man, tho' he done her wrong."

Now it wasn't murder in the second degree; it wasn't murder
    in the third;
The woman simply dropped her man, like a hunter drops a
    bird.
  He was her man, but he done her wrong.

"Oh, bring a thousand policemen, bring 'em around today,
Oh, lock me in that dungeon, and throw the keys away,
  I shot my man, 'cause he done me wrong.

"Oh, put me in that dungeon; oh, put me in that cell;
Put me where the northeast wind blows from the southeast
    corner of hell.
  I shot my man, 'cause he done me wrong."

Frankie mounted to the scaffold as calm as a girl can be,
And turning her eyes to heaven, she said, "Good Lord, I am
    coming to Thee.
  He was my man, but he done me wrong."

This story's got no moral; this story's got no end;
This story only goes to show that there ain't no good in men.
  He was her man, but he done her wrong.

AUTHOR UNKNOWN

Kentucky Belle

Summer of 'sixty-three, sir, and Conrad was gone away—
Gone to the county town, sir, to sell our first load of hay.
We lived in the log house yonder, poor as ever you've seen;
Röschen there was a baby, and I was only nineteen.

Conrad, he took the oxen, but he left Kentucky Belle;
How much we thought of Kentuck, I couldn't begin to tell—
Came from the Bluegrass country; my father gave her to me
When I rode north with Conrad, away from the Tennessee.

Conrad lived in Ohio—a German he is, you know—
The house stood in broad cornfields, stretching on, row after
row;
The old folks made me welcome; they were kind as kind
could be;
But I kept longing, longing, for the hills of the Tennessee.

O, for a sight of water, the shadowed slope of a hill!
Clouds that hang on the summit, a wind that never is still!
But the level land went stretching away to meet the sky—
Never a rise, from north to south, to rest the weary eye!

From east to west, no river to shine out under the moon,
Nothing to make a shadow in the yellow afternoon;
Only the breathless sunshine, as I looked out, all forlorn,
Only the "rustle, rustle," as I walked among the corn.

When I fell sick with pining we didn't wait any more,
But moved away from the cornlands out to this river shore—
The Tuscarawas it's called, sir—off there's a hill, you see—
And now I've grown to like it next best to the Tennessee.

I was at work that morning. Someone came riding like mad
Over the bridge and up the road—Farmer Rouf's little lad.
Bareback he rode; he had no hat; he hardly stopped to say,
"Morgan's men are coming, Frau, they're galloping on this
way.

"I'm sent to warn the neighbors. He isn't a mile behind;
He sweeps up all the horses—every horse that he can find;
Morgan, Morgan the raider, and Morgan's terrible men,
With bowie knives and pistols, are galloping up the glen."

The lad rode down the valley, and I stood still at the door—
The baby laughed and prattled, playing with spools on the
floor;
Kentuck was out in the pasture; Conrad, my man, was gone;
Near, near Morgan's men were galloping, galloping on!

Sudden I picked up baby and ran to the pasture bar:
"Kentuck!" I called; "Kentucky!" She knew me ever so far!
I led her down the gully that turns off there to the right,
And tied her to the bushes; her head was just out of sight.

As I ran back to the log house at once there came a sound—
The ring of hoofs, galloping hoofs, trembling over the ground,
Coming into the turnpike out from the White-Woman Glen—
Morgan, Morgan the raider, and Morgan's terrible men.

As near they drew and nearer my heart beat fast in alarm;
But still I stood in the doorway, with baby on my arm.
They came; they passed; with spur and whip in haste they
       sped along;
Morgan, Morgan the raider, and his band six hundred strong.

Weary they looked and jaded, riding through night and
       through day;
Pushing on east to the river, many long miles away,
To the border strip where Virginia runs up into the west,
And for the Upper Ohio before they could stop to rest.

On like the wind they hurried, and Morgan rode in advance;
Bright were his eyes like live coals, as he gave me a sideways
       glance;
And I was just breathing freely, after my choking pain,
When the last one of the troopers suddenly drew his rein.

Frightened I was to death, sir; I scarce dared look in his face,
As he asked for a drink of water and glanced around the place;
I gave him a cup, and he smiled—'twas only a boy, you see,
Faint and worn, with his blue eyes; and he'd sailed on the
       Tennessee.

Only sixteen he was, sir—a fond mother's only son—
Off and away with Morgan before his life had begun!

The damp drops stood on his temples; drawn was the boyish
   mouth;
And I thought me of the mother waiting down in the South!

O, plucky was he to the backbone and clear grit through and
   through;
Boasted and bragged like a trooper; but the big words
   wouldn't do;
The boy was dying, sir, dying, as plain as plain could be,
Worn out by his ride with Morgan up from the Tennessee.

But, when I told the laddie that I too was from the South,
Water came in his dim eyes and quivers around his mouth.
"Do you know the Bluegrass country?" he wistful began to say,
Then swayed like a willow sapling and fainted dead away.

I had him into the log house, and worked and brought him to;
I fed him and coaxed him, as I thought his mother'd do;
And, when the lad got better, and the noise in his head was
   gone,
Morgan's men were miles away, galloping, galloping on.

"O, I must go," he muttered; "I must be up and away!
Morgan, Morgan is waiting for me! O, what will Morgan say?"
But I heard a sound of tramping and kept him back from the
   door—
The ringing sound of horses' hoofs that I had heard before.

And on, on came the soldiers—the Michigan cavalry—
And fast they rode, and black they looked galloping rapidly;
They had followed hard on Morgan's track; they had followed
   day and night;
But of Morgan and Morgan's raiders they had never caught
   a sight.

And rich Ohio sat startled through all those summer days,
For strange, wild men were galloping over her broad high-
   ways;

Now here, now there, now seen, now gone, now north, now
    east, now west,
Through river valleys and corn-land farms, sweeping away
    her best.

A bold ride and a long ride! But they were taken at last.
They almost reached the river by galloping hard and fast;
But the boys in blue were upon them ere ever they gained the
    ford,
And Morgan, Morgan the raider, laid down his terrible sword.

Well, I kept the boy till evening—kept him against his will—
But he was too weak to follow, and sat there pale and still;
When it was cool and dusky—you'll wonder to hear me tell—
But I stole down to that gully and brought up Kentucky Belle.

I kissed the star on her forehead—my pretty, gentle lass—
But I knew that she'd be happy back in the old Bluegrass;
A suit of clothes of Conrad's, with all the money I had,
And Kentuck, pretty Kentuck, I gave to the worn-out lad.

I guided him to the southward as well as I knew how;
The boy rode off with many thanks, and many a backward
    bow;
And then the glow it faded, and my heart began to swell,
As down the glen away she went, my lost Kentucky Belle!

When Conrad came in the evening the moon was shining
    high;
Baby and I were both crying—I couldn't tell him why—
But a battered suit of rebel gray was hanging on the wall,
And a thin old horse with drooping head stood in Kentucky's
    stall.

Well, he was kind, and never once said a hard word to me;
He knew I couldn't help it—'twas all for the Tennessee;
But, after the war was over, just think what came to pass—
A letter, sir; and the two were safe back in the old Bluegrass.

The lad had got across the border, riding Kentucky Belle;
And Kentuck she was thriving, and fat, and hearty, and well;
He cared for her, and kept her, nor touched her with whip
    or spur:
Ah! we've had many horses, but never a horse like her!
                —CONSTANCE FENIMORE WOOLSON

Casey at the Bat

It looked extremely rocky for the Mudville nine that day;
The score stood two to four, with but one inning left to play.
So, when Cooney died at second, and Burrows did the same,
A pallor wreathed the features of the patrons of the game.

A straggling few got up to go, leaving there the rest,
With that hope which springs eternal within the human breast.
For they thought: "If only Casey could get a whack at that,"
They'd put even money now, with Casey at the bat.

But Flynn preceded Casey, and likewise so did Blake,
And the former was a pudd'n, and the latter was a fake.
So on that stricken multitude a deathlike silence sat;
For there seemed but little chance of Casey's getting to the
    bat.

But Flynn let drive a single, to the wonderment of all.
And the much-despised Blakey "tore the cover off the ball."
And when the dust had lifted, and they saw what had oc-
    curred,
There was Blakey safe at second, and Flynn a-huggin' third.

Then from the gladdened multitude went up a joyous yell—
It rumbled in the mountaintops, it rattled in the dell;
It struck upon the hillside and rebounded on the flat;
For Casey, mighty Casey, was advancing to the bat.

There was ease in Casey's manner as he stepped into his place,
There was pride in Casey's bearing and a smile on Casey's
    face;
And when responding to the cheers he lightly doffed his hat,
No stranger in the crowd could doubt 'twas Casey at the bat.

Ten thousand eyes were on him as he rubbed his hands with
    dirt,
Five thousand tongues applauded when he wiped them on his
    shirt;
Then when the writhing pitcher ground the ball into his hip,
Defiance glanced in Casey's eye, a sneer curled Casey's lip.

And now the leather-covered sphere came hurtling through the
    air,
And Casey stood a-watching it in haughty grandeur there.
Close by the sturdy batsman the ball unheeded sped;
"That ain't my style," said Casey. "Strike one," the umpire
    said.

From the benches, black with people, there went up a muffled
    roar,
Like the beating of the storm waves on the stern and distant
    shore.
"Kill him! kill the umpire!" shouted someone in the stand;
And it's likely they'd have killed him had not Casey raised his
    hand.

With a smile of Christian charity great Casey's visage shone;
He stilled the rising tumult, he made the game go on;
He signaled to the pitcher, and once more the spheroid flew;
But Casey still ignored it, and the umpire said, "Strike two."

"Fraud!" cried the maddened thousands, and the echo an-
    swered "Fraud!"
But one scornful look from Casey and the audience was awed;

They saw his face grow stern and cold, they saw his muscles
    strain,
And they knew that Casey wouldn't let the ball go by again.

The sneer is gone from Casey's lips, his teeth are clenched in
    hate,
He pounds with cruel vengeance his bat upon the plate;
And now the pitcher holds the ball, and now he lets it go,
And now the air is shattered by the force of Casey's blow.

Oh, somewhere in this favored land the sun is shining bright,
The band is playing somewhere, and somewhere hearts are
    light;
And somewhere men are laughing, and somewhere children
    shout,
But there is no joy in Mudville—mighty Casey has struck out.

                    —ERNEST LAWRENCE THAYER

John Henry

When John Henry was nothin' but a baby
    Sittin' on his mammy's knee,
He said, "De Big Bend tunnel on de C. & O. road
    Is gonna cause de death of me."

De cap'n said to John Henry,
    "Gonna bring me a steam drill aroun';
Gonna take dat steam drill out to de tunnel
    An' gonna mow de mountain down."

John Henry tol' his cap'n
    A man ain't nothin' but a man;
But befo' he'd let dat steam drill beat him
    He'd die wid a hammer in his han'.

John Henry said to his cap'n,
    Lightnin' was in his eye:

"Wid my twelve-poun' hammer an' a four-foot handle
  I'll beat dat steam drill or die."

John Henry went to de tunnel;
  Dey put him in de lead to drive.
De rock so tall an' John Henry so small,
  He put down his hammer an' he cried.

John Henry started on de right side,
  Steam drill started on de lef';
"Befo' I'd let dat steam drill beat me down
  I'll hammer my fool self to death."

Steam drill started workin',
  Was workin' mighty fine;
John Henry drove his fifteen feet,
  An' de steam drill only made nine.

Cap'n said to John Henry,
  "I b'lieve de mountain's sinkin' in."
John Henry said to his cap'n,
  "It's just my hammer suckin' win'."

De hammer dat John Henry swung
  Weighed over thirteen poun'.
He broke a rib in his lef' han' side
  An' his intrails fell on de groun'.

John Henry had a li'l woman,
  Her name was Polly Ann;
On de day dat John Henry drop down dead,
  Polly Ann hammered steel like a man.

Dey took his body to Washin'ton;
  Dey carried it over the lan'.
People f'om de Eas' and people f'om de Wes'
  Dey mourned for dat steel-drivin' man.

AUTHOR UNKNOWN

INDEX

OF AUTHORS, TITLES AND FIRST LINES

457

❧ WASHINGTON SQUARE PRESS CLASSICS ❧

A new and growing series presenting distinguished literary works in an inexpensive, well-designed format

• • • • • • • • • • • • •

Anthologies of Short Stories, Poetry and Essays Now in Washington Square Press Editions

CHAUCER, GEOFFREY, *The Canterbury Tales.* Translated by R. M. Lumiansky, Preface by Mark Van Doren. Illustrated. W 567 (60¢)

CRANE, STEPHEN, *Maggie and Other Stories.* Selected and with an Introduction by Austin McC. Fox. W 133 (45¢)

FROST, ROBERT, *A Pocket Book of Poems.* Edited by Louis Untermeyer. Illustrated. W 556 (60¢)

HAWTHORNE, NATHANIEL, *Twice-Told Tales and Other Short Stories.* Introduction by Quentin Anderson. W 580 (50¢)°°

MILLAY, EDNA ST. VINCENT, *Collected Lyrics.* Introduction by Norma Millay. W 550 (60¢)

MILLAY, EDNA ST. VINCENT, *Collected Sonnets.* Introduction by Norma Millay. W 551 (60¢)

PETERSON, HOUSTON, ed., *Great Essays.* W 598 (60¢)

POE, EDGAR ALLAN, *Great Tales and Poems.* W 246 (45¢)

SHAKESPEARE, WILLIAM, *The Complete Sonnets, Songs and Poems.* Edited by Henry W. Simon. W 131 (35¢)°

SPEARE, M. EDMUND, ed., *A Pocket Book of Short Stories.* W 255 (45¢)

SPEARE, M. EDMUND, ed., *The Pocket Book of Verse.* W 241 (45¢)

WILLIAMS, OSCAR, ed., *Immortal Poems of the English Language.* W 553 (60¢)

WILLIAMS, OSCAR, ed., *A Pocket Book of Modern Verse.* W 554 (60¢)

°Price will be changed to 45¢ at the time of the next printing.

°°Price will be changed to 60¢ at the time of the next printing.

• • • • • • • • • • • • •

If your bookseller does not have the titles you want, you may order them by sending retail price, plus 5¢ per book for postage and handling, to: Mail Service Department, Washington Square Press, Inc., 1 West 39th Street, New York 18, N.Y. Please enclose check or money order—do not send cash.   WSP-1 (B)